RADICAL ARISTOCRATS:

London Busworkers from the 1880s to the 1980s

KEN FULLER

CHAMPION!

THE LONDON FOREST STRIKE OF 1991

BY

KEN FULLER

ISHI PRESS INTERNATIONAL

Radical Aristocrats
London Busworkers
from the 1880s to the 1980s

by Ken Fuller

First published in 1985
in England by Oxford University Press

Champion! - The London Forest Strike of 1991
by Ken Fuller
First published in 1992

This Second Printing of both in March, 2011
by Ishi Press in New York and Tokyo

with a new preface to the Second Editions

ISBN 4-87187-675-6
978-4-87187-675-9

Ishi Press International
1664 Davidson Avenue, Suite 1B
Bronx NY 10453-7877
USA
1-917-507-7226

Printed in the United States of America

AN AFTERWORD MASQUERADING AS A PREFACE TO THE SECOND EDITION

Below, I attempt to provide the reader with an update regarding the events following 1985, when *Radical Aristocrats* was first published. It will be noticed that after the mid-1990s my account becomes somewhat sketchy, and there is a reason for this. In 1995, I was appointed as the TGWU's Regional Organiser for London, the Southeast and East Anglia (then called Region 1), meaning that I was tasked with overall responsibility for the union's organising efforts in the region and, thus, no longer had direct experience of the London Bus Section. Then, to compound the difficulty, in 2003 I moved to the Philippines.

Since arriving here, I have spent my time writing, submitting occasional feature articles to the *Morning Star* and *Tribune* in London, and also writing commentaries published in *BusinessWorld* (yes, don't ask me why, but they published my sometimes obviously left-wing material without a murmur – or payment) and *Daily Tribune* over here. Since mid-2008 I have written a weekly column for the latter newspaper. Aside from this, I have been engaged on several book projects. In 2007, University of the Philippines Press published my *Forcing the Pace: The Partido Komunista ng Pilipinas, From Foundation to Armed Struggle* (a finalist in the 2008 National Book Award), and in a few months' time a second volume, *A Movement Divided: Philippine Communism, 1957-1986*, will appear under the same imprint. A third volume is (I hope!) nearing completion.

In addition, I have written a couple of novels for which a publisher (or, should I say, an agent, this being a requirement for fiction with both UK and US publishers) is still required. When, therefore, I received a text from Bob Hall, a Romford man who runs a bar in Tagbilaran City, telling me that a US publisher was on the premises, I drove into town with the novels uppermost in my mind.

"Do you publish fiction?" was my first question to Sam Sloan, and when he replied in the negative I feared that my journey had been wasted. But then we got talking, and Sam explained that although he publishes the occasional new work, his New York-based Ishi Press (originally a Japanese company) deals mostly with reprints. "Well," I said, "there's a labour history of London busworkers I had published 25 years ago…" Sam was interested and by the following day we'd agreed that he would incorporate the pamphlet I'd written about the London Forest strike of 1991, and that bulk supplies to London busworkers would be made available at a heavy discount.

Such swift progress is previously unknown to me or, I suppose, the vast majority of authors. It was possible because Ishi Press is not encumbered with the substantial up-front costs facing traditional publishers. Instead, there is an arrangement with Sam's printers that they produce only what is ordered. If Amazon requires ten copies, ten copies are printed. If a bulk order comes in from London, the London printer will run the copies off and deliver them. And so on with each order.

The chances of Sam and I ever meeting were practically non-existent. He was only in the Philippines, visiting an old friend, for a week. He's a non-drinker and yet, persuaded by an acquaintance he'd met in the Internet café around the corner, he entered a bar. And the guy behind the bar happened to know me and my literary pursuits.

First of all, then, I owe thanks to good fortune for that unlikely occurrence. Secondly, thanks to Sam for his no-nonsense approach and ready acceptance of my wares. Thanks are also due to Sally Davison who, when I discovered that my contract with Lawrence & Wishart required me to give that company, as the original publisher of *Radical Aristocrats*, nine months' notice of republication or reissue, readily waived that clause.

*

As indicated in the text, when *Radical Aristocrats* was first published in 1985 the London Bus Section of the Transport & General Workers' Union (TGWU) was facing its most challenging period for decades, perhaps ever. Much has happened in the last quarter of a century.

The Greater London Council (GLC) was abolished in 1986, and London Regional Transport (LRT) thereafter reported directly to the Department of Transport. Former GLC leader Ken Livingstone moved across the Thames to the House of Commons, where he sat as a Labour MP. However, due to the fact that the GLC had been able to introduce a variant of the low-fares policy declared unlawful by the Law Lords, bus patronage in London went on increasing year after year, while in the rest of the country it declined.

For London's busworkers, however, the news was not so good. Gradually, the routes operated by LRT subsidiary London Buses Ltd. (LBL) were put out to tender. Inevitably, the early tendered routes were lost to private operators, as LBL's bids were based on current wages and conditions. LBL therefore decided that in future it would bid on lower wages and worse conditions, without consulting the TGWU beforehand. This tactic was first employed at Potters Bar garage, and when LBL succeeded in retaining the routes by this method, the existing workforce was offered a severance package which, being relatively generous, meant that the employer was able to avoid strike action. The union then faced the task of recruiting the replacement staff and integrating them into the London Bus Section.

Next time around, LBL adopted a different tactic, setting up a new low-wage subsidiary, Westlink, in Hounslow, which then bid for and won routes formerly operated by the "mainstream" Hounslow garage just down the road. Once again, the union was faced with an organising task, as the workforce at Westlink was obviously new. That task fell to me, and in the period preceding privatisation I was assigned responsibility for negotiating on behalf of the staff at all of LBL's low-wage units – Potters Bar, Westlink, Orpington, London Coaches and Norbiton – and then some of the first private operators to win routes, like Grey-Green and Capital Citybus.

While it was possible to achieve high-percentage wage-increases at these garages, the gap between them and the "full-wage" garages was still considerable. Neither was I fooled into thinking that the increases achieved were solely a result of my negotiating ability, as the managers at these lowly outposts were swiftly faced with the dismal realisation that while low wages might allow them to win tenders, they did nothing to aid staff retention: the level of staff turnover was appalling.

The first negotiations at Norbiton garage, just outside of Kingston, took place in the wake of a "successful" tendering exercise, in which Norbiton had won its routes based on worsened wages and conditions. A bitter industrial dispute ensued. The initial stance adopted by the union's London Bus Committee, supported by the Norbiton membership, was that there should be *no* negotiations, as the fleet agreement on wages and conditions should be defended at all costs. At this stage, I made myself unpopular by taking a different view.

For where would such a stance lead? Eventually, surely, LRT would simply withdraw the routes from Norbiton and award them to Len Wright Travel which, although it came second in the bidding process, paid even lower wages. If we saw our task as that of defending wages and conditions in London's bus industry, where was the sense in contributing to a situation which would worsen them still further? Complicating the situation was the fact that some of our members at Norbiton actually wanted the routes to be re-awarded so that they would qualify for the severance package. The atmosphere was less than healthy. Eventually, however, negotiations were renewed and, after several improvements to the original proposals the members voted to accept.

The situation in the London Forest dispute of 1991 was quite different. By this time, LBL had been split into thirteen operating subsidiaries. London Forest Travel retained the tendered routes at its Walthamstow garage on the basis of drastically lower wages. Having discovered that Capital Citybus, the private company (originally called Ensign CityBus) which had come second in the bidding for the bulk of the routes, was prepared to pay more than the London Forest rate, our members conducted the longest bus strike since the seven-week dispute of 1958, while the negotiating team gained every concession possible from the company directors.

But it wasn't enough. London Forest never matched the Capital Citybus rates, so our members stayed out until LRT re-awarded the routes. We had gained an assurance that Capital Citybus would recognise the union, so while our members would still be working for somewhat less than previously, they had avoided the very low Forest rates and they would take their union cards with them. In fact, it worked out even better than we had hoped because LBL, anxious to avoid handing over a trained workforce to a private competitor, managed to reallocate every member who wished to stay within its own network. In effect, the union membership had re-tendered the routes and London Forest management had lost. We then organized the Capital Citybus workforce and negotiated a recognition agreement.

The London Forest story was told in a booklet I wrote after the strike. This was entitled *Champion!* and originally published by the union's London Forest Operating Staff Committee. Copies were sold for £1 apiece to our members throughout London, with the proceeds going to our union's campaign against the government's proposal to deregulate bus services in London. Copies of this pamphlet must now be quite rare (possibly explaining why a copy for sale on the Amazon website is priced at £10!), and therefore thanks are due to Sam Sloan of Ishi Press for making it available here

It wasn't just the busworkers who suffered during these years. Due to the effects of first tendering, then a combination of tendering *and* privatization, the infrastructure of the industry was vandalised, with garages being closed all over London. As early as 1983, a London Transport "garage strategy" document had spoken of eight garage closures by 1993, and another ten by 2003; the only assurance the document gave was that 30 "core garages" were safe. In 1985, there were 61 LBL garages. That document, having been drafted by the kind of grey, unimaginative management that would, by its servile adherence to government diktat, eventually preside over the demise of London Buses Ltd., proved to be somewhat pessimistic. This was due to the fact, noted above but apparently unforeseen by these "strategists," that public demand for London's bus services would register a steady increase. But the damage was bad enough, with even structures like Norbiton garage, built fairly recently at a cost of millions, eventually closing. And, of course, the world-famous Chiswick Training Centre, with its "skid-pan," would be bulldozed. There is little doubt that this led to a deterioration of driving standards as, particularly when faced with rapid staff turnover, the privatised companies – to say nothing of the independent operators - relaxed the requirements.

The damage went deeper still, as some of the small private operators entering the field (no pun intended) simply parked their buses on open land. As the bottom line dictated everything, and because lost mileage meant reduced contract payments from LRT, some operators cut corners – a blind eye was sometimes turned to vehicle safety standards, and the drivers' hours regulations were often breached.

*

In preparation for privatisation, the LBL subsidiaries all put forward wage-cut proposals, leading to strikes affecting most of London (only one subsidiary, East London, set its wage-rates at a level our members found acceptable). At the same time, the Tory government was considering deregulating London bus services. The Transport Act, 1985, which deregulated services in the rest of the country, contained a clause enabling deregulation to be introduced into London without further legislation, so this was a real danger.

Outside of London, deregulation had led to chaos. Busy routes were over-bused, with drivers sometimes racing to get to stops ahead of the opposition. In city centres, traffic jams caused by this over-busing were a regular feature. On the other hand, the rural areas, and even urban areas at unprofitable times of the day or week, saw a reduction of services. Unlike London, in the rest of the country bus-ridership continued to decline.

With the attention of the public already focused by the strikes against wage-cuts, the union used this opportunity to campaign against the prospect of deregulation and call for an inquiry into London's bus services. During the course of this campaign, our activists distributed some 250,000 leaflets to the travelling public; on one side, we denounced the wage-cuts; on the other we called upon the public to stand alongside our members in opposing deregulation. Eventually, the House of Commons Select Committee on Transport announced that it would be holding an inquiry. Led by Passenger Services Secretary Graham Stevenson, the Union gave oral evidence to the inquiry and presented written testimony in the form of a document entitled *Code Red* (written by me, with an appendix by union executive member Martin Mayer, a Sheffield bus driver), detailing the horrific results of deregulation elsewhere in the country.

Although we had also hoped to persuade the committee (which, of course, had a Tory majority) to recommend changes in the current London regime, particularly regarding the "race to the bottom" of tendering, it would only go as far as recommending that deregulation not be introduced to the capital. However, when considered against the consequences that would have ensued if they had recommended otherwise, it was clear that we had won a major political victory.

The strikes against the wage-cuts, meanwhile, had continued until both sides in each of the companies had reached a basis for settlement – not as good as many of our members had desired, but probably as much as was realistic in the circumstances. The struggle over wages would rumble on into the 21st century.

*

One of the problems encountered during this period concerned the consciousness of many of our members, activists and, dare I say it, some of the old-school full-time officers. Certainly, the level of class consciousness in the London Bus Section had declined compared to the militant 1930s and 1940s. The left now was not as organised as it had been then, although in the early 1980s a number of us put forward the progressive line in a rank-and-file journal called the *London Busworker*, thousands of copies of which were sold across London every month. Briefly, as an attempt was made to reach out to activists in the rail unions, this became *Transport Worker*, but the journal eventually folded.

There were also objective factors as work: whereas, for example, London busworkers at an earlier time had tended to remain in the job until retirement, there was now high staff turnover, and consequently it became more difficult to build a group consciousness; many of our newer members had no knowledge, let alone experience, of the superior wages and conditions their forerunners had enjoyed and which were now being eroded.

Moreover, those who had such knowledge and experience often tended to adopt a counterproductive stance. To an extent, this was to be expected, for we were experiencing entirely new problems. For example, some of our members looked upon the staff at the low-wage garages (who were, once we had organized them, their fellow-members) as very much the poor relations, to be regarded with disdain. The drivers employed by the private operators were sometimes considered the "enemy," for they were now working on what had once been "our" routes. In effect, members who acted in this way were more loyal to their employer rather than to their class.

Attempts – eventually successful – to organise the unorganised sometimes met problems. I remember, one Friday afternoon as I was recruiting drivers employed by a private operator at Hounslow bus station, receiving a telephone call from our London District Secretary instructing me to drive across to Southall garage, where the branch officers were threatening to pull their members out of the union if I continued to recruit drivers in the private sector. It took some time before it was widely accepted that such drivers were more of a threat if they were outside of the union, and that it was in everyone's material interest for London busworkers to stand together, regardless of employer. Within a few years, we were forming teams of lay activists to go out recruiting.

Another lesson that had to be learned was that in this new situation, new tactics were required. Norbiton, discussed above, was a case in point. In the case of London Forest, while our members in that company fully understood and supported the tactics we adopted, heads were often scratched elsewhere. This was new ground, striking against a publicly-owned employer when a private operator would probably benefit. We did it because it was in the interests of our members. It was a mistake, anyway, to look upon the publicly-owned London Buses as some kind of socialist paradise. Here, the publicly-owned employer was behaving no differently from his private counterparts, and we knew anyway that privatisation was on the horizon, so let this be an object lesson to any employer who wished to reduce our members' wages and conditions!

Even the strike itself needed some new thinking. I remember, having spoken at a meeting of Walthamstow Trades Council, being asked by a delegate whether the local community should boycott those bus companies which were "scabbing" by covering some of London Forest's routes during the dispute. No, I said, because this was a new kind of dispute. Our immediate enemy was London Forest. The aim of the strike was to deny it revenue. Unlike disputes in the past, when one company had covered the whole of London, it frankly didn't matter if other garages (now in other companies) were plying the routes. While we had opposed the break-up of LBL into separate subsidiaries, here we were turning that situation to our advantage. Divide and rule could work for us as well as for the employers.

On deregulation, the view we took was that it would be bad for everyone – the travelling public and the companies, whether private or public. We thus began to put together an alliance with the directors of some LBL subsidiaries and their counterparts in the private sector. (The Tory government would, in any case, be more likely to listen to the arguments of the private sector.) As part of the strategy, we hosted meetings between these directors with Labour's John Prescott and Joan Ruddock when they held the shadow transport portfolio, putting forward arguments in an attempt to influence a future Labour government's transport policy for London. (Alas, it was 1997 before Labour was elected, by which time much of the damage had been done – and with Tony Blair in Number 10 it was obvious that little of it would be repaired.)

At a certain point in the campaign against deregulation we held a rally (at, I believe, Central Hall, Westminster) where, with our private sector allies in the audience, even our general secretary Bill Morris, the main speaker, demonstrated that he had failed to adjust to the new situation. In the speech his office asked me to write for him, I laid out the disastrous consequences of deregulation elsewhere in the country, the importance of ensuring it was never introduced to London, and the perspective of building as broad as possible an alliance, including the private sector, for this campaign. Well, our leader (now Baron Morris of Handsworth) seemed to be unacquainted with the concept of the tactical alliance, for he completely ignored the speech I'd written and issued a call for a return to public ownership! Possibly he was repositioning himself on the left in preparation for his 1995 re-election and had overlooked the fact that there were employers in the audience.

*

Privatization of London Buses came in 1994, and although there were originally three management buyouts and one management-employee buyout, these were short-lived. As things stand in 2011, big business (at least in terms of the bus industry) rules the roost, with one former LBL subsidiary being owned by First while Arriva, Stagecoach, Go-Ahead, ComfortDelGro and Transdev own two apiece. Transdev is currently in the process of selling London United to RATP, which runs the Paris Metro.

Preface to the Second Edition

As indicated above, Labour swept to victory in 1997, but by then the Blair leadership's "new Labour" project had triumphed, sweeping away the party's former commitment to public ownership and diluting the influence of both trade unions and constituency parties within the its structures. There would, therefore, be no return to public ownership under such a regime, but there were positive developments. London Regional Transport was replaced by Transport for London. A new Greater London Authority, along with the position of London mayor, was created. Ken Livingstone, having adopted an anti-Blairite stance, was elected mayor as an independent in 2000, and then as the Labour candidate in 2004. Thus, London was once again governed by a pro-bus administration.

In 2008, Livingstone was defeated by the Tory Alexander Boris de Pfeffel Johnson, who in his blundering way has attempted to unpick much of the good that the Livingstone administration did. Since May 2010, the whole country has been saddled with the Con-Dem coalition, and it would be surprising if its ideologically-driven public expenditure cuts did not impact on London busworkers. Once again, challenges lie ahead.

But busworkers have demonstrated that they have learned the lessons of the past couple of decades. There is a high degree of cross-company unity, and the divisions introduced by tendering and wage-cutting have been largely overcome. In recent years, not only has a London busworker been elected for successive terms onto the union's Executive Council, but the member in question is none other than John Murphy from Potters Bar – no longer the "poor relation."

In recent years, London busworkers, ably led by Pete Kavanagh, the senior regional officer for the passenger transport sector, have hammered out a number of common demands in a "London Busworkers' Charter," and in 2008 they embarked upon a campaign to eliminate the differences in wage-rates across the city. Although bedeviled by the judiciary's ever-more creative interpretations of the previous Tory government's raft of anti-union legislation, our members have undertaken strike action in support of their demands and, given the vision and determination, will surely make further progress. Unfortunately, it seems that some employers also wish to eliminate wage differences, but by a somewhat different method: East London and Selkent, both owned by Stagecoach and hitherto the highest payers, have confronted their staff with a demand for a wage-cut of 15 percent or an increase of four hours in the working week.

Our members' determination to oppose such outrages and carry forward the struggle for a more civilised regime will be strengthened if it is based on an understanding of what went before, and an appreciation of the fact that today's struggling London busworkers are part of a proud tradition stretching back more than a century. Although obviously welcoming the general reader with an interest in labour history, it is with this in mind that *Radical Aristocrats* and *Champion!* are republished here. At the end of the day, however, the ongoing "race to the bottom" engendered by the tendering system must be terminated by political means, so our members must struggle on that front also.

The TGWU is no more, having merged with Amicus to form Unite the Union, the UK's largest trade union. The name of the new union is appropriate, for unity has been the indispensable precondition for the victories London busworkers have won in the past, as it will be for their achievements in the future.

Tagbilaran City, March 2011
Ken Fuller

Contents

Illustrations

Foreword

A great deal of research is essential to any portrayal of historical events, and this examination of the never-ending struggle between London busworkers and their powerful opponents – a major employer often supported by both the government and a narrow-minded, authoritarian union leadership – is a good example of scrupulous, painstaking research.

Other participants in the events described here, particularly those of the post-war period, might place a different emphasis on certain issues. One example is the failure to elect representatives direct to the union's General Executive Council (GEC) following the retirement of Bill Jones, the undisputed leader of the London busworkers even in the years when he was not in office. Another is the failure to forge stronger links with the rail unions operating the Underground network before the 1958 strike; if all the unions in London Transport had stood united at that time the outcome would have been very different.

It is considered by some that the London Bus Section, once the most powerful body in the TGWU, is too insular, with an excessive pride in its militant history for its leaders to be able to lift their members in the current struggle against an employer working at the government's bidding and committed to privatisation and a drastically reduced labour force.

During the 1950s and 60s busworkers nationally played a major role in every important union committee and conference: thirteen members of the GEC (a third of the total); four, or half the GEC's so-called 'inner cabinet', on the Finance and General Purposes Committee. More than one third of all TGWU officers, including five of the Regional Secretaries, were busworkers. The London Bus Section provided many of the main speakers at the Biennial and Rules Conferences. They enjoy a special privilege arising from the amalgamation in that they have direct access to the GEC and can call on the General Secretary to lead their pay negotiations, although no talks have been held at that level since 1965.

The running battle between the lay leadership and some of the regional and national officials is recorded in this book, and it is astonishing that while the lay leadership of the London busworkers, with its domination of the union's policy-making bodies, was highly organised and effective, it did not produce leaders at a national level.

The one exception to this was Sam Henderson, the only person to be appointed twice from being a lay member to a national official, first from being a driver on the Glasgow trams and then from being a London bus conductor. Although Sam had comparatively short periods of office, the first less than two years and the second just over six, he was involved in important inquiries into each of the major sectors of the bus industry, culminating in the London Phelps-Brown Inquiry in 1963; he died shortly afterwards at the age of 62.

Many London busworkers, especially those who have lived through the events chronicled in this fascinating book, will recognise the accuracy and honesty of Ken Fuller's account. Students and other readers without direct personal experience of industrial relations in London Transport will find it informative and descriptive of a major section of union lay members in their long fight to achieve social and economic justice against overwhelming odds.

Larry Smith,
Executive Officer, TGWU
March 1985

Acknowledgements

This study was initially undertaken as the author's project while a student on the Distance Learning Course inaugurated by Region 1 of the Transport and General Workers' Union in conjunction with the University of Surrey. Thus my first debt is to the TGWU for enabling me, first as a lay member and then as a full-time officer, to participate in this course. Particular thanks are due to Barry Camfield, John Fisher and John Holford for their unstinting assistance and encouragement.

I am also indebted to the following who, during the course of my research, were generous with their time and with materials: Terry Allan, Noreen Branson, Frank Cosgrove, Max Egelnick, Kerry Hamilton, Bill Jones, Bill Morris, Harry Selmes, Larry Smith and John Stevens. It is a convention in the pages preceding a work such as this to thank one's spouse for exhibiting patience, understanding and all the other qualities which make that person the ideal partner for the Great Literary Figure. When the spouse concerned is married to such a foul-tempered, inconsiderate (and hardly important) scribbler as the present author, such an appreciative gesture is even more appropriate: thank you, Minah.

Responsibility for any shortcomings of the study which follows must, of course, rest solely with the author.

Introduction

> In 1923, we were the aristocrats of labour. Our top wage then was £4 7s. 6d. a week. My father was getting 29s 6d as a building labourer. Other sections of the working class respected us as being the leaders. What the busmen did today, somebody else would want to do tomorrow. We took the lead with everything.[1]

These words come from Harry Selmes, who joined the London General Omnibus Company in 1923 and remained a London busworker until his retirement 40 years later. In those days employment on London's buses offered security for life, the second highest wage for semi-skilled workers in the country and the respect of one's peers. In this sense, London busworkers did indeed constitute an 'aristocracy'. It is important, however, that from the outset we distinguish London busworkers from the traditional 'aristocracy of labour'. The latter developed in the middle decades of the nineteenth century and was confined to the skilled 'trades', mainly in engineering. This 'aristocracy' was characterised by long apprenticeships, regulation of the work upon which each man could be employed and various other practices which, by restricting entry into these occupations (some skilled unions even provided funds for emigration), kept wages as high as possible. London busworkers were obviously not skilled in this sense and, besides, developed as a cohesive industrial force much later. Moreover, whereas the traditional 'aristocrats' were politically conservative, the dominant tendency among London busworkers from 1913 until the 1960s was far more radical.

Thus the term 'aristocrats' used in the title and throughout this work must not be confused with the earlier phenomenon – even though, as we shall see, there were some points of similarity.

The study which follows quite deliberately concentrates on the present London Bus Section of the TGWU and its forebears; that is, during the period when the London Passenger Transport Board and later London Transport comprised of three road sections (Central Buses, Trams and Trolleybuses and Country Services). This study takes the Central Bus

Section as its subject – this, after all, was the 'aristocratic' Section. In the interests of clarity, I have also taken liberties with the nomenclature of various parts of the London Bus Section machinery. Thus, for example, the careful reader will notice that reference is made to the 'Central Bus Committee' and the 'London Bus Conference' during periods when these, although performing the same functions, were known by slightly different names.

The history of London's busworkers falls approximately into four distinct phases, roughly corresponding to the four Parts of this work.

Part One chronicles the struggle to achieve trade union organisation and then, in a brief historical period, 'aristocratic' status. The achievement of these goals was made possible both by the objective changes in the nature of the occupation caused by the introduction of motor buses, and by the subjective activity of the London and Provincial Union of Licensed Vehicle Workers (LPU). This organisation quickly gained a reputation for militancy, wearing its sobriquet of the 'red button' union with considerable pride. Shortly after the formation of the LPU, the First World War broke out, and the nature of this conflict had a significant influence on the development of socialist ideas and understanding within the ranks of London busworkers.

Despite two amalgamations, first into the United Vehicle Workers and then, in 1922, into the Transport and General Workers' Union, this combination of industrial militancy and political radicalism was maintained. In this period, however, London busworkers came up against a formidable force for moderation in the person of Ernest Bevin. Their own short tradition of fiery independence was confronted by the TGWU's intention, personified in Bevin's tough centralist approach, to create a single, unified structure from a host of disparate trade groups. Above all, however, Bevin's approach to industrial relations, exemplified by his role in the Mond-Turner talks of 1928, was incompatible with the desire of the London Bus Section to maintain its aristocratic status through improvements in wages and conditions. The strains of these early years of amalgamation are considered in Part Two.

As the militancy of the London Bus Section was unable to gain official expression this led, in 1932, to the formation of the London Busmen's Rank and File Movement, which proved to be one of the most effective unofficial movements the British trade union movement has ever seen. This movement, which is dealt with in Part Three, was really a reflection of the Section's aristocratic status and reaffirmed the link between industrial militancy and socialist politics.

Part Four describes the decline of the London busworkers' status which began with the defeat of the 1937 Coronation Strike. However, the major contribution to this decline was made by the changed circumstances which followed the Second World War. The deep changes which affected British society in the post-war period would, in the course of lowering the busworkers' status, first depoliticise the Section and then rob it of its militancy. This process was accentuated until the mid-1950s by the influence of Arthur Deakin. Thenceforth the TGWU leadership would, ironically, become steadily more progressive as the London Bus Section lost its radicalism.

Throughout the post-war period the size of the Section has been whittled down as the scale of London Transport's bus operation contracted. Now numbering less than 20,000, London busworkers find themselves faced with a political threat to their future in the form of the London Regional Transport Act. By yet another ironic twist, such a situation requires the re-establishment of both industrial militancy and political radicalism. Whereas previously these had their base in the aristocratic status of the 'trade', they are required now in order to safeguard its future. There is no reason to believe that the membership is not capable of rising to this challenge or that, despite the present dangers and difficulties, the future will in the long run be anything other than healthy.

It is hoped that this study will appeal to the general reader with an interest in labour history, and also assist members of the London Bus Section of the TGWU to rediscover their militant heritage. If the Section as a whole now embarks upon a determined defence of the industry and the jobs, wages and conditions of those who work in it, each and every member will justifiably be able to claim that heritage as his or her own.

Notes

1. Harry Selmes, interviewed by the author, 18 August 1984.

PART ONE

London Busworkers Before 1922

CHAPTER ONE

Sutherst's Union

For most of the nineteenth century membership of the British trade union movement was largely drawn from the skilled occupations – the 'labour aristocracy'. Unskilled and semi-skilled workers were seen as a threat to the wages and conditions of these groups and considered virtually unorganisable. In 1889, however, 'New Unionism' burst upon the scene, with the unskilled and semi-skilled organising into trade unions and achieving improvements (short-lived though these were in some cases). At the forefront of this new development were the London gasworkers and dockers.

In the same year, Thomas Sutherst, a barrister, organised between two and three thousand London tram men 'and some from the omnibuses' into their first trade union.[1]

Certainly, a trade union was needed in the horse-drawn era. Omnibus crews worked a fifteen or sixteen-hour day, completing six return journeys, seven days a week. It was possible for crews to take a day's unpaid leave, with 'odd' men covering the duties, 'but such days were few and far between'.[2] Not surprisingly in view of these hours, earnings were higher than those of the average worker, with conductors able to earn between £4 and £5 a week, although the average appears to have been between 35s. and £2. At this time, an unskilled worker received an average of £1 a week and a skilled worker 30s.

The fact that London omnibus crews were 'among the highest-paid sections of the working classes'[3] had its drawbacks: management could afford to be selective in recruitment and strict in discipline. The General Manager of the London General Omnibus Company (LGOC), by far the largest company, remarked in 1877 that when 'we want six conductors, we probably have sixty or eighty candidates.'[4] Crews were expected to contribute to a fund to cover accidents and repairs, and fines were levied for a host of misdemeanours. The 'slightest cause for complaint ... led to instant dismissal. Omnibus crews were hired by the day and fired on the spot.'[5] Henry Hicks, later an LGOC director, claimed that some 75 per cent of conductors 'left' within a year. Further, crews were expected to dress themselves appropriately, as no uniform was provided. This entailed the purchase of a 'hard-wearing black suit';[6] for headwear, most drivers preferred a top hat, while conductors purchased bowlers.

John Atkinson, later a trade union official, claimed that upon the formation of the union in 1889

> most of the companies gave the men better conditions of labour and the inspectors ... treated the men with more civility and altogether better than they did previous to any union being formed and furthermore the system that had been in vogue of fining the men excessive fines was practically abolished from the first agitation.[7]

It would seem, however, that many of the companies referred to were tram companies, and that the impact of the new union on omnibus crews was minimal.

Nevertheless, the LGOC men felt sufficiently confident to enter into a major dispute when, in 1891, their employer decided to introduce ticket machines. For some time, the LGOC had been concerned about the proportion of takings being pocketed by conductors. For their part, the conductors looked upon the practice as traditional – and it was, in fact, inherited from the coaching era. The company too had been aware of the practice for many years, and turned a blind eye to it. Although conductors could be sacked for low takings, the company knew the approximate earnings of each route and if a conductor collected more than this 'nothing was said if he pocketed some of the difference'.[8] Even after the London Road Car Company (LRCC), the LGOC's chief rival, had introduced ticket machines, the LGOC's managing director A.G. Church held back.

Church retired in February 1891, and three months later the machines were introduced. In recognition of the fact that the crews' earnings would suffer, the Company increased the driver's wage from 6s. to 7s. per day and that of conductors with less than three years' service to 4s. 6d., rising to 5s. thereafter. The introduction of the machines, however, provided the new union with the opportunity to air some long-held grievances.

In the first week of June a late night mass meeting of between 3,000 and 4,000 LGOC men was held at Fulham Town Hall, with Sutherst in the chair. Sutherst complained that many of the men were being worked fifteen or even twenty hours a day. Their demands were for a twelve-hour day, one clear day off every fortnight, a week's notice for dismissal, the abolition of stoppages for accidents and a daily wage of 8s. for drivers, 6s. for conductors and 5s. for horse-keepers and washers.

The meeting heard that the LRCC had been willing to concede the twelve-hour day a year earlier had the LGOC also been agreeable to its implementation. It was resolved that a strike should commence from midnight on Friday if the demands were not met.

> Great excitement prevailed during the whole meeting, and speeches were frequently interrupted with snatches of song. Brakes and private 'buses conveyed the men to their different districts of London in broad daylight.[9]

The following night at midnight, a further meeting was held at the Great Assembly Hall, Mile End Road.

> When Mr Sutherst, who presided, asked: 'Are you determined to see that no 'buses leave the yard if you do strike?' hats were flung in the air, and the men cheered wildly for several minutes. Such a spirit exists now as has never been roused amongst the men before, and if they strike whilst the iron is hot they stand to win. It is reported that the Commissioner of Police has expressed his readiness to provide 'temporary licences' in the event of a strike without delay or formality; but he and the companies may rest assured that any blackleg 'buses that are about will be boycotted by all decent citizens, and will be safer indoors.[10]

Certainly, the strike appears to have been prosecuted with some determination, for as Moore records:

> Some men remained loyal to their employers, but their efforts to take their omnibuses out were frustrated by the angry mobs of strikers gathered at the stable gates. Day after day the strike dragged on, and for a week the London streets looked quite unfamiliar – devoid of the omnibuses which lend so much life to them.[11]

Crews employed by the LRCC and other companies came out in sympathy, although Tillings continued to run, that company having 'conceded Sutherst's terms'.[12] Pirate buses*

* Pirates had first appeared shortly after the formation of the LGOC in 1855. They were masters of sharp practice, going off their line of route in search of passengers, leaving no stone unturned in their efforts to maximise profits. 'The pirate,' said Moore, 'is naturally of a roving disposition, and by no means restricts himself to one route: a 'Kilburn' may be seen at Blackwall, or a 'Bayswater' at Bethnal Green ... During shopping hours, pirates are continually running to and from Oxford Circus, but it is interesting to notice that the name of their destination very rarely appears on them. 'Regent Circus' is put up instead, and the public having doubts as to where Regent Circus really is, the pirates obtain passengers for both Oxford Circus and Piccadilly Circus, and turn them out at whichever they like.'[13] Moore concluded that pirates – the 'pests of the streets of London – although

were comparatively few in numbers, and were scarcely noticed. Every day, the pirates contributed more to the strike fund, conscious that the longer the strike lasted, the more profitable it would be for them ...[15]

On the second day of the strike Sutherst met the LGOC and LRCC directors. The twelve-hour day was conceded, but at the expense of wages. The result is summarised in the following table:

	Strikers' Demands	*Employers' First Offer*	*Employers' Final Offer*
Hours	12 hours	—	12 hours
Drivers, per day	8s.	7s.	6s. 6d. after one year
Conductors, per day	6s.	5s. after 3 years	5s . after year
Horsekeepers, per day	5s.	?	5s. 6d.

The other demands were not conceded. The men remained on strike for the rest of the week, but the employers refused to improve their offer.

Sutherst admitted that the union had 'very few members' during the strike,[16] but it was only after the strike that the true weakness of its position was revealed. At the Fulham Town Hall meeting Sutherst had secured an undertaking that there would be no resumption of work until every union member was reinstated. This was not adhered to, however, and some strikers were dismissed. When the Lord Mayor made representations on their behalf he was told:

> Directors regret that the Lord Mayor's sympathy should have been devoted to men in custody for breaking the law on the one hand and those discharged for dishonesty or incapacity on the other.[17]

Scabs who had remained at work were, in contrast, awarded a gratuity of two guineas.

The main achievement of the strike – the twelve-hour day – did not last for long, for within a few months the LGOC 'allowed' some of its crews to work fifteen hours one day and nine hours the next – an early example of flexible rostering! The following year the pre-strike hours were being worked by all willing to do so in return for an extra shilling.

---

not quite as numerous as once they were, continue, practically unchecked, to defraud ladies, children, foreigners and other unsuspecting persons whom they succeed in enticing into their travelling plunder-traps.'[14]

The other successful outcome of the strike – the increase in conductors' wages – fell victim to the high rate of turnover. The qualifying period of one year meant that many conductors would never achieve the full rate. Indeed, only 607 of the 1,047 conductors employed at the time of the strike remained in service eleven months later.[18]

Some of the strikers who did not return to work attempted to form a company of their own – the London Co-operative Omnibus Company. As the name implied, this was to be a co-operative venture with all the drivers, conductors and horsekeepers involved being shareholders. It commenced operations with a single omnibus, to the front of which was attached a broom symbolising the determination of the co-operative to sweep the LGOC, the LRCC and the other companies off the road. But that

> single omnibus never had a companion, and, after a brief career, it disappeared from the roads, and was bought, it is rumoured, by one of the companies it was intended to smash.[19]

The union fared little better. Hibbs remarks that 'its short life was a useful one and it was responsible for considerable improvements in working conditions of bus and tram crews ...'[20] There appears to have been a lull in trade union activity by busworkers between the demise of Sutherst's union and the formation, in the early years of the twentieth century, of the London Bus, Tram and Motor Workers' Union.[21] The latter appears to have made little impact, however, and it was not until the formation of the London and Provincial Union of Licensed Vehicle Workers (LPU) on the eve of the First World War that London busworkers began to organise effectively.

As we have seen, Sutherst's union was formed in the watershed year of 1889. In that year the New Unionism spread all over the country and into Ireland. But many of the gains were not lasting. Even before the year was out the South Metropolitan Gas Company had spent £100,000 to smash the Gasworkers' Union and abolish the eight-hour day (the main agitational point of the time and the issue around which the union had been formed). The shipowners fought back by organising themselves into a Shipping Federation to smash the seamen's and dockers' unions. Morton and Tate write that

> By 1893 it is probably true to say that most of the 'unskilled' and general unions of 1889 were mere shadows of what they had been, and lucky to escape total annihilation.[22]

Thus, the demise of Sutherst's union was part of a general pattern of a counter-attack which was being waged by the employing class throughout industry. Indeed, the introduction of ticket machines may well have been the instrument chosen by the LGOC to test the strength of, and if possible to destroy, the new union. The company would certainly have been aware that the union would have been unable to present its basic case – the loss of 'illegal' earnings – to the public. Had the dispute lasted longer it is quite feasible that the LGOC itself would have done so. The fact that this step was not taken suggests that the employer was aware not only of the weakness of the union's position but of the possibilities for clawing back any concessions it made.

Most of the other 'new unions' recovered from the employers' counter-offensive. The fact that London busworkers did not recover for at least a decade indicates that there were special factors at work within the industry which hindered the development of trade union organisation.

The high earnings available (despite the conditions which made them possible) and the method by which they were earned would have encouraged an individualistic outlook in crews, and one which would have resisted attempts to organise for the pursuit of *collective* demands. Although 'among the highest-paid sections of the working classes', busworkers in London, in common with some sections of the traditional 'labour aristocracy', experienced an element of self-employment in their relations with the employer. Barker and Robbins deduce this from the method by which fares pocketed by conductors were apportioned, with the conductor giving a certain amount to the driver who, in turn, passed a share to the horsekeeper and the water-man (the latter in fact received nothing from the company).[23] 'To this extent, even though the proprietors paid their men a formal wage, they were, in reality, hiring out their omnibuses to them.'

No matter how defective this deduction may appear, it is important that this is how the relationship seems to have been perceived by the crews themselves and, so long as it continued to turn a blind eye to the illegal pocketing of fares, by the company. This perception would have been strengthened by the fact that crews contributed to the accident fund and bought their own working clothes. This petty-bourgeois outlook is further illustrated by the fact that some dismissed strikers formed their own company (even though this did bear the name of a co-operative); to them this would have been a logical step following their quasi self-employed status with the LGOC. Of course, some busworkers would have progressed beyond this 'false consciousness', as evidenced by the fact that one of the union's demands had been for the *abolition* of contributions to the accident fund.

Ironically, the decision of the LGOC to introduce ticket machines may well have had the long-term effect of proletarianising the conductors' views of themselves, thus removing one of the subjective obstacles to trade union organisation.

To summarise, it might be said that by the latter part of the nineteenth century, London busworkers were still looked upon (and continued to view themselves) as semi-skilled, quasi self-employed workers. To the extent that they were able to achieve relatively high earnings they had a toe-hold in the labour aristocracy. With the coming of the motor age they would achieve full aristocratic status – and permanant trade union organisation.

Notes

1. T.C. Barker and M. Robbins, *A History Of London Transport*, Vol.I, London 1975, p.283.
2. Ibid., p.280.
3. Ibid., p.279.
4. Ibid., p.280.
5. Ibid., p.281.
6. Ibid., p.279.
7. Ibid., p.284.
8. Ibid., p.278.
9. *The Trade Unionist*, 6 June 1891, quoted in *The Busman's Punch*, July 1933, p.10.
10. Ibid.
11. H.C. Moore, *Omnibuses and Cabs*, London 1902, p.112.
12. J. Hibbs, *A History of British Bus Services*, Newton Abbot, 1968, p.40.
13. Moore, op.cit., p.171.
14. Ibid., p.164.
15. Ibid., p.112.
16. Barker and Robbins, op.cit., Vol.I, p.287.
17. Ibid.
18. Ibid.
19. Ibid.
20. Hibbs, op.cit., p.40.
21. T. Cooper, *A Simple Case of Unpatriotism?*, unpublished paper, 1976, copy in possession of author.
22. A.L. Morton and G. Tate, *The British Labour Movement*, London 1979, p.206.
23. Barker and Robbins, op.cit., Vol.I, p.278.

CHAPTER TWO

The 'Red Button' Union

The capital's cabdrivers had been organised in the London Cabdrivers' Trade Union since 1894. It was this union which in 1913 absorbed the London Bus, Tram and Motor Workers' Union (or, suggests Cooper, another union derived from it[1]) and turned its hand to the organisation of London's bus and tramworkers, renaming itself the London and Provincial Union of Licensed Vehicle Workers (LPU). By the late summer of that year 9,000 out of a possible 12,000 busworkers had been recruited.[2] Over the next five years the LPU distinguished itself as a militant, highly politicised trade union.

Two questions arise here: what changes were responsible for this remarkable transformation, and why did London busworkers respond so positively to organisation by the cabdrivers when the Amalgamated Association of Tramway and Vehicle Workers (AAT) had been organising tramworkers in London (and presumably attempting to organise busworkers) for some time?

The way was paved by certain developments which had taken place within the passenger transport industry in London. In the early years of the twentieth century the horse-drawn omnibus began to be replaced by the motor bus. Not many drivers of the old horse-buses survived the transition. In 1913 only 1,098 out of a total of 4,346 in service with the LGOC had been employed by the company for more than three years; of these, it is estimated that only 502 had driven horse-buses.[3]

To a considerable extent this development in technique called forth a new, rather more skilled workforce. Certainly, at a time when motor vehicles were still something of a novelty, the driver of a motor bus would have enjoyed far greater status than his predecessor. With this would have gone a greater measure of *self*-esteem and professional pride. This greater sense of his own worth would have produced in him a readiness to defend and, where possible, to improve his working conditions and earnings. Also, of course, it is quite possible that the higher standards required for driving a motor bus would have reduced the number of serious applicants for each vacancy, thus increasing the work-force's bargaining power.

In the utterances of some LPU officials of the period there is detectable a strong vein of 'labour aristocratic' thinking. For example, there are constant references to 'the trade', giving the impression that the members (or their leaders) looked upon the occupation as being rather more than a means of earning a living. This would certainly tally with sentiment in the traditionally 'aristocratic' industries such as engineering where, important though wages and conditions were, there was also a concern for standards of workmanship and training. Again, we will see that the LPU was active in resisting wartime dilution, and it was primarily the 'aristocratic' trades which were subject to this measure. The fact that they were licensed by the Commissioner of Police would have tended to strengthen the busworkers' notion that they belonged to an élite. This point should not be pressed too far, though, because, as we have seen, such licensing was also the case with horse-bus drivers. The introduction of motor buses would, however, have increased concern for public safety and observation of the relevant laws.

All such factors which contributed to the sense of 'aristocracy' would also have fuelled the urge towards trade union organisation as a means of safeguarding status.

The motor bus had another significant effect in that it contributed to the virtual monopoly position held by the LGOC. This company, which from its foundation in the 1850s had always been by far the largest, was hesitant in its approach to the motor bus. By March 1907, it owned a mere 171 out of a total of 984 then on the road.[4] Even so, the new buses were being introduced faster than the horse-buses were being withdrawn, resulting in over-capacity. A fare-cutting war developed, and in the first half of 1907 the LGOC lost £62,679; in the year to June 1908, a gross loss of £147,253 was recorded. In 1907 the LGOC's chief rival, the London Road Car Company, made a loss of £24,077. Both companies increased their capital by just less than one-third. The LGOC Vice-Chairman told shareholders in 1907 (a year in which no dividend on ordinary shares was paid) that 'when the smash came', the company, 'which was in a better position than any other would be somewhat crippled but it would still be alive and kicking'.[5]

The smaller companies gradually went to the wall, and by 1913 Albert Stanley, the Detroit businessman who had become managing director of the LGOC (who later became Lord Ashfield), admitted that Tillings 'were the only people to retain a vestige of independence'.[6] This was due to the fact that Tillings had entered into an agreement with the LGOC in

1911 whereby the former would not run more than 150 buses. In 1912, in fact, the LGOC had merged with the Underground Electric Railway Company, which had been founded by American interests just after the turn of the century. This merger formed the basis for the monopolistic Traffic Combine which, apart from those periods which saw an upsurge of pirate competition, controlled London's passenger transport industry with the exception of the cabs and the trams operated by the London County Council and individual London boroughs.

Thus, when the LPU was founded in 1913 it found that it had, in effect, a single employer with which to negotiate for its busworkers. This obviously strengthened its position. Had the London busworkers been split, as previously, among several employers, each with its own rates of pay and conditions, those employers would have been able to play off one section of employees against another. The fact that the LGOC had gone over completely to motor buses by the time of the LPU's birth, meant also that the strike weapon acquired more power than hitherto, for the company would have been anxious to recoup its heavy capital outlay as quickly as possible.

There is a sense of historical irony in the fact that the internal combustion engine played such a large part in raising the status of London's busworkers, for half a century later it would, with the massive growth in individual car-ownership, make a considerable contribution to lowering it once again.

Discussing the outbreak of New Unionism in 1889, Engels had written that the new organisations

> were founded at a time when the faith in the eternity of the wages system was severely shaken; their founders and promoters were Socialists, either consciously or by feeling; the masses, whose adhesion gave them strength, were rough, neglected, looked down upon by the working-class aristocracy; but they had this immense advantage, that their minds were virgin soil, entirely free from the inherited respectable bourgeois prejudices which hampered the brains of the better situated 'old' unionists.[7]

While London's busworkers' place in the ranks of the aristocracy of labour would be consolidated during the short lifetime of the LPU, they were never 'aristocrats' in the traditional sense; their own New Unionism may be seen partly as a belated continuation of the developments of 1889 and, as with the dockers and gasworkers, the minds of many would have been virgin soil in which the socialists among their own ranks would sow their political seeds.

It is also possible, of course, that given the high turnover of staff during the period of conversion to motor buses many of the new drivers may have come from occupations where they had experienced trade union organisation and therefore brought with them their trade union attitudes. (Barker and Robbins record that in 1913 80 per cent of all applicants for driving jobs with the LGOC were carmen or drivers of heavy commercial vehicles.)

All members would, to a greater or lesser degree, have been influenced by the changes in the political climate which had taken place since the previous attempt at organisation. As British capitalism had moved into its imperialist stage in the last quarter of the nineteenth century it had become only too apparent that the 'boundless' expansion which had characterised the previous forty years did, after all, have bounds. As the rival capitalisms of Germany and the USA began to replace British imports with domestic goods, and then to challenge Britain on the international market, economic crises once again became deep and protracted; the Great Depression lasted, apart from brief recoveries in 1880 and 1888, from 1873 to the mid-1890s.

It was in this climate that Marxism and other socialist trends began to put down roots in the British working-class movement. Marx's daughter Eleanor, and her husband Edward Aveling, played an important part in the formation of the Gasworkers' Union and the Dockers' Union; Tom Mann and John Burns of the Marxist Social Democratic Federation were called in to assist in the development of the latter union. Apart from the Marxist organisations, moves were afoot in these years to form a mass party of the working class, based on the trade unions. At the turn of the century the Labour Representation Committee, which was to evolve into the Labour Party, was established.

Industrially, the class war was raging. The formation of new unions continued into the twentieth century. The Transport Workers' Federation was formed in 1910, presided over by the ubiquitous Tom Mann. The following year Mann was helping to rebuild the Seamen's and Firemen's Union. In Liverpool he was the chairman of the transport workers' strike committee when thousands of railway workers struck. A lock-out by the port authorities led to a general transport strike involving 80,000 workers. Then the London dockers struck. In 1912 a million miners were out.

The years 1910-14 are known as the period of 'the Great Unrest'. The spirit of revolt was everywhere, amongst all sections of the working class, including women. The suffragette movement was agitating for the vote while, during the 'Bermondsey Rising', women workers in the jam, glue and pickle factories took to the streets, forcing eighteen out of twenty factories to raise wages within three weeks.

There was, however, no political party capable of channelling this tidal wave of revolt into a force for real change. The Marxist groups turned their backs on potential support by preaching that capitalism would collapse on its own and believing that all that they had to do was to prepare the workers for the eventuality by the dissemination of socialist ideas. The Labour leaders, on the other hand, betrayed the working class by their adoption of the by-now traditional 'don't rock the boat' attitude following the first election of 1910 when, along with Irish MPs, they held the balance of power in the Commons. In its eagerness to save the Liberal government the Labour Party alienated support, thus contributing to a massive slide in its vote in the second election of that year.

This lack of a clear political direction contributed to the rise of syndicalism which, in a sense, was *anti*-political in that it believed that each industry could be taken over by its respective trade union and that socialism could be achieved by trade union action alone.

The LPU was thus formed during the height of 'the Great Unrest', at a time when Marxist and other socialist ideas had been abroad in the labour movement for almost a quarter of a century, and when the crisis of the economic system had grown deeper than ever. This climate had its inevitable effect on London busworkers. Just as Marxists had participated in the formation of the 'new unions' in 1889, it is quite likely that socialists of one trend or another assisted in the birth and development of the LPU (George Sanders, an early full-time organiser, was certainly a socialist).

The pages of the LPU journal, the *Licensed Vehicle Trades Record* (referred to hereafter as the *LVT Record*), betray an eclecticism tending to indicate that the political activists within the union were influenced more by the general climate of radical ideas than by a firm political line. Certainly, there was a regular column contributed by 'Members of the National Guilds League', and an Organiser on one occasion defined Guild Socialism as 'to get control via the Industrial Unions of all the industrial centres and to exist in relation to the State, and the key to it is the abolition of wages'.[8] More characteristic of the line of political argument, at least until the October Revolution in Russia, was an article entitled 'Socialism and the State' which appeared in the 9 January 1918 issue of the *LVT Record.* This commenced by advancing the syndicalist notion that 'the mission of the trade union is to be ready to take over production at the revolution'. The same article promised that since

> the state, in the name of the community, finds it necessary to take over an industry, we can be absolutely sure of economic progress, for state-owned

property only needs the workers to seize control of the state to be controlled democratically.

The date of this article is important, for the writer appears to have encapsulated within himself the contradictions between syndicalism and communism which, following the Russian Revolution, occurred within the politically-conscious sections of the union as a whole. It would seem that Archie Henderson, an Organiser, was under the influence of syndicalism when he claimed: 'We hope, some day, when strong enough, to be able to manage our own trade without the assistance of the profiteer.'[9] If disenchantment with the Labour leaders could be taken as a symptom of either syndicalism *or* communism, George Sanders was certainly exhibiting it in October 1917, when he wrote that:

> the EC decided to run candidates under the auspices of the so-called Labour Party ... These men we have showered money on in the past have aped the master class's habits, have got bestial and luxurious ... they have fallen so low that what little energy they possess they use in kidding the flower of the manhood of the country to go and be slaughtered.[10]

Then again, the LPU would have been influenced by its links with the Transport Workers' Federation (TWF). The union discussed affiliation to the TWF in December 1915, with the decision finally being taken 'with the approval of the branches.'[11] Later, as we shall see, the TWF was called in to assist during the wage negotiations of 1919 and 1921.

Several factors contributing to the level of organisation and militancy of London busworkers have been mentioned by other authors. Allen characterises the group as:

> excitable, volatile, and, like the dockers, group-conscious. Their conditions of work bring them together in garage and depot canteens where they can discuss grievances; the garage as a unit of organisation is compact and manageable; and there is easy and rapid communication between garages.[12]

Clegg says that at the time of the negotiations which led to the formation of the TGWU, 'there was a considerable agitation in favour of the "small union" and the benefit thereof in rapid and effective action.'[13] This 'small union' outlook would, in the years prior to 1922, have had the effect of emphasising the group-consciousness mentioned by Allen, encouraging a sense of internal solidarity.

Having identified the factors which both prepared London busworkers for organisation and contributed to their militancy, there remains the question of why the AAT not only failed to organise them in the first place but, after 1913, saw many London tramworkers desert its own ranks and join the LPU.

In 1914, the AAT had four London branches: London No.1, North-East London, South-West London and South London.[14] These branches, as their names indicated, covered geographical areas rather than specific workplaces. Possibly the desire for a London-based organisation by the busworkers told against the AAT, which had its headquarters in Manchester. A weightier consideration, however, seems to have been the lack of militancy and consistent negotiated terms achieved by the tram union in London and elsewhere. For example, the AAT's Report for 1914 reveals that while the London No.1 Branch had 'achieved improved conditions of labour ... at West Ham of 4s. per week to men only', AAT members at Leyton, East Ham, Walthamstow and Ilford had received increases of 3s.3d., 3s., 2s.6d. and 2s. respectively.

During the few years of its existence, the LPU became known as the 'red button' union, while the AAT was referred to as the 'blue button' union, and although these labels had their origin in the colours of the two unions' badges, they were not without political significance. There were frequent quarrels between the two, perhaps the most bitter of which occurred during the tram strike of 1915. By this time the LPU represented about half of all tramworkers employed by the London County Council, mainly south of the river. On 12 May it commenced a series of meetings all over London, agitating the membership over demands for a shorter spreadover (the time from signing-on to signing-off). The second meeting, at the Gaiety Theatre in Brixton, was attended by men from New Cross, where feeling was particularly high. In the next issue of the *LVT Record*, one of the men wrote:

> We have had the screws put on us for a long while ... Walking home from Brixton after a midnight mass meeting, we decided to call out the men, and at three o'clock we started. In an hour over a hundred men were out with us, and by seven o'clock the pavement was blocked with strikers. We began to feel a new sense of freedom and manliness come over us.[15]

The following day notices were posted in all LCC depots dismissing all who did not present themselves for work on 15 May. An AAT deputation visited the LCC's Chief Officer, Aubrey Llewellyn Coventry Fell, to assure him that it was purely an LPU strike, although the AAT men were becoming agitated over their wages demand. On 15 May London south of the river – the union's stronghold – was devoid of trams. That night, at a mass meeting at the Euston theatre of Varieties, the AAT men decided to join the strike.

The LPU made the strike official from the first Saturday. Despite the fact that this action was not immediately followed by the AAT, the latter's London District Secretary, C. Watson, agreed reluctantly to the formation of a Joint Strike Committee. For a week after the Euston meeting, Watson did nothing, leading Cooper to conclude that he was 'undermining the determination of the strikers'.[16] Although the AAT declared the strike official on 19 May, no strike pay was paid until 26 May.

On 22 May Fell posted a notice in all depots instructing strikers of military age to return their uniforms to the depots. Four days later, after some men had drifted back to work, he instructed depot officials to bar men of military age from resuming. Large numbers of men now returned, and on 1 June the Joint Strike Committee recommended a full return. For his part, Fell held to his threat not to re-engage men of military age, although some exceptions were made.

Tacitly admitting its dishonourable role, the AAT conducted an inquiry into the actions (or lack of them) of its London District Secretary. The LPU, on the other hand, increased its membership. Archie Henderson, an AAT Organiser, joined the LPU and 'urged all AAT members to put on the "red button" '.[17] According to Cooper, the AAT had few branches in London by the end of the year.

This episode illustrates the difference in style of the two organisations and provides a clear indication of why busworkers resisted organisation by the AAT. This must surely strengthen the possibility that there were among the busworkers (or among the cabdrivers who eventually organised them) a core of highly motivated individuals who were able to persuade their colleagues that their interests were best served by membership of a tightly-organised, militant organisation.

Ironically, the LPU's first confrontation was not with the LGOC but with Tillings. In September 1913 a dozen Tillings men were suspended for refusing to remove the union's red button from their uniforms. Although at the time the Company denied that it had any objection to union membership, this claim was shown to be a sham when, during negotiations, it refused to receive a deputation organised by the LPU. By the third week of September LGOC workers had become involved as well, and six hundred buses were off the road – although (an interesting precursor of things to come) the union's official leadership intervened in order to restrict the dispute to Tillings. After both sides had agreed to arbitration a settlement was reached whereby both companies granted recognition, although the union was prohibited from involving itself in 'questions of discipline and management'.[18] According to Barrett the union gained 2,700 members during the course of the dispute, with the result that the LPU now contained 90 per cent of all London's busworkers within its ranks.[19]

By 1918 the LPU had 20,000 members organised in 60 branches, 'some over 500 strong'.[20] This reflected developments in the trade union movement as a whole, which enjoyed one of its sharpest periods of growth during and immediately after the war. Unlike the tram branches of the AAT, the LPU's bus branches were based on 40 garages. Full-time officials were elected every two years which, in the opinion of Archie Henderson, meant that 'I can afford to ignore the bureaucrats of Gerrard Street [the LPU head office] and do what I am told by the democrats of the East End of London.'[21]

At grass-roots level power and control was diffused throughout the organisation by a system of road stewards:

> We have a shop system that devolves responsibility for a particular road. If he is on the 10 road, he collects the grievances on that road. ... Even spare men have their own steward, who will say what the men's conditions are, and how they are treated. They have a right to raise difficulties in the garages. If not satisfactorily dealt with it goes to the District Committee, which meets the Company with the District Organiser.[22]

There appears to have been a clear conception of the union as an organisation which existed to fight for the membership. Archie Henderson told the Amalgamation Conference in 1918 that the

> expenses of my 14 branches does not approach 33½ ... Our money does not go in management. We spent £72,000 in four years on strikes. I think it is the finest investment we could have made with the money.[23]

The method of the LPU's organisation obviously had a great deal to do with the level of militancy displayed by the union. We will see that the elected leadership, both the Executive Committee and the top full-time officers, were sometimes lukewarm in their support of policies decided by the membership, but that the latter succeeded on several occasions in imposing their wishes on them. In this, the rank and file were supported by the full-time Organisers, especially George Sanders and Archie Henderson. Both organisers were actively involved in the *LVT Record*, Sanders as editor for the last few years of its life. That journal was obviously an invaluable tool with which to agitate the rank and file and criticise the leadership's shortcomings. That full-time officials should play such a role may be surprising today – but, as mentioned earlier, they were *elected*, and thus sanction lay with the membership, not with the General Secretary or the EC.

Notes

1. Cooper, op.cit.
2. J.R. Barrett, *The Busman's Punch: Rank and File Organisation and Unofficial Industrial Action Among London Busmen, 1913-1937*, University of Warwick 1974, p.3.
3. Barker and Robbins, op.cit., Vol.II, p.314.
4. Ibid., p.133.
5. *Railway Times*, 7 September 1907, quoted in ibid., p.135.
6. In his evidence to the Select Committee on Motor Traffic, 1913, ibid., p.181.
7. Letter to Sorge, 12 December 1889, quoted in Morton and Tate, op.cit., pp.194-5.
8. Ben Smith, quoted in 'Report of the Amalgamation Conference Between the Executive Councils of the London and Provincial Union of Licensed Vehicle Workers and the Amalgamated Association of Tramway and Vehicle Workers Held at Secular Hall, Humberston Gate, Leicester on the 30th and 31st January and 1st and 2nd February, 1918. Also Adjourned Meeting Held on 26th and 27th February, 1918.' Hereafter, this will be referred as simply '1918 Amalgamation Report'.
9. *LVT Record*, 25 October 1916.
10. 'Notes by the Editor', *LVT Record*, 14 October 1917.
11. LPU Annual Report, 1916.
12. V.L. Allen, *Trade Union Leadership*, London 1957, p.57.
13. H.A. Clegg, *Labour Relations in London Transport*, Oxford 1950, p.14.
14. AAT Annual Report, 1914.
15. Cooper, op.cit.
16. Ibid.
17. Ibid.
18. Barrett, op.cit., p.5.
19. Ibid.
20. W.J. Hammond in '1918 Amalgamation Report'.
21. Ibid.
22. Ben Smith in ibid.
23. Ibid., p.195.

CHAPTER THREE

Wages and Conditions, 1914-1919

On the eve of the First World War hours of work for London's busworkers were still extremely onerous. Although crews were paid for only nine hours a day, the total time from sign-on to sign-off (the spreadover) was between ten-and-a-half and twelve-and-a-half hours on the early shift and between eleven and thirteen hours on the late shift. The 'relief' shift, spanning both early and late shifts, was spread over fifteen or sixteen hours.[1] Wages were paid not on an hourly basis but on one of mileage. This was a constant source of grievance, for it meant that the length of the spreadover bore no necessary relationship to payment, as time spent at a terminus, for example, was not paid. Moreover, although constrained by the daily minimum payment, the mileage-rates differed for each of the LGOC's three Divisions, which meant that crews in the less congested 'A' Division would cover more mileage per day than their colleagues in the central 'C' Division.

In June 1914, the fledgling LPU signed the first-ever written agreement with the LGOC and Tillings. (Subsequently, with the exception of 1916, the two companies always negotiated common agreements with the LPU and its successors, although Tillings were notorious for straying from their provisions.) It contained several advances: for the first time staff were provided with a free uniform and, more significantly, the agreement stated that no 'contributions to the Accident Club by Drivers and Conductors shall be enforced after the 1st day of July 1914, and thereafter no cash stoppages shall be made in consequence of any accident'. Each member of staff received a travel pass. A small area of control was ceded by the companies in that all new schedules were to be received by the union's schedules steward three days before they were posted for operation. If the schedule was not to the men's liking, the local union representative could, within seven days, request a meeting with the Company.

The main provisions of the agreement are, along with those of 1916 and 1919, summarised in the table on page 37. It will be seen that, as

Features of Agreements Negotiated by the LPU, 1914, 1916 and 1919

Year	*Drivers' Wages*	*Conductors' Wages*	*Spare Drivers' Wages*	*Spare Conductors' Wages*	*Spreadover Maximum*	*Spreadover Alliance*	*Paid Holidays*	*Overtime Rate*	*Working Week*	*Maximim Time on Duty*	*Minimum Meal Relief*
1914	6s. 8d. per minimum, but based on mileage, with varying rates for each of three Divisions.	5s. 8d. per minimum, with same conditions as drivers.	Weekly minimum of 30s. if standing by for up to 4 hours each day.	Weekly minimum of 25s. if standing by for up to 4 hours each day.	None	1s. for each daily duty with a spread-over in excess of 12 hours.	None	Time-and-a-quarter	Six days; working week based on hours not specified.	None	Not specified
1916	7s. per day, with conditions as in 1914.	6s. per day, with conditions as in 1914.	Not available (n.a.)	n.a.	14 hours, 20 20 minutes on some duties, 15 hours, 10 minutes on others.	1s. for each daily duty with a spreadover in excess of 12 hours.	n.a.	n.a.	As above.	None	Not less than 1 hour for dinner; approx. 30 minutes for tea. 2½ hours break for duties over 15 hours.
1919	56s. per week, plus 34s. 'war wage'. Mileage system abolished.	44s. per week, plus 34s. 'war wage'. Mileage system abolished.	Guaranteed week of 42 hours (35 for women), based on drivers' wages.	Guaranteed week of 42 hours (35 for women), based on conductors' wages.	10 hours, with an average of 9 hours.	None	6 days	Time-and-a-quarter for first two hours over 48, time-and-a-half thereafter.	Six days, based on 48 hours.	None, but constrained by maximum spreadover of 10 hours.	From 20 to 40 minutes.

regards hours of work, much remained to be done. Perhaps the most important thing about the agreement was the fact that it had been signed. The companies had recognised that they could no longer impose conditions on their work-force, but that these would have to be negotiated with the union. The actual terms of the agreement were probably seen by the LPU (and were certainly seen as such by the membership) as a starting-point upon which improvements could be made.

Speaking of the 1916 agreement the 22nd Annual Report of the LPU states that:

> We were successful in fixing up an agreement with the LGOC which embodied practically all the concessions of the former agreement, together with certain additions, and we have endeavoured to get similar conditions from Messrs. Tillings, Ltd. They were reluctant, however, to conform to our request, and ultimately agreed to go to arbitration.

The fact that Tillings resisted this agreement would seem to testify to the fact that it did, indeed, embody 'certain additions'. The rank and file, however, were of the opinion that it was they, and not the agreement, which had been 'fixed up'. Their grievances arose from the intensification of labour due to wartime conditions.

As will be seen in the table on page 37, the agreement permitted a maximum spreadover of fifteen hours ten minutes. A crew working such a duty were entitled to a minimum of two-and-a-half hours meal-relief between 'spells' of duty, but this meant that they could still find themselves in charge of the vehicle for twelve-and-a-half hours. Another aspect of the agreement which grated on the increasingly militant sensibilities of London busworkers was the fact that it contained a provision for compulsory arbitration.

Since the formation of the LPU, there had been a degree of tension between the leadership and the busmen. As early as November 1913, Alfred 'Tich' Smith, the union's President, had complained after a schedules dispute that the membership's attitude was 'not a loyal one'.[2] He went on to describe his own model of industrial relations thus:

> If the company issues an order or regulation that, in the opinion and judgement of the drivers and conductors is of an unsatisfactory nature, their duty as trade unionists is very clear: they must obey it and at the same time report the matter at once to us ... if you are going to take steps such as were suggested at some of the garages last week, you not only do an injury to yourselves, but make the position for us much more difficult to handle.[3]

As Ernest Bevin and Arthur Deakin were to discover in later years, any trade union leader who expected London busworkers to conform to such an approach would be in for a few sleepless nights, for as Barrett points out, the busworkers had discovered that

> the 'frontier' of job control was actually at the garage level [and] the crucial problems of scheduling and discipline had to be dealt with on the spot if the workers' collective power was not to be totally undermined.[4]

For the same reasons, Barrett might have added that, at least in the LPU days, the 'frontier' of control within the union itself also lay at garage/branch level.

The 1914 agreement itself had been the occasion for criticism of the leadership, as it apparently came nowhere near the rank-and-file demand for the nine-hour day, and it was only accepted on the third ballot. Indeed, the worse the negotiated terms, the more likely the unofficial strike: this simple dictum was to hold good for at least the next 25 years. Certainly Alfred Smith was to complain frequently of such actions throughout his period of office.

It was due to these tensions that during the First World War a Vigilance Committee was formed, and in this way London busworkers evolved a form of rank-and-file organisation for what may be called 'inner-union struggle' which was to persist for many years. George Sanders and Archie Henderson played a leading role in this Committee, whose aim it was to force progressive change within the union so that the whole organisation might prosecute the struggle against the employer (and the employing class generally) more effectively. The signing of the 1916 agreement greatly increased support for the Vigilance Committee and led, to judge from the pages of the *LVT Record*, to a state of almost open warfare within the union.

On 21 November there was a Special Delegate Meeting at the Club and Institute Hall, Clerkenwell Road, where the Executive Committee 'were absolutely overwhelmed by the flood of antagonism towards them'.[5] They sought endorsement for the practice of signing agreements without resort to the membership and were decisively defeated, with only one branch – Putney – voting for the proposal.

On 3 January 1917 E. Fairbrother wrote in the *LVT Record* that of:

> the many blunders committed by the late EC, the one that stands out is the signing of the 'Charter' ... [the increased] physical strain on the men in consequence of the intensification of their labour, i.e. darkened streets, overloading of 'buses, etc. alongside the great increase in money taken per

'bus, and at a time when there was a shortage of labour ... What have they got in the way of concessions? [An increase] out of all proportion to the increased takings and the rise in living, and the three months' notice [to terminate the contract] is a distinct advantage to the masters, enabling them to defeat us in a dispute by giving them more time to prepare.

The agreement had serious consequences. The LGOC,

emboldened by the easy way the agreement was accepted ... have since got the EC to agree to let them employ women to wash and clean the 'buses at a cheaper rate than the men, and now they are making another attack on the Inside [i.e. engineering] Staff regarding their conditions of labour. But the crowning crime or blunder was the signing of this agreement behind the backs of the members. Not even the delegates were consulted as to the advisability of signing same without putting it in front of the men, as was done with the previous Charter, although even then an attempt was made by the EC of that time to sign it without submitting it to the men, and when they did the men very wisely turned down the 13 hours spreadover that the officials wished to foist upon them.

The strength of feeling concerning the EC's actions may be gauged from George Sanders' 'Notes by the Editor' in the 20 December issue of the journal, in which he states that

In spite of the resolution at the Euston Theatre calling upon them to resign, and the proceedings at the Special Delegate Meeting, it was not, I regret to state, until violence had been threatened that they agreed to clear out.

* * *

During the First World War many employers attempted, with varying degrees of success, to 'dilute' labour, i.e. to introduce semi-skilled labour into skilled, and unskilled labour into semi-skilled, occupations. London busworkers were faced with attempts by the LGOC to introduce women workers. Such attempts, especially concerning women drivers, were resisted, as they were seen as a threat to their wages and conditions, at least in the long term.

The LPU Annual Report for 1916 records that:

As far back as October 1915 the question of female labour in the Trade caused a certain amount of uneasiness among our membership, and a resolution was received from the Telford Avenue Branch requesting us to oppose it.

The union received an assurance from Sir John Simon that 'nothing of the kind would take place', but following discussions between the

Commissioner of Police and the bus and tram companies concerning the issuing of licences to women conductors, the union felt it necessary to denounce the suggestion in a letter to the Home Secretary and the Commissioner on 25 October.

> We communicated with the companies concerned, and while protesting at the employment of women, because it was not a fit occupation for them, we were, however, if it was proved that a real shortage of labour existed, prepared to agree to their employment, subject to them doing exactly the same work, and at the same remuneration, and that their employment should be terminated at the conclusion of the war.[6]

The question was put before a series of midnight branch meetings called for the purpose. On 18 January 1916 the LGOC stated that it had exhausted every effort to secure male washers and that it was obliged to resort to female labour; the company eventually met the union's demand for women workers to receive the male rate of pay.

There seems to have been no question, at least at official levels of the union, of this policy being anti-women. Archie Henderson, replying to a critic of the policy in the *LVT Records1* on 25 October 1916, pointed out:

> *You* know that our resolution is not aimed at them but at the employer, who might, otherwise, after the war, take advantage of the glutted labour market to pit his women workers against the men coming home, and during the ensuing scramble reduce the status of the whole trade ... The underlying objection we have to women in the industry is this: We hope, some day, when strong enough, to manage our own trade in some sort of partnership with the community and without the assistance of the profiteer. If we allow our trade to be flooded with competing labour, that would weaken us.

Such objections paralleled those of the other 'aristocratic' trades: 'competing labour' threatened not only wages, etc., but 'the whole status of the trade'.

In December 1916 Ben Smith and George Sanders addressed a London District Meeting of the Transport Workers' Federation, after which it was unanimously decided to

> support the agitation against the employment of women drivers and coloured labour being introduced ... if the members of the respective unions involved are alive, we should win outright against any further dilution of our trade.[7]

On 14 February 1917 the *LVT Record* reported that the Home Secretary had agreed to issue driving licenses to women.

> With regard to omnibuses, if it is the intention of the authors to apply the licenses to them, the dangers are obvious. The power of the above ranges from 40 to 60 horsepower, and are driven continually on the heaviest traffic roads, necessitating continuous de-clutching, thus rendering the work highly strenuous and sufficient to try the strongest of men ... during the year 1916 approximately 700 persons lost their lives, and 35,000 were injured by accidents owing to the abnormal darkening of the streets, and with vehicles driven by experienced men ... We agreed to the introduction of women conductors, and they have to the extent of more than 75 per cent replaced male conductors called to the Colours.

On 8 February a protest meeting was held at the Euston Theatre, with 2,000 present. The resolution, carried by a large majority, was moved by Ben Smith:

> That this mass meeting of the licensed vehicle workers of London views with the greatest alarm the recent decision of the Home Secretary to give permission to the Commissioner of Police to grant licences to women to drive public carriages, and we hereby pledge ourselves to resist their employment at all costs, both in the interests of the licensed vehicle workers themselves and to public safety.

Although he seconded the motion, it was reported that in the *LVT Record* Archie Henderson was of the opinion that 'the members would not resist these women at all costs'. The meeting, however, 'would not have it, and he was subjected to frequent interruption ... Archie was not himself, and he can and will make a better show than he did on this occasion.' D.J. Davies, a member of the new EC, then moved that

> this meeting ... calls upon the EC to take a ballot on the question, that on the appearance of a woman upon a licensed vehicle as a driver all licensed vehicle men to cease work until she is taken off the road.[8]

The ballot was subsequently held, showing a strong majority in favour of this hard line. The 14 March issue of the *LVT Record* reported that a

> further series of midnight and special branch meetings have been held with a view to getting a further opinion of the members regarding the women drivers, and they have been as emphatic as the ballot.

The stand taken by the union had the desired effect: no women drivers were employed.

Once employed as conductors, however, women seem to have been as willing as their brothers to defend the terms negotiated by the union, and the union, in turn, proved just as willing to defend them. The Annual Delegate Meeting in 1917 agreed by a large majority to take action in defence of six men and four women at Palmers Green who had been dismissed for

> taking their buses in because they refused to be a party to the LGOC breaking the agreement, they having refused to pay them for standing by for 104 minutes, when the agreement states the maximum stand by time should be fifteen minutes ...[9]

(Standing by: 'spare' staff are employed to cover sickness, etc.; some spare staff will stand by at a garage in order to cover duties falling victim to staff absence, lateness, etc. However, what is *actually* referred to here is not stand by time, but *stand* time, i.e. periods when the bus is at a terminus, for the 1916 agreement provided a maximum of fifteen minutes for this.)

This case became entangled with the claim by the whole membership for a 10s. war bonus (during the war, all such increases were agreed by the Government's Committee on Production), and a dispute with the LGOC and Tillings over the companies' withdrawal of recognition after the union had voted to terminate the clause forbidding sympathy strikes. The whole fleet came out on strike, in violation of wartime regulations. Later, Ben Smith was to boast with regard to regulations that:

> We have had strikes in spite of [them] and none of us are in 'stir'. In the past strike they made us sign a document to the effect that we understood Clause 42 of the Defence of the Realm Act. We had the strike nevertheless.[10]

On 17 May courtesy of the Board of Trade, a settlement was reached entailing the reinstatement of the members at Palmers Green and the submission of the war bonus claim to the Committee on Production. For its part, however, the union was forced to recognise the agreement concerning sympathy strikes. In less than a month the Committee agreed a war bonus of 5s. per week for bus and tram workers.

There was just one snag: the award applied to men only.

In July the following year a similar award was made, with the women once more excluded. According to Barrett, the Committee justified this on the grounds that the equal pay principle applied only to wages, not to war bonuses awarded by the Committee.[11] If this was indeed the Committee's position, it was one lacking in consistency, for on 18 October 1917, it had agreed a 4s. award for all drivers and conductors, male and female.[12]

Despite the fact that the union had arranged a meeting with the Commitee on Production, the women struck, supported by their male colleagues. By the time the leadership was forced into recognising the strike it had spread to the South Coast, and women workers on the London underground were out, too.[13] The strike secured the inclusion of women in the Committee's awards.

There is some evidence that women, at least in some branches, entered fully into the life of the union. For example, a report from Seven Kings in the *LVT Record* of 28 November 1917 notes: 'Our meetings are continually on the increase, more so with the ladies, who are taking a great interest in the work and doings of our organisation.' Barrett notes that there was a politically-conscious minority among women conductors, one of whom signed her letters 'Bolshevik'.[14] 'Jeanny D'Arker' contributed regularly to the *LVT Record*, writing full-blooded articles on topics such as 'War and Revolution'.

All in all, London's male busworkers had no grounds for qualms about their women colleagues.

The actions taken by the LPU members during the First World War must be seen as part of the resistance which spread throughout the trade union movement as the real nature and consequence of the war became apparent, and this will be discussed in the following chapter. Thus, brave though the LPU was in disregarding the Munitions of War Act and the Defence of the Realm Act, it was not alone in doing so. A general trade union offensive, commencing during the latter stages of the war, surpassed the peak of the Great Unrest in the immediate post-war years, amid police strikes and mutinies in the armed forces. It is in this context that the great advance of the 1919 agreement must be seen.

As has been seen in the table on page 37, this agreement, which was negotiated with the assistance of the Transport Workers' Federation, saw the final abolition of the mileage system and the introduction of a maximum spreadover of ten hours – a tremendous advance which, since its loss in 1921, has never been recovered. Even so, the agreement was far from perfect as the companies were able to work staff on more than one service in one day and, if no work could be found, staff might be transferred to other garages or employed upon

> such other work as tree-cutting, special traffic or queue regulating, transfer of buses, special lorry work, taking cashiers to bank, etc., so long as such work is temporary, and does not interfere with the regular work of any other employee.

Having said this, the 1919 agreement was a milestone – one to which

London busworkers would look back fondly during the employers' offensive which, commencing in 1921, continued into the 1930s. Perhaps more importantly for our purposes, it was also the last agreement negotiated by the LPU, and thus would become associated in the minds of the rank-and-file militants with the 'red button' image.

Then, too, the agreement strengthened the busworkers' claim to 'aristocratic' status. According to Routh in 1906 bus drivers in Britain had been the second highest-paid group of semi-skilled workers, earning £93 as against an average of £72 for the whole category (and, of course, London earnings were probably higher still).[15] By 1924 London bus and tram drivers were still the second highest group, earning £190 compared to an average of £158 for the whole category.[16] During the earlier period, as we have seen, this level of earnings was achieved by extremely long hours. The abolition of the mileage system in 1919 placed considerable constraints on the companies for, due to the complexities of scheduling, it would have been impossible for six weekly duties to add up to a neat total of 48 hours. Thus, while receiving *payment* for 48 hours, London busworkers actually *worked* considerably less than this, the difference being made up by paid 'build up time'.

Thus, from 1919 onwards London busworkers were paid more, and worked shorter hours, than most other groups of semi-skilled workers. They had arrived.

Notes

1. Barker and Robbins, op.cit., Vol.I, p.314.
2. Barrett, op.cit., p.7.
3. Ibid., pp.7-8, quoting *LVT Record*, 26 November 1913.
4. Ibid., p.8.
5. *LVT Record*, 6 December 1916.
6. LPU Annual Report, 1916.
7. *LVT Record*, 20 December 1916.
8. Ibid., 28 February 1917.
9. Ibid., 16 May 1917.
10. 1918 Amalgamation Report, pp.434-5.
11. Op.cit., p.15.
12. *LVT Record*, 31 October 1917.
13. Barrett, op.cit., p.16.
14. Ibid., p.15.
15. Guy Routh, *Occupation and Pay in Great Britain, 1906-1979*, London 1980, p.106.
16. Ibid., p.107.

CHAPTER FOUR

Imperialist War and The 'Red Button' Union

During the war years there was one issue by which the political commitment and class outlook of any trade union or political organisation could be measured: the war itself.

As early as 1907 the Socialist parties affiliated to the Second International had resolved at the Stuttgart Conference to oppose militarism and war and, in the event of war breaking out, to utilise the crisis to bring about the downfall of the capitalist class in their respective countries. War was seen as the means by which the capitalist nations would attempt to effect a redivision of the world. This approach received further endorsement at the Basle Conference in 1912. But when the chips were down, it was only in Russia that this was translated into practice, and there only after three years of slaughter. In Britain, after an initial show of opposition, Labour and the majority of the trade union leaders became collaborators in the war effort. By 24 August 1914 they were calling for an 'industrial truce', in effect relaxing terms and conditions previously won by the movement so that 'their' capitalists might conduct the war more effectively.

By contrast, the LPU appears to have been opposed to the war from its very outset. Certainly by 1916 the leadership could see the war for what it really was. The Annual Report for that year commented:

> the very perspective of him who cannot see that finance, power and influence are the only parties that can benefit, as a result of the war, is indeed very dim ... in the midst of a world war, organised labour finds itself more or less impotent to withstand the encroachments of many of its treasured liberties and customs, by the higher authorities charged with the government of the country.
>
> A military and repressive atmosphere pervades the workshop and the home ...
>
> If the workers – comprising organised labour – deplore it, we feel and

claim that the remedy lay partly in their own hands prior to the outbreak of hostilities ...

The whole deplorable circumstances of the War points to the necessity of improving and internationalising the Trade Union movement, as by that means alone can an effective brake be placed upon the highly complex machinery of capitalist exploiters, and their companions in crime, the government diplomats who negotiate international strife, in order to bring about territorial aquisition, and the expansion of the commercial octopus.

Earlier, in 1915, the branches had been circulated with the request that they call special meetings to discuss the question of conscription. 'The Branches were unanimously against conscription in any form.'[1] At some stage an Anti-Conscription Committee was formed, out of which evolved the Vigilance Committee referred to earlier. Also in 1915, attempts were made to get cab drivers and bus and tram conductors placed on the list of reserved occupations, but the government's Reserved Occupations Committee refused. The union urged its members against the wearing of war badges.

The LPU gave short shrift to anyone, no matter how senior, who did not adhere to the anti-war position. Brothers Laurence Russell and H.A. Bywater, Organising Secretary and General Secretary respectively, discovered this the hard way after they enlisted in the army.

On 5 August 1914, Russell, as editor of the *LVT Record*, had written in that journal:

The workers of the world are now faced with the greatest calamity ever known in the history of civilisation. At the present moment all our Continental trains are crowded with men of various nationalities who are hurrying back to their own country to take part in the coming fight. Many of these men have been working side by side, and are on terms of the closest intimacy and friendship, and yet in a few days' time they may be shooting each other in cold blood. For what reason? Why, simply to satisfy the ambition and lust for power of the governing classes.

Russell was – initially – just as firm in the defence of workers' rights during the war. When a dispute broke out at the National Steam Car Co. in 1915, he wrote in the *LVT Record* of 3 March that this

attack on the rights of trade unionism must be resisted at all costs. We therefore look to every member to do his part by supporting the 300 men who are fighting in the interests of all licensed vehicle workers to enjoy a living wage.

A fortnight later he wrote:

> It is more than possible that the dispute may continue, but, however long the fight may last, we shall never be a party to lowering the standard rates of wages, which have only been obtained through the unity of the busmen of London.

Less than a month later, Russell was attested at the War Office

> and a week or two after is holding recruiting meetings as a full-blown Sergeant, and appealing to the men who were locked out and other of our members to join the army, which naturally had the effect of weakening the men's forces.[2]

By 31 January 1917, Sergeant Russell's degeneration had progressed so far that he was complaining in a letter to the *LVT Record* (now edited by the progressive George Sanders) that: 'We find the *Record* being used for the purpose of most grossly insulting employers of labour with whom we have agreements.'

If the members detected a note of sour grapes in Brother Russell's tone at this stage, they also knew the reason for it.

At the 1915 Annual Delegate Meeting a resolution was passed calling for nomination papers to be issued for the posts occupied by the two defectors. A. 'Tich' Smith, now not only President but also acting General Secretary, and Ben Smith, acting Organising Secretary, then resigned on 2 November. Smith explained that 'loyalty to his comrades, viz., Messrs Bywater and Russell, would not permit of him holding office after the passing of such a resolution.'[3] In similar vein, Ben Smith argued that he 'could not approach the employers of labour to keep open the positions of men serving in the forces, in face of this resolution'.[4]

The EC then refused to implement the ADM decision, assuring the Smiths that the positions of Bywater and Russell would be kept open, following which the former withdrew their resignations. A Special Delegate Conference in April 1916 decided nevertheless that the positions should be filled at the elections in May. In these elections Bywater and Russell were returned, and on 10 June the EC granted them leave of absence for the duration of the war. This was subsequently rescinded, whereupon 'Tich' Smith tendered his resignation yet again.

A Special General Meeting was called for 12 November at the Euston Theatre to discuss the resignation. Despite the fact that 12,000 leaflets had been distributed, only 400 members turned up. Furthermore, a good proportion of these seem to have been cabdrivers, and of these a majority were owner-drivers. This raises the possibility that the busworkers had attempted to organise a boycott. Certainly, the theatre received a telephone call just before the meeting saying that it had been cancelled. A further possibility is that the busmen had abstained from the ballot held earlier in large numbers, possibly on the grounds that the nominations of Russell and Bywater were improper. 'Tich' was himself an old cabdriver. In his address he levelled criticism at the Vigilance Committee, although as George Sanders commented in his report of the meeting,

> it is hardly good taste to chide members for meeting together for what they consider is the best interests of the society (especially when they invite all members to attend their meetings) when 'Titch' himself engineered a 'private and confidential' committee at the time of the last election ...[5]

Significantly, it was the secretary of the Owner-Drivers' Cab Section, a man named Blundy, who moved the motion calling upon the EC to rescind its own motion accepting the resignation and requesting Smith to reoccupy the position of President. D.J. Davies then moved an addendum calling upon the EC to resign. Both were carried, with one vote against. For good measure the meeting then went on to pass a resolution condemning the Vigilance Committee.

According to Sanders,

> the meeting reflected no credit on the society – the poor attendance, the interruptions, the interjections about a 'busmen's union, which I hope the 'busmen are too sensible to notice, as they are only the opinions of a very few of our taxi members.

From this it would seem that the anti-progressive tenor of the meeting reflected the petty-proprietorial outlook of a very vocal group of owner-drivers.

The final position emerged at the Special Delegate Meeting held at the Club and Institute Hall, Clerkenwell Road, on 21 November 1916, where, as stated earlier, the EC was 'absolutely overwhelmed by the flood of antagonism displayed towards them'. Right from the start things went badly for the EC. When they attempted to place one of their own number in the chair, threatening to close the meeting unless he was allowed to preside, 'almost riotous protests from practically every delegate present, brought his career to a speedy but quite conclusive termination'.[6] George Sanders was elected from the floor to chair the meeting. An attempt to have Organisers appointed by the EC rather than elected by the membership was defeated by 17,400 votes to 300. When the EC then recommended that the nominations of Bywater and Russell be considered valid, they were defeated by 13,000 to 5,000. 'Tich' Smith and Ben Smith were then returned as General Secretary and Organising Secretary and the office of President was abolished. In securing the abolition of the post of President the membership were displaying a keen sense of tactics, for this had been 'Tich' Smith's position; by electing him as General Secretary they were guarding against the possibility of him continuing to campaign for the return of Bywater to that position!

With the ousting of Bywater and Russell the LPU's anti-war position was confirmed. This policy appears to have been much firmer, and rather more internationalist in tone, than elsewhere in the labour movement. On 3 January 1917 the *LVT Record* went as far as publishing a report from Germany concerning German transport workers:

> During the first eighteen months of the war in Germany, the labour organisations and, not least, the trade unions, underwent a severe time of trial. We are able to state, however, with great joy and satisfaction, that the trade unions in general, and the German Transport Workers' Union in particular, splendidly proved their power of resistance ...
>
> The German Union of Transport Workers endeavoured to steer clear of all chauvinist and bellicose machinations, to which, unfortunately, so many sister unions appear to have fallen victim.

Upon the introduction of conscription some members were willing to stand by their principles. Private R. Tipping wrote from the guard-room cells at Warminster:

> I am sending greetings to all my comrades, both men and women, in the Licensed Vehicle Workers' Union. I am awaiting trial by District Court Martial charged with being a deserter from something which I refused to join, and that after the Hammersmith Tribunal had agreed that I had proved to them the sincerity of my beliefs ... Whatever my sentence, I will never become a soldier to capitalism.[7]

Reuben Tipping was subsequently sent to Dartmoor, from where he wrote on 19 September 1917: 'I must tell you that I have been afraid of receiving news of your arrest under the Defence of the Realm Act for your outspokenness in the journal ...'

The anti-war position of the LPU, and certainly some of its members, was far from being a pacifist one. 'Hendonian' wrote in the 18 April 1917 issue of the journal that:

> We are being enslaved by bureaucracy; we are daily being crushed by the heel of a vile tyranny that has wiped out nations and peoples, and has stifled

the word liberty in their mouths ... Our brothers in Ireland have for years been awake to the ever-growing tentacles of this vile octopus, whose birthplace is London, and they have kept his tentacles well cut so that he may not suck their blood. Well done the Irish! ... Our Russian brothers have found their strength; and what strength it is! How glorious their victory! The tyrant rulers pulled from their pedestals, and the people's own elect established thereon in a few days.

I put it to you, what Ireland and Russia can do, are we not also capable of doing?

... There is one answer, Revolution, and then lasting peace ...

As a final word, brothers, I would say that I am a man who has seen active service in France, and therefore no milk and water pacifist. I appeal to those of my brothers who possess time, money and influence to organise themselves for the coming war, which must be soon and short.

Like Russia, like Britain. Stand firm, we cannot fail!

Another member, serving on a submarine in Russian waters, seems to have attempted to pick up a little practical knowledge to further this aim:

I'm trying to get in touch with some of the people here to find out how their revolution was engineered ... it certainly would be something if I could get the idea, eh?[8]

Members serving in the forces (those who took the trouble to write to the journal, at least) were just as strong in their opposition to the war and in their desire for social change as those who went to prison. Replying to a member of the Battersea branch in September 1917, T.A. Dance wondered, as he wrote from France:

what the 'heads' will think when they know the true feeling that exists today among the Tommies out here. I reckon that Ticehurst of the Dogs' Home would have a shock. So he thinks that the *Record* is too much of a revolutionary character, does he? Well, the boys out here are just thirsting for a revolution in dear old Blighty. We out here don't intend to come back to the old conditions of life ...

The two reactions to the events in Russia mentioned above relate to the February Revolution, when the liberal-capitalist forces gained control, deposing tsarism. When the alliance of workers and peasants led by Lenin and the Bolsheviks swept to power in October, however, those writing for the LPU's journal appeared undismayed by the sharp about-face executed by the capitalist press:

> The news of the Russian Revolution was hailed with delight by our capitalist press when it was thought that it was a revolt against pro-Germanism. They hailed it as a great democratic movement for freedom until it was really discovered that this was true, then their attitude changed to one of fear, lest the workers of the world took the example set by the Russian peasants.[9]

It is impossible to gauge how far the strong anti-war and pro-socialist policies of the *LVT Record* were shared by the membership. One indicator would be the circulation of the journal, given that its political content was (at least under the editorship of George Sanders) substantial. We know that in 1917 the Battersea branch was taking 250 copies each fortnight and that, even after the price was doubled from 1d. to 2d., Merton actually succeeded in increasing its sales.[10] As most branches enjoyed 100 per cent membership it may thus be assumed that several thousand copies were sold each fortnight. This would certainly indicate that a substantial proportion of the membership maintained a strong interest in the politics of the journal.

It might be argued that the strong class line of the journal merely reflected the views of Sanders and Henderson. This hardly stands up, however, because the LPU's Annual Reports reveal a similar left-wing attitude. Had the membership found the politics of Sanders and Henderson objectionable they surely would not have re-elected them to their positions. Moreover, after 1917 it was the official policy of the union to politicise the membership. A motion carried by an overwhelming majority at that year's Annual Delegate Meeting instructed 'the EC to utilise the Political Levy Fund for the purpose of educating the members up to their class position'.[11]

When it came to translating the anti-war policies into action, however, the results were sometimes disappointing – at least to regular columnist 'Jeanny D'Arker' who in a piece entitled 'War and Revolution' in the issue of 14 October 1917 asked:

> What do you care? I submit to you that you do not care! Week after week you meet to discuss trivialities ... The state has sapped from you your manhood; its laws have brutalised you and made you callous and frightfully timid. You have stood by and seen hundreds torn from their wives – yea, and from their children. Yes, you have protested at your branch meetings, which are safe places ... Some of you are already equipped for battle; what keeps you back?

This slightly hysterical reproof notwithstanding, it may be said that by the end of the war there had been established within the 'red button' union a political culture which was quite firmly anti-capitalist. To a certain extent this would have been due to the developments within the working-class movement mentioned earlier, and to the small, tightly-organised nature of the union. The efforts of George Sanders would have made a considerable contribution to the development of such a culture, especially after he began editing the *LVT Record*. And the war itself would have opened the eyes of many to the real nature of capitalism.

Thus, London busworkers as an organised group achieved an 'aristocratic' status and a strong political identity virtually simultaneously. To a large extent, of course, industrial militancy and political radicalism would have fed off each other, especially during the war, when trade union rights were under *political* attack. The combination of these two characteristics would provide many a headache for trade union leaders during the following two decades when, first within the United Vehicle Workers and then within the Transport and General Workers' Union, London busworkers found themselves in entirely different circumstances.

Notes

1. LPU Annual Report, 1916.
2. *LVT Record*, 14 February 1917.
3. LPU Annual Report, 1916.
4. Ibid.
5. *LVT Record*, 22 November 1916.
6. Ibid., 6 December 1916.
7. Ibid., 2 May 1917.
8. Ibid., 31 July 1917.
9. 'T.U.G.' (a serviceman on leave), ibid., 23 January 1918.
10. Ibid., 17 October 1917.
11. Ibid., 16 May 1917.

CHAPTER FIVE

Interregnum: From LPU to UVW

In a brief period the 'red button' union had succeeded in creating a trade union and political culture among London busworkers that made it 'one of the most militant unions in the country'.[1] The Amalgamated Association of Tramway and Vehicle Workers (AAT), on the other hand, was, as we have seen, not only renowned for its moderation but was frequently at loggerheads with the LPU. Nevertheless, by 1918 the two were talking of amalgamation.

At the Amalgamation Conference in Leicester in early 1918 two of the major points of contention were the site of the head office (London or Manchester?) and the question of full-time officials (should they be elected, as in the LPU, or appointed, as in the AAT?). On the latter point the LPU was willing to compromise to the extent of having elections every three years. But Stanley Hirst, the AAT General Secretary, was of the opinion that 'the man who is elected for a short notice has to make as many friends as he can to retain his position. The man who runs straight makes enemies.'[2] It was during this debate that Archie Henderson, until 1915 an AAT Organiser himself, made his memorable rejoinder: 'I can afford to ignore the bureaucrats of Gerrard Street and do what I am told by the democrats in the East end of London.' According to Henderson, who was in a position to know, hundreds of LPU members 'have been members of the AAT and have experienced your methods and ours. They are absolutely wedded to our system.' Ben Smith was adamant that 'our members when they see in the Rules that the officials shall be permanent there will be no amalgamation.' Finally, it was agreed that the question be put to the members in a ballot.[3]

In 1919 a new pressure group, the Rank and File Committee, was formed when the EC of the LPU amended a Whitley Council scheme which had been rejected by ballot in late 1918 and forced it through a hastily-convened Special Delegate Meeting.[4] The rank and File Committee took the extreme step of taking the EC to court over the issue, as a result of which London busworkers were excluded from the scheme. The unofficial body made little progress with its demand for recallable officials, however. Although the Committee was short-lived, it was an augury of future developments among London busworkers and 'provided a base of support for the Minority Movement ...' which would arise in the 1920s.[5]

The amalgamation of the 'red button' and 'blue button' unions went ahead in 1920. The new organisation was to be known as the United Vehicle Workers, but although the two were united in organisational terms, they were far from united in belief.

Corfield points out that the LPU had always had its eye on a national organisation for all passenger transport workers and that the unfortunate experience of the 1915 tram strike had 'emphasised the need for amalgamation'.[6] This contradiction between the organisational needs of passenger workers and the fierce independence of London busworkers was to prove a constant source of tension in coming years. In the UVW's First Annual Report, Stanley Hirst, now General Secretary of the new union, remarked that the amalgamation:

> brought together men holding opinions and ideas which varied considerably. Whether the best ideas have prevailed is purely a matter of opinion, and I leave that for the members to decide for themselves.
>
> Occasionally, I have found, to my regret, that although we are now one union, there is still a tendency to discuss certain matters in terms of 'reds' and 'blues'.

On another occasion Hirst stated the problem with rather more frankness by way of the following allegory:

> A husband claimed that he had never quarelled with his wife. Whenever anything occurred upon which they could not agree they compromised. For example, in choosing the wallpaper for their drawing-room he selected red, his wife blue, but after a short argument they compromised. When asked what colour they compromised upon the man replied 'blue'.[7]

During the amalgamation negotiations of 1918 the size of the LPU had been 24,000, as against the AAT's 28,000. By the end of 1919, the AAT was claiming 56,979 members, although this figure probably included members still in the armed forces.[8] The UVW started life the following year with 109,425 members. The discrepancy of some 28,000 members would have been accounted for by the fact that a third organisation, the Lorrymen's Union, was included in the amalgamation and that the LPU benefited from the general trend towards growth of union membership.

Nevertheless, London busworkers were clearly outnumbered in the new union. Just months previously they had had their own union, of which many would have been founder-members. Now their proud achievement, the 'red button', was no more and they were part of an organisation dominated by the lower-paid tramworkers. Within the UVW there seemed to be a deliberate policy of moving the old 'red button' officials away from their base of support. George Sanders was promoted to National Organising Secretary of the Omnibus Section; Charles Carter was made Financial Secretary; Ben Smith and Archie Henderson were shunted into the Commercial Section, the former as National Organising Secretary and the latter as National Organiser; 'Tich' Smith was made Parliamentary Secretary. On the other hand Stanley Hirst, the lacklustre leader of the AAT, was made General Secretary. John Cliff, who had been Chairman of the AAT's Executive Council for six years, was now Joint Secretary of the newly-formed Joint Industrial Council for the tramway industry. In later years he was to swiftly climb the promotion ladder within the TGWU. Thus, while the old 'red button' men were being moved away, the 'blue button' men appear to have gained control of the union nationally and would, in later years, be moved into positions giving them responsibility for the London Bus Section.

The LPU was successful in securing the location of the new UVW head office in London, but the old LPU practice of opening the doors to rank-and-file members during EC meetings was discontinued, and the office at Emperor's Gate was soon dubbed 'Traitor's Gate' by an increasingly cynical London membership. When a group of busworkers attempted to enter an EC meeting in 1920 Hirst took the unheard-of step of calling the police.[9]

Despite these negative developments the official journal, that great source of strength to the LPU, survived the amalgamation, appearing now as simply *The Record.* (As the TGWU journal was also to bear this name, the UVW journal will be referred to in these pages as the *UVW Record.*) It seems to have lost none of its freedom under the editorship of J. Gill. As before, the policy was to encourage contributions from the membership. Revolutionary politics continued to receive a generous airing although, as mentioned earlier, these now tended to move away from syndicalism towards Communism.

In 1921, the UVW recorded that:

> ... trade unionism at the present moment is at the lowest ebb it has ever been in our lifetime. Owing to various causes we find that the master class holds

the winning hand at the moment. On every hand we find that the workers are being beaten on the industrial field, mainly owing to the fact of faulty machinery, and also to the weaklings in our midst. Most of the large unions are negotiating or have agreed to decreases in wages without any effective protest. These various sections that are submitting to these reductions must have a bearing on the sections that are willing to fight. The miners have just been beaten after a most heroic struggle, and during the past two years the workers have been gradually receding from the position they held during the war.[10]

In 1919, when the LPU had negotiated its last agreement, unemployment had stood at a mere 2.4 per cent and wages and earnings (taking 1906-1910 as the base-line of 100) had risen to 223-8. Two years later unemployment reached 16.6 per cent as the post-war restocking boom came to an end.[11] In 1919 the whole labour movement had been on the offensive, with strikes rolling across the country; on Clydeside the authorities had feared a rising. In 1921 the employers staged their counter-offensive.

By February 1921 unemployment had passed the one million mark. The mine-owners seized their opportunity and demanded a wage-cut of 20 per cent on the 1914 level. The miners called upon their partners in the Triple Alliance (the railwaymen and the Transport Workers' Federation, of which the UVW was a member), and a transport strike was called for 12 April. Lloyd George's government invoked the Emergency Powers Act, causing the *UVW Record* of 13 April to report that:

The Triple Alliance declared a strike and Mr George declared a state of emergency, called out the Army and the Navy, the Air Force, and the Middle Classes Union. Once again the 'good old country' required saving, and the capitalist press made the astonishing discovery that those who quite recently it denounced as 'won't-works' and 'scallywags' were jolly fine, law-abiding patriotic citizens, literally falling over one another to ensure that the food supply, from which they have been barred since they have been out of work, should still go to the people who have been getting it all the time. A learned judge binds an offender over because he thinks he may be wanted to help in the 'saving'. The London parks are armed camps, and three times three round the streets dash stage batteries of artillery, while lumbering up and down Oxford Street, twice daily and one performance in the evening, are the various breeds of tanks.

This piece in 'Editorial Notes' concluded that:

it is clear that on the question of national agreements and the threatened wage reductions, the miners' cause is our cause. If, by the time this appears, a

> Triple Alliance strike is in progress, every member of the UVW will do his duty and stand by his class.

This was not to be. Panicking, the Triple Alliance leaders persuaded the Miners' Federation of Great Britain to talk to the government on 12 April, postponing the strike until Friday the 15th. Then, using as a pretext a loose statement made by Frank Hodges, the miners' Secretary, which gave the impression that a settlement had been reached, the Alliance called off the strike. The 27 April issue of the *UVW Record* advanced the view that the facts 'build up a case which clearly and irrefutably show that our leaders, from the beginning of the crisis, were seeking every means to call the strike off'. The miners were betrayed. The employers took this as a signal for pressing their attack throughout industry, and by the end of the year six million workers had suffered wage-cuts averaging 8s. a week. 15 April 1921 entered labour history as 'Black Friday'.

Significantly, the response of the London busworkers to the impending strike had been to organise support by unofficial means, thereby indicating – even before the betrayal – their distrust of the UVW leadership. Along with rank-and-filers from other unions during the first fortnight of April they established the South East District Vigilance Committee, which planned picketing and agitated in the branches. A series of late-night mass meetings were called officially by the UVW for the night of 14/15 April, only to be called off at almost literally the last minute, leaving thousands of busworkers waiting in the rain. Furious, the South East District Vigilance Committee attracted 10,000 members to a protest meeting, from which a deputation was despatched to the UVW head office.[12] On arrival they occupied the building and locked out the officials. Predictably, the police were called once more, but the protesters insisted that all they were guilty of was the occupation of their own property.[13]

As a result of the leadership's involvement in Black Friday, the branches at Merton, Old Kent Road and Nunhead withheld their contributions and 'so explosive was the situation that the United Vehicle Workers did not dare to discipline them outright'. At the Sheffield Annual Conference it became apparent that a major revolt would occur unless the leadership treated the matter tactfully, and George Sanders warned of the dangers involved in a breakaway.[14]

It was in the climate created by the miners' defeat that the LGOC and Tillings demanded amendments to the 1919 agreement. Originally they posted notices to the effect that a wage-cut of 3s. per week would operate from October 1921, but these were withdrawn following the intervention of the Transport Workers' Federation.

Nevertheless, concessions were wrung out of the busworkers. The maximum spreadover of ten hours, the jewel in the crown of the 1919 agreement, was swept aside for 25 per cent of all duties; the new maximum was twelve hours, although an allowance of 12. 6d. was agreed for all duties with a spreadover in excess of ten hours. After 4 April 1922, wages would be cut by a farthing per hour for drivers and one-eighth of a penny for conductors for every five points the government's cost of living index fell below 135. If the index fell below 85 both grades would lose a farthing per hour for each subsequent fall of five points until the index fell to 70.

Surprisingly, the agreement contained some improvements. Holiday entitlement was increased from six days to eight and the disciplinary system was redrawn to give the membership well-defined rights. During negotiations, the union requested that the companies ensure that all new entrants join the UVW.

'You tell them now that they have to be members of the Union,' George Sanders pointed out.

'Yes,' replied George Shave, the LGOC's Operating Manager, 'but we cannot put it in an agreement. We have done that, and Lord Ashfield has told you that it is being carried out; but I do not want to put it in the Agreement. There is no need to emphasise it.'

The eventual agreement permitted the union to have collectors 'within the shelter of the garages' provided that they were employees of the companies and that 'the privilege is not abused'.

The 1921 agreement was not as bad as it might have been. The fact that it contained improvements at a time when employers all over the country were tearing up collective agreements can only be seen as a testimony to the strength of London's busworkers. 'Suffice it to say,' Stanley Hirst wrote in the UVW's Annual Report for 1921, 'that by the strength of our organisation we were able to maintain most of what had been previously won, and in comparison with employees in other trades, our members generally are favourably situated.'

While it must be borne in mind that the agreement was hardly a victory, Hirst's estimation seems about right. At the time many London busworkers saw it as a further betrayal, further colouring their reaction to the recent amalgamation. More importantly, it was to greatly influence their attitude to the proposed amalgamation into the Transport and General Workers' Union.

Notes

1. Tony Corfield, 'The History of the Union', *The Record*, July 1963.
2. 1918 Amalgamation Report.
3. Ibid.
4. Barrett, op.cit., p.28.
5. Ibid.
6. Corfield, op.cit.
7. Corfield, op.cit., August 1963.
8. AAT Annual Report, 1919.
9. Corfield, op.cit., August 1963.
10. 'Proposed Modification To The Existing Agreement Between the London Bus Companies and the United Vehicle Workers', UVW, 1920.
11. Routh, op.cit., p.134.
12. Barrett, op.cit., pp.30-1.
13. Corfield, op.cit., August 1963.
14. Ibid.

PART TWO

The Strains of Amalgamation

CHAPTER SIX

Amalgamation

For a decade various attempts had been made to bring some semblance of unity to the transport unions. As we have seen, the National Transport Workers' Federation had been formed in 1910. Two years later the TWF joined the National Union of Railwaymen and the Miners' Federation to form the Triple Alliance. However, the TWF had its limitations in that decisions taken by its General Council were not binding on the constituent unions. In March 1920 the attempt to form one large transport union began. The leading figure behind these efforts was Ernest Bevin.

Born in 1881, Bevin had been a carter for a number of firms and, briefly, a tram conductor, before joining the Dockers' Union in 1910. He quickly set up a carmen's branch on the Bristol Docks, becoming its first chairman. The following year he became a full-time official at the Bristol office of the Dockers' Union, and by 1914 he was the National Organiser. By the time he commenced the task of hammering together the organisation which was to become the TGWU Bevin was Assistant General Secretary of his own union.

The two unions which began the amalgamation process were Bevin's own and the National Union of Dock Labourers. They formed an amalgamation committee, making Bevin the provisional secretary of the new organisation. The first meeting convened by the committee, held at Anderton's Hotel, Fleet Street, on 18 August 1920, was attended by 59 delegates from 13 trade unions. Here the new union's trade group and territorial structure was agreed. This allowed the affairs of each trade group (such as dockers, passenger transport workers, etc.) to be run, subject to approval by the General Executive Council, by trade group committees. The country was divided into Areas (now called Regions), with the local affairs of all trade groups within each Area being conducted by an Area Committee. The General Executive Council would comprise some members elected by the whole membership within each Area and others elected from each of the National Trade Group Committees.

The amalgamation scheme was approved in December 1920, and over half a million ballot papers were sent out. By the middle of March 1921 the UVW had secured a majority for amalgamation. This may have been due in large part to the tramworkers, who according to Corfield were impressed by Bevin's successful presentation of their case at a Court of Inquiry concerning wages in the same year.[1] The new union was assured of 362,000 members and a delegate conference was called at the Venetian Rooms of the St Pancras Hotel on 11 May. Stanley Hirst was nominated for General Secretary, receiving his own union's 130,000 votes, but Bevin sailed home, having been nominated by nine of the amalgamating unions and receiving 225,000 votes. Hirst was then elected Financial Secretary.

The founding unions were:

Amalgamated Society of Watermen, Lightermen and Bargemen
Amalgamated Carters, Lorrymen and Motormen's Union
Amalgamated Association of Carters and Motormen
Associated Horsemen's Union
Dock, Wharf, Riverside and General Workers' Union
Labour Protection League
National Amalgamated Labourers' Union
National Union of Docks, Wharves and Shipping Staffs
National Union of Ships' Clerks, Grain Weighers and Coalmeters
National Union of Vehicle Workers
National Amalgamated Coal Workers' Union
National Union of Dock, Riverside and General Workers
National Union of British Fishermen
North of England Trimmers' and Teemers' Association
North of Scotland Horse and Motormen's Association
United Vehicle Workers
Belfast Breadservers' Association
Greenock Sugar Porters' Association.

Asked to give their views on the amalgamation scheme, several UVW officials did so in the *UVW Record* of 5 January 1921. The old LPU personalities all spoke in favour, although with important qualifications. Charles Carter was of the view that amalgamation, 'not only of like Unions, but of all Unions, national and then international, is the only method of keeping a check upon the inquisition of capitalism and to bring about its demise'. Ben Smith felt that, given capital's high degree of organisation, 'We must, therefore, create such a machine that will effectively resist any encroachment of our position, such a machine that will give us the power of attack.' Archie Henderson took an historical view:

> Whenever and wherever the workers fail it is because they lack power and strength. These are the keys that open the door to the promised land. The land More dreamt of, Owen slaved for, Morris pictured, Hardie died for, Smillie works for, and all good, thoughtful men hope for. Our first step to power and strength is amalgamation.

By far the longest contribution came from George Sanders. Given his consistent socialism, his following among London busworkers and the part he was to play in the British Bureau of the Red International of Labour Unions, it is worth quoting him at length.[2] He began by stating his agreement with the principle of amalgamation providing that it was not approached 'from any ulterior or underhand motive, or to foster the ambition of individuals who wish to loom large on the horizon'. This, as we shall see in a moment, was almost certainly a reference to Bevin. He continued:

> I want to state quite frankly that I should have been much more enamoured of the scheme that is now in front of the members had the National Union of Railwaymen and the Associated Locomotive and Firemen's Union (*sic*) been included in the list of Unions for the proposed amalgamation. Whether they have been approached or not I am unable to state, but at any rate if at all possible to get them in it ought to be done without delay. It appears to me that an amalgamation of transport Unions is not complete without these two bodies, and instead of rushing the present scheme every effort should be made to persuade these two Unions to come into the scheme, or if they have refused, it ought to be made quite clear to the members of the constituent Unions who are asked to support the new scheme.
>
> One more point ought to have the careful consideration of our members before voting, and that is that the officials of some of the Unions that we are asked to amalgamate with went over to the side of the capitalist class while the late war was in progress. Seeing the terrible state this country is reduced to, they may be sorry for what they have done, but there is no guarantee that in the face of a crisis they would not do exactly the same again, and as the majority of the members of these Unions probably acquiesced in their attitude, it is a point that must be looked at. It does not follow that because you ask a man a question such as: 'Are you in favour of amalgamation?' if he answers, 'Yes' it does not mean that he is in favour of amalgamating with everything and everybody. On the same principle that oil does not amalgamate with water, we ought to be assured that whatever fighting powers we may possess will not be deadened by close alliance with bodies which would stultify our efforts towards emancipation.
>
> ... If the members on looking into these questions will feel confident that our interests are guaranteed, then, of course, they will vote for this amalgamation scheme. If, on the other hand, they consider that more time

should have elapsed before the vote is taken then, of course, they will refuse to vote until such time as a proper comprehensive scheme is put in front of them, embracing the whole of the passenger and goods system.

We may take it from these overwhelming qualifications that Sanders was opposed to the scheme. There can be little doubt that one of the 'individuals who wish to loom large on the horizon' was, to Sanders' mind, Bevin himself. Later, in the *UVW Record* of 30 March, Sanders put his name to an article accompanying a cutting from the *Weekly Dispatch.* The *Dispatch* story, under the headline 'Capital's Hand To Labour' and subheaded 'Secret Dinner To Leaders. Seeking Industrial Peace', revealed that a dinner had been given by an organisation called the National Alliance of Employers and Employed.

The founder of the Alliance is the Right Honourable F. Huth Jackson, a director of the Bank of England, and among the members are such prominent employers as Sir Vincent Callard (Messrs Vickers, Ltd.), Sir Robert Hadfield, Bart., FRS (Messrs Hadfields), and the Right Hon. Sir George Murray (Armstrong, Whitworth, Ltd).

On the Labour side of the Alliance are ranged such men as Mr W.A. Appleton (General Federation of Trade Unions), Mr Charles Duncan, MP (the Workers' Union), Mr. Arthur Pugh (Iron and Steel Trades' Confederation), Mr Ben Tillett and Mr Bevin (Dock, Wharf and General Labourers' Union), and Mr J. O'Grady, MP (Furnishing Trades' Association).

The dinner, continued the *Dispatch,* was called to

discuss the industrial depression and informally to discuss means of creating a better understanding between capital and labour so as to remove the existing obstacles to the advancement of British world trade ... The moderate men in the labour movement appreciate the difficulties of the industrial position, and are anxious to meet the employers in a mutual endeavour to remove them, but the wild men prefer the coercion of the strike threat to the round table method of conciliation.

The dinner might be 'interpreted as an appeal to the moderate men to use their influence to curb rash confreres.'

In his own piece Sanders expressed no surprise at some of the names mentioned by the *Dispatch,*

but the name that interested me most was E. Bevin, who on several occasions has come into close contact with the vehicle workers ... If it is true that Mr Bevin accepted the invitation to dinner with the idea, as it states, of using his influence to curb rash confreres, it does not appear to fall in line with the

> views expressed by E. Bevin on the Council of Action* ... I do think that Ernie Bevin ought to let us know whether the account as written in the *Dispatch* is a true one from his point of view ...

It is not known whether Bevin responded to this taunt. The point to note here is that Sanders' piece appeared just after the UVW had secured a majority for amalgamation; hence the amalgamation process itself could not be stopped, and opponents would have to look to other means.

London busworkers were soon to be deprived of their most valuable weapon – the *UVW Record.* The last issue appeared on 6 July 1921. A front-page article related that 'up to Monday 27 June we were not aware ourselves how near *The Record* was to its end.' On that day the editors of the journals of all the amalgamating unions were called to a meeting where it was decided that all of them should fold up forthwith. A new TGWU journal was to be published on 1 August.[4]

Grave doubts were being expressed by London busworkers concerning the amalgamation which was due to commence legally on 1 January 1922. There was talk of seccession; a secessionist conference was called and a TOT (Trams, Omnibuses and Tubes) Union promoted.[5] Given the doubts expressed in the two quotations above, it must be considered possible that Sanders was feeding the discontent given that, due to his position, he could not lead such a movement.

Several branches called for a special conference of the Section so that the accumulating grievances could be aired. Apparently paralysed, the UVW did nothing. When the list of branches demanding the conference had grown to more than twenty the Provisional Executive of the TGWU stepped in. In a circular sent to all Branch Secretaries in the London Bus Section Bevin, Harry Gosling (President) and Ben Smith (Acting Organiser for the Omnibus Section due to the fact that Sanders had met with a serious motorcycle accident) noted 'the amount of discontent prevalent in the ranks of the omnibus workers' and that 'there have been threats of secession from one or two branches'. They recognised that 'a good deal of the prevalent grievances are very real'. Thus, a special conference comprising three delegates from each London bus branch was held at Anderton's Hotel on 13 December.

* The Council of Action was set up by the TUC and the Labour Party in 1920 to stop Poland's war of aggression against Soviet Russia (in which Britain was becoming involved on the Polish side) 'by any and every form of withdrawal of labour'. Bevin had stated that 'this question you are called upon to decide today – the willingness to take any action to win world peace – transcends any claim in connection with wages or hours of labour.'[3]

Here the grievances mentioned in the previous pages were aired, with delegates demanding the formation of a special section of the new union for London busworkers. The handling of the 1921 agreement came in for especially bitter criticism. Strong feelings were expressed over the fact that even though the agreement stated that 'there shall not be any systematic overtime', the LGOC was forcing the men to work a seven-day week. Lloyd of Palmers Green complained that when route 20 was opened up 22 of his members had been sent to Chalk Farm to work their rest days and that there had been, in fact, no rest days that year. Likewise, Adams of Battersea pointed out that when summer schedules were being operated the company, by forcing crews to work their rest days, could put on 200 extra buses without employing a single extra man.[6]

Some members felt that the UVW had had no business to negotiate over the LGOC's demands for amendments to the 1919 agreement anyway. Cassomini of Forest Gate reminded the meeting that

> Negotiation, was no use unless they had the men behind them, and if they had the men behind them then negotiation was unnecessary. The men were dissatisfied with the incompetence of the officials, and were claiming that there was no mandate to undertake negotiations.

Criticism of UVW officials was widespread. Adams of Battersea said that

> one of the grievances was the question of the officials, the high salaries they received, and the expenses they drew, which were sometimes more than their salaries. The busmen themselves had no control over the officials, and what was needed was rank and file officials with rank and file control.

Similarly, Lancaster of Holloway claimed that 'the men were losing constitutional control' and that the 'Busmen's position had been weakened through the amalgamation with the old AATV'. Warne of Croydon declared that officials should be

> stronger men who would carry out the mandate of the men and not be swayed by this section or that. If Croydon failed to get satisfaction they would have to say: we are sorry, but we must adopt our own methods, just as we did when the union was a red union.

Many members felt that insult had been added to injury because the LGOC, perhaps thinking that the days of the 'red union' were over, had instructed the men to carry five standing passengers in the S and N type buses, without reference to the union.

It is difficult to gauge how widespread the secessionist movement was. The ballot of UVW members on the amalgamation had resulted in 65,407 for, with 5,455 against. It is possible that a majority of votes against had come from London. Some 60,000 members had not voted at all, and many of these abstentions may have been in the London Bus Section, especially in view of Sanders' advice to 'refuse to vote until such time as a proper scheme' was put in front of them. It is clear, anyway, that the movement was far wider than the 'one or two' branches mentioned in the circular. The delegate from Plumstead claimed that 'the secessionist movement had been going on for some time, and the Executive had done nothing.' Ben Smith stated that there were threatened secessions from 'a great many of the Lodges'.

For his part, Bevin

> wondered whether any of them had read Upton Sinclair's *100%*. If they did they would find that the men who boasted of being extremists were often on the side of, or inspired by, employers. He made no accusations, but he knew that some of the inspiration of the secessionist movement came from Electric Railway House [the LGOC's head office].

Besides, it was 'absolutely unnecessary to have such things as "unofficial" movements. In his ten years' experience in the dockers' movement' he had found them unnecessary 'because if grievances arose he got with the men and thrashed out the difficulties with them as pals.' It is impossible to say whether Bevin really believed that some of the secessionists were knowingly working on behalf of the LGOC. Bearing in mind his tendency in later years to brand all dissenters as 'Communists', it is possible that this was a calculated smear.

Nevertheless, Bevin knew that concessions had to be made. After an adjournment, he explained that the

> Executive wanted to find a way to link the busmen with the tram-men, a real coalition, so that a combined effort might be brought into being, not to drag down the busmen to the trams, but to raise the trams up to the busmen's level.

Thus buses and trams would all be members of the same trade group. Even so, the leaders present would 'recommend to the Executive that specially for London a bus sub-section should be created'.

It was decided that a committee of twelve would be elected by ballot which would then discuss the grievances aired at the Conference and report back to a further delegate conference. This was held in June 1922, when it was agreed that a nine-strong Bus Sub-Section Committee would be established for London and that, following the precedent set by the election of the National Group Secretary, all London bus officers would be elected.[7]

The principle of election did not survive for long. In the election for National Passenger Secretary John Cliff defeated George Sanders by 23,000 votes to 8,000, although the latter polled well in London.[8] Thus, the very principle for which the London busworkers had clamoured robbed them of their staunchest champion. Sanders was later appointed National Officer to the General Workers' Section, a post he held until his death in June 1932 at the age of 61.* In 1923 J.J. Mills was elected as London District Secretary to the London Bus Section, comfortably defeating W.J. Hammond, an old LPU Organiser. Mills was considered left-wing in these early days.[9] As the contradictions between Bevin and the London Bus Section became sharper, however, he obviously had no alternative – other than resignation – to acting as instructed by Bevin and the GEC. The following year a London Tram Secretary was elected. In 1925, however, the General Executive Council (GEC) attempted to short-list candidates for a further officer's post in the London Bus Section before conducting an election. In protest, the London Bus Sub-Section Committee (the body established in 1922) refused to appoint its representatives to the examining panel; three candidates withdrew for the same reason. The GEC then relented and all candidates were allowed to stand. Cassomini of Forest Gate was accordingly elected as Schedules Officer. At the 1927 Biennial Delegate Conference Bevin settled the matter once and for all by insisting that motions calling for the election of officers be debated; he then secured their defeat.[10]

However, the GEC made further organisational concessions to the Section. In 1925 the Section was divided into three Districts (paralleling the LGOC's three Divisions), each with a committee which would meet monthly. A Central Bus Committee would at first be elected from these District Committees and then, after 1931, by direct ballot of the membership in each of the Districts. An additional full-time official (the post to which Cassomini was elected) would be provided. In 1929 the

* Sanders' obituary in *The Record* the following month noted that throughout his illness he 'remained true to his rebel creed. When he knew, soon after his operation at the Cancer Hospital – much as they tried to keep the news from him – that he could not hope to get better, his spirit rebelled against such a cruel fate, and with the courage, the good cheer and merry wit with which he waged all his industrial battles he fought for his life.'

GEC agreed to appoint three additional officials to the Section, as well as utilising the services of a fourth to cater for busworkers in the outer ring of London. Two years later, although the number of District Committee meetings was reduced to eight per year, expenses were paid by the Union and the practice of Quarterly Delegate Conferences was institutionalised. In 1934 the Section was again re-organised, allowing the Quarterly Delegate Conferences to occupy a full day (previously they had been held in the evening), with the payment of £1 expenses per delegate (this had been 3s.).

Thus members of the London Bus Section were recognised as the 'aristocrats' of the TGWU, with their own sub-section, committee and conferences. But London busworkers also considered themselves to be 'aristocrats' of the whole working class, and if they were to continue to occupy this élite position, their wages and conditions would not only have to be protected but, where possible, improved. It was Ernest Bevin's refusal to lead the struggles to secure such improvements which was to bring him into a series of confrontations with the Section and, eventually, to the appearance of a phenomenon he had been most anxious to avoid: an effective unofficial movement.

Notes

1. Corfield, op.cit., August, 1963.
2. See *UVW Record*, 2 February 1921 for an enthusiastic report of a visit made by Sanders to Dalston. The branch President writes that the visit on 21 January was 'the signal for an outburst of enthusiasm by the members who had packed the room to hear this stalwart on the most important questions of the day ... It was a great night in the annals of Dalston, and all those who were present left the meeting feeling that the time had not been spent in vain, that there was still something to hope for, work for and live for.
3. A. Hutt, *British Trade Unionism*, London 1975, p.89.
4. *UVW Record*, 27 June 1921.
5. Corfield, op.cit., August, 1963.
6. All references and quotes from this Conference are taken from the minutes.
7. Corfield, op.cit., October 1963.
8. Ibid.
9. Bill Jones, interviewed by the author, 18 February 1984.
10. Corfield, op.cit., October 1963.

CHAPTER SEVEN

The 1924 Tram Strike

As the economic recession continued and the trade union movement attempted to recover from the betrayal of Black Friday, the LGOC, in common with other employers, demanded still more concessions from its workers. In the latter part of 1922 the Company announced that with the introduction of winter schedules a large number of drivers and conductors would have to be dismissed. In fact this was due in some measure to the busworkers' resistance to the working of compulsory overtime in the summer period, which meant that extra men had to be employed for this period. However, a London Bus Conference on 1 November agreed that, rather than see the men unemployed (and walking the streets with licenses in their pockets, available for employment by the 'pirates'), 500 men would be considered 'spare' (i.e. available to cover for holidays, sickness and absenteeism) with a guaranteed week of 40 hours, as opposed to the 48 hours stipulated by the agreement. This would last until April 1923, after which time the full guaranteed week would be restored to them.[1]

In January 1923 the LGOC and its associates put forward a modification of the sliding scale negotiated as part of the 1921 agreement, whereby the wages of drivers would be cut by 2s. per week and those of conductors by 6d. per week. When this was put to a ballot at the end of January, 8,803 members of the London Bus Section voted for rejection, while a mere 1,501 voted for acceptance.[2] A further meeting with the companies succeeded in reducing the proposed wage-cuts and another ballot was held in early February, with approximately the same results.[3] When notified of this decision the companies agreed to withdraw notice of the reductions and to continue with the existing agreement.

Nine days after the second ballot a late night mass meeting was held at the Albert Hall to consult with the membership and advise them of the progress of the negotiations.

> Nearly 10,000 men came from all parts of the Metropolitan area, being conveyed to and from the meeting by nearly 200 special omnibuses.
>
> ... The knowledge that the companies had withdrawn the notice to vary the agreement had not been divulged until the General Secretary made the announcement at the meeting. The result was received with great cheering.
>
> Regarded as a meeting, the rally was not a success. The great majority of the men had come to the meeting for the purpose of hearing a report of the negotiations, but were prevented from so doing by a small minority of the men who were plainly bent on disruptive tactics, and were clearly out to spoil the meeting.
>
> The General Secretary succeeded, by a very masterly effort, amidst much interruption, in giving a report of the negotiations, but after this had been done further business was impossible.[4]

The nature of the dissidents' complaints is not known, but it is possible that now that the Section had demonstrated that it could frighten off further encroachments on its working conditions without taking action, they were demanding a return to the provisions of the 1919 agreement or, at least, the shortening of the maximum spreadover. It was a demand that was to come up regularly over the next few years. It is also possible that lingering secessionist sentiments were expressed, for the *Record* concludes its report of the meeting by protesting that:

> We are convinced that the rally demonstrated that the great majority of the members have implicit confidence in their Negotiating Committee, and that their loyalty to the Union is beyond question.

We must question the assertion that the disruption was caused by a 'small minority', for had that been the case they would hardly have been able to render further business impossible in a meeting of 10,000.

The tramworkers were less fortunate than their comrades on the buses. Between October 1922 and October 1923 wage-cuts totalling 5s. per week were made. Despite the fact that the Court of Inquiry in 1921 had recommended the standardisation of wage-rates on London's trams (the legacy of the AAT), nothing had been done in this regard. In June 1923 the three private tram companies (the London County Council was the major employer) announced a further reduction, arguing that this was necessitated by losses incurred through the competition of motor buses.

There was certainly some truth in this. Throughout these years the tram companies were all in financial difficulties. The competition came from the LGOC and its associates and also from a new generation of 'pirates'. On 5 August 1922 Arthur George Partridge was first into the field with his 'Chocolate Express', which ran from Shepherds Bush to

Liverpool Street. Within a year he was followed by another 150 pirate buses. Like their predecessors in the nineteenth century, they indulged in a number of malpractices. Some carried a supply of destination-boards on the top deck so that they could change route at will; some were even known to execute U-turns if the queues on the opposite side of the road appeared to 'justify' it. In that they tended to operate over profitable sections of route at profitable times of the day, they were, of course, a threat to the LGOC, as they impaired its ability to cross-subsidise its loss-making suburban routes.

The London Bus Section, too, had good reason to oppose them, for they represented a threat to its aristocratic status. The *Record* of May 1923 wrote:

> We are experiencing considerable difficulty in securing from these companies the full observance of our trade union agreements. One of the larger companies, Messrs. Frost Smith, Ltd., has not yet agreed to sign our agreements. The representative of this company has right throughout the negotiations pursued a policy of evasion.

And further:

> The number of owner drivers has considerably increased during the past three weeks. These men have no regard whatever for an eight-hour day or the observance of trade union conditions.

Some members of the London Bus Section took a keen interest in combatting the pirates; one such member was fined £3 and ordered to pay three guineas costs following an incident in which he had deliberately blocked a pirate who was attempting to pass him.[5] The LGOC responded by flooding 'many streets with a larger number of buses than the actual traffic requires' which meant that 'a journey through the City is neither more nor less than a funeral procession.'[6]

The answer, said the union, was a single traffic authority, and numerous representations to the Ministry of Transport were made to this effect. Finally, the Ministry announced that legislation would be introduced in the autumn of 1923. The union appealed

> to our London members to take every opportunity of making their voice heard upon this question, which so vitally affects their own economic interests. The Union's MPs are paying special attention to the problem.[7]

The position of the tramway companies, meanwhile, was worsening. In July 1923 the general manager of the London and Suburban Traction

Company (Lord Ashfield's holding company for his Traffic Combine's tramways) notified the TGWU of the proposed reduction in wages.

> Owing to the large and rapidly increasing number of omnibuses which are working the areas served by the tramways, the earnings of my company are being seriously affected and tend to become worse and worse.[8]

Justifiably, Bevin pointed out that the companies were all part of the Combine, and so it was really nonsense to talk of loss of earnings being captured by the same Combine's motor buses (in fact, Lord Ashfield was chairman of both the London and Suburban Traction Company and the LGOC). In giving notice that the union would fight Bevin once more urged the government to form a single traffic authority, a measure which had been recommended by a Select Committee in 1919 and, before that, by a Royal Commission in 1905.

The companies' notices expired but the prevailing wage-rates continued to be paid. In August the tramworkers asked the District Joint Industrial Council to consider the wages question, the need for legislation to control passenger transport in the capital, and to make progress on the standardisation of wage-rates. With considerable boldness, in view of the fact that the companies were demanding wage-*cuts*, in December the TGWU put in a claim for a *rise* of 8s. per week, emphasising the wide disparity in the wages of a bus driver (86s. 6d. at the top rate) and a tram driver (67s.), added to which the busworkers achieved the top rate after six months while tramworkers had to wait two years. The claim was made on all the tram companies, including the London County Council.

In February a mass meeting of tramworkers instructed their committee to strike on 15 March if agreement had not been reached. Meanwhile, the busworkers authorised their own committee to strike in sympathy. Both actions were endorsed by the General Executive Council. Harry Gosling, President of the TGWU and Minister of Transport in the first Labour government (which had been elected in the meantime), requested that the strike be delayed for six days. On 20 March both sides met at the Ministry of Labour. The private companies offered to go to arbitration, while the LCC put 5s. on the table. Despite the fact that a Court of Inquiry was ordered, the strike began at midnight that night. The following day the capital's 16,000 tramworkers and the LGOC's 23,000 busworkers were out solid; the Underground trains and 300 pirate buses were heavily laden.

On 24 March the Court of Inquiry reported that the merits of the union's case could not be faulted and that 'the present crisis has, in the main, arisen through the tramway undertakings in the metropolitan area being unable to earn sufficient to meet the claim ...'[9] Not only was there competition from motor buses, but the tram companies were saddled with the cost of maintaining track. The Inquiry offered no solution to the dispute, apart from 'reproving both sides for the protraction of the negotiations'.[10] All the witnesses were agreed, however, on the need for a single traffic authority.

The government announced its intention to bring in a Bill to provide for such an authority. In fact, this went through its first reading the following day, being the same Bill prepared by the previous Tory administration. The resulting London Traffic Act of 1924 regulated the number of buses and the routes along which they might travel; the vast number of 'restricted streets' implied an effective restriction of new 'independents', thus giving the LGOC the green light to go ahead and buy up its pirate competitors. (There would have been little sense in it doing so before, as no sooner than it had bought them out, new ones would have appeared.) The Act established a Licensing Authority under the Ministry of Transport which approved routes, vehicles and frequencies. As a result the number of pirates decreased and the trams were afforded a 'stay of execution'.[11]

Most of the companies now came into line with the LCC's offer of 5s. per week increase and a proposal that the remainder of the claim be submitted to arbitration. This was rejected by the TGWU and Bevin sought the support of the rail unions. Mass meetings of the Underground members organised by the National Union of Railwaymen agreed to strike in sympathy, and ASLEF instructed its members to strike from 28 March.

The Labour government now threatened to invoke the Emergency Powers Act and set up a Cabinet Committee to prepare emergency action. This move provoked a joint resolution from the TUC General Council and the National Executive Committee of the Labour Party, deploring the government's measures and urging it to take control of London's transport and pay the wage increase by means of a subsidy. The employers finally agreed to pay an increase of 6s. per week. The Underground strike was called off and the tramworkers accepted the offer in a ballot on 29 March. The buses and trams returned to the streets.

After the dust had settled the union replied to those who had criticised it for taking official strike action while a Labour government was in office. An article in the April issue of the *Record* noted that the employers had made use of the recession to drive down conditions and that a movement to improve them was inevitable once the economy showed signs of improvement.

> These movements could not have been checked, nor would it have been wise to have held them up because a Labour government had assumed office ... to check the movement would be to dispirit the workers, to weaken their faith in industrial action, and to encourage the employers to encroach still further on the present standards.

The editorial in the same issue declared that

> Governments may come and governments may go, but the workers' fight must go on all the time, in every possible way. A strong industrial army is the best support a Labour government can have ...

Throughout the strike Bevin had attracted the kind of press treatment to which trade union leaders have since become accustomed: 'Boss' Bevin he was called, as if the action had been a result of a whim of his own and not called for by the members. No amount of public criticism – not even the fact that a Labour government was in office – seems to have affected him. When Prime Minister Ramsay McDonald wrote him a personal letter arguing that responsibility would, in the eyes of the public, fall upon the government, Bevin retorted curtly that 'the demand was before the employers before ever we knew there was a likelihood of a Labour government coming in ...'[12]

Bullock suggests that Bevin's pugnacious attitude and this blank refusal to bend to the wishes of a Labour government was dictated by his need to consolidate his position as leader of the budding giant, the TGWU.[13] 'His reputation as a tough and successful negotiator shot up – and so did the Union's recruiting figures.' Certainly his attitude to the government does not seem to have been determined by doctrinal differences. By calling out the busworkers in support of their colleagues on the trams he may have wished to demonstrate to the busmen his determination to build 'a real coalition ... not to drag down the busmen to the trams, but to raise the trams up to the busmen's level'.

Undoubtedly, the strike was a triumph for Bevin. He had completely turned around the companies' intention to cut wages and gained an *increase* for the tramworkers. The action had hastened the introduction of legislation to regulate the passenger transport of London. It is curious, however, that in that very same year, Bevin 'used all his influence to prevent the militant leaders of the London busmen from staging another hold-up of London's traffic'.[14]

Notes

1. *The Record*, November 1922.
2. Ibid., February 1923.
3. Ibid., March 1923.
4. Ibid. This kind of reporting clearly illustrates the change of style in the new *Record*, for its predecessors would at least have reported the demands of the dissidents – and quite possibly have supported them!
5. Ibid., April 1923.
6. Ibid., January 1924.
7. Ibid., May and November 1923.
8. Clegg, op.cit., p.25.
9. Ibid., p.26.
10. A. Bullock, *The Life and Times of Ernest Bevin*, Vol.I, London 1960, p.240.
11. Barker and Robbins, op.cit., Vol.II, p.211.
12. Bullock, op.cit., p.241.
13. Ibid., pp.239-40.
14. Ibid., p.246.

CHAPTER EIGHT

The Roots of Disaffection

> If any one thing consolidated the London road passenger transport membership into the Transport and General Workers' Union it was the strike of March, 1924. This strike at once showed the new Union had a fighting leadership ready to put its members' interests before any other loyalty ...[1]

This assessment of the 1924 strike is seriously defective. If anything, the very success of the tram strike led to greater tension between Bevin and the London Bus Section, for he then refused to lead the busworkers into a struggle to improve their own wages and conditions. His reluctance to do so, which continued throughout the 1920s, placed increasing strains on the London busworkers' loyalty to the TGWU and prepared the ground for the London Busmen's Rank and File Movement.

In October 1923, following the LGOC's retreat on its proposal to introduce further wage-cuts for busworkers, the Bus Committee requested the General Executive Council to apply for a renewal of the existing agreement for one year. The LGOC refused the application, preferring the agreement to continue, subject to one month's notice by either side. Following their part in the tram strike the Bus Committee wrote to the GEC on 24 April 1924 to request that one month's notice to terminate be given from the first of May. The GEC replied that notice could not be given without the formulation of alternative proposals. Accordingly, the Bus Committee proposed the practical abolition of spreadovers;* that membership of the TGWU be a condition of employment; the abolition of voluntary rest-day working and the regular rotation of rest-days and, by no means least, an equal rate of 92s. for

* Although, as explained previously, the technical meaning of 'spreadover' is the period between signing-on and signing-off, when used colloquially, as here, it indicates a duty of up to twelve hours which contains several hours relief separating the two 'spells of duty'. This enables the employer to utilise a number of crews to cover both morning and afternoon peaks.

drivers and conductors (an increase of 5s. 6d. for drivers and 12s. 6d. for conductors).

These demands were not greeted favourably by Bevin, and certainly not by the LGOC. It was not the demands themselves to which he objected, but to their inconsistency. How, he asked, could they at first request the continuation of the existing agreement and then, when this was refused, demand substantial improvements? What was the sense in first supporting a movement to narrow the differential between tram and bus rates, and then demanding its widening? Dismissing the demand for a wage-increase he urged:

> We should confine ourselves to an attempt to grapple with the whole problem of duties and spreadover, and bend all our energies to securing a satisfactory settlement of the question.[2]

The General Executive Council established a Sub-Committee to confer with the Bus Committee. The Bus Committee, meeting on 22 May was of

> the opinion they were the competent body to decide the terms of the application and the terms of the Agreement. They desired to enter a very strong protest against the action of the Officials and the EC in not tendering the requisite notice to the Company, terminating the Agreement. They declared that they had already notified the members that the Agreement would be terminated as and from May 1st, 1924 and that the Committee had been belittled in the eyes of the members by reason of the fact that no such notice had been given.[3]

The Bus Committee went on to explain that the refusal to extend the agreement for a year had worsened schedules and subjected the members to speed-up, in which case there was no inconsistency in their demand for a higher rate of pay to compensate for this.

It should be borne in mind that this was the first time the London Bus Section had called upon the TGWU to renegotiate its agreement with the LGOC. The Section had the clear impression, in line with its understanding of the undertakings given at Anderton's Hotel in 1921 and 1922, that the Bus Committee was the appropriate body to formulate claims on the Company. Had Bevin agreed to this the Section would have been, at least for negotiating purposes, a union within a union, and in a circular on 17 June he made it clear that as

> the termination of an agreement affecting the livelihood of our members involves policy and, ultimately, a financial obligation, the taking of such a step is the prerogative of the Executive Council both in accordance with Rule and practice.

The Bus Committee gave notice of its intention to resign unless the agreement was terminated. When the GEC Sub-Committee refused to do this they made good their threat. At a London Bus Conference on 2 June the GEC Sub-Committee argued that the Section should concentrate on improving conditions as the application formulated by the Bus Committee would 'in our belief, resolve itself into bartering conditions of work for wage increases'.[4] They advised that the Section should attempt to get wages stabilised.

The Conference refused to accept the resignation of the Bus Committee and, moreover, decided that a month's notice of termination *should* be given. The GEC Sub-Committee argued that the Bus Committee's proposals were impossible to achieve and would 'mislead the members'.[5] After the Conference it formulated a series of demands, including the stabilisation of wages and the revisions in conditions sought by the Section, although it would 'not pledge the Executive to obtain the whole of the proposals'.[6] The Bus Committee advised the leadership that, unless the month's notice was given, 'responsibility on our part is at an end'.[7]

On 17 June, the same day that Bevin met the LGOC to open negotiations, the union's Finance and Emergency Committee directed Bevin to inform the London Bus Section that 'they have no desire to enter into a quarrel, neither will they be dragged into a quarrel' and that '*they are only anxious to do the right thing in the interests of the membership*' (emphasis in the original). This statement by Bevin continued:

> The Finance and Emergency Committee further advise me to appeal to the members not to look at this question from the point of view of one of conflict with them but rather as one of co-operation in endeavouring to do the best in the interests of the London 'Bus Section and of the Union as a whole ...
>
> ... In the opinion of the Finance Committee, nothing has done so much harm to the Movement as lifting up the hopes of sections of workers and then dashing them to the ground ...

Indicative of the regard in which Bevin was held by some members was

> ... A further statement has been brought to the notice of the Financial Committee to the effect that certain officers of the Union are under some pledge not to ask for a further increase in wages. This is a ridiculous statement and a foul suggestion. No Officer or Committee would be fit to hold any position if they were party to such a private arrangement, and the members may take it as an absolute lie ...[8]

Despite the conciliatory tone of this circular, Bevin and the GEC had succeeded in denting the pride of the London Bus Section. Five years previously they had conducted their own negotiations; now they had to ask the General Executive Council. This was hardly the way to treat proud aristocrats and could only lead to trouble.

The negotiations with the LGOC took place during the course of seven meetings spread over two months. The first meeting between the two sides opened with George Shave, the LGOC's Operations Manager, remarking drily, 'I had no idea, Mr Bevin, what it was you wanted to speak to me about.'

Bevin: 'But you made a rough guess.'

Shave: 'No, I do not think so.'[9]

It is quite apparent from the record of the negotiations that Bevin was far from trusted by the London Bus Section, or at least by some members of it. At the opening of the second meeting on 9 July, Shave enquired whether 'the constitution of the Committee' had been settled. Bevin replied sharply that this 'really ought to be settled within our own circle'.

Shave: 'I was only anxious to save time and to clear the air. (Document handed to Bevin.) That is why we are perturbed. Is that a true copy of what has been sent in?'

Bevin: 'I have not seen this resolution ... May I ask you how you came by this?'

After Bevin had questioned him closely Shave claimed that the document (and we may only guess at its contents) had been sent to him anonymously, and that he would make investigations as to its origins.

Shave: 'Further on I will mention other communications in connection with one of the clauses, that we have received.'

Bevin: 'I dare say.'

Shave: 'Not one, but a number of them.'

It is quite possible that the branches did not trust Bevin to put their arguments forcefully enough, or at all, and that in sending their resolutions to Shave they were seeking to ensure that they were raised. It is equally possible that Shave had come by the documents by other means (and we shall see in later Chapters that the LGOC's successors certainly had their own intelligence systems) and that he was setting out to disarm or embarass Bevin.

Bevin and Mills, the London District Secretary, argued that conditions had worsened, thus necessitating a relaxation of the agreement. Bevin warned that

> If you try to screw the Union by means of super-organisation over a given

> point, then you lead to revolt: the men will not submit. You will have to join the Institute of Psychology that I have been asked to join. It is worth joining, so they say.

Shave denied that the men had been subjected to intensification. Bevin argued that before the war there had been '50 per cent less intensification' whereas today the

> development of petrol propulsion has grown with such rapidity that every vehicle which comes on the road is an intensification of the one already there ... some of your older men, with your big type of buses, have the whole guts taken out of them with a day on the road ... It is the same front and back. You have intensified it, in my opinion, to the last point.

Bevin contended that the fall in the cost of living index in June would mean a loss of 1s. per week in wages for the membership, due to the sliding scale. This fall, however, was largely a result of the Budget, which had included a 'remission of taxation intended to benefit the home', so the company should not really claim it. Shave, with his wicked sense of humour, replied that it 'certainly is a very novel point that you should bring forward that the Budget was framed purely and essentially for the assistance of the working classes and that they should benefit by it'.

Shave conceded that schedules could be arranged along the lines requested by the union but that the problem was 'absolutely costs – coming down to pounds, shillings and pence'. In reply to Shave's suggestion that a joint working party be set up to consider schedules, Bevin snapped back: 'Why do we want to waste time going into schedules, when it is a question of costs and not of practicality?'

By the sixth meeting on 15 August Frank Pick (then a Director, Pick became Managing Director of the LGOC in 1928) was suggesting that the time was inopportune to revise the agreement and that a further meeting should take place in January 1925. He was willing to agree that the current agreement would not be used to reduce wages below their present level, although if the cost of living index justified it an upward movement would be acceptable.

At the final meeting it was agreed that the current agreement continue in force until 1925. In the meantime, as an interim measure, wages would be stabilised; not less than 75 per cent of all duties would have a maximum spreadover of nine hours, with a maximum time on duty of eight-and-a-half hours; a further 15 per cent of all duties could have a maximum spreadover of ten hours. Thus, 90 per cent of all duties would now come within the terms of the 1919 agreement.

The Company refused to make union membership a condition of employment. This must have been a touchy subject for Bevin, for as we shall see later the union was losing membership in the London Bus Section. In mid-1927 the Section asked the GEC to support strike action in order to enforce union membership, and although this request was denied,[10] it is possible that an approach by Bevin was responsible for the following notice which appeared in all LGOC garages in the same year:

> Whilst there is no obligation on the part of any employee to belong to a Trade Union, the company find it mutually convenient to have some organisation to represent the staff collectively on their behalf. The Company therefore recognise the Transport Workers' Federation (*sic*!) for drivers and conductors and Inside Staff (other than craftsmen).[11]

In 1929 the Operating Manager

> issued a statement which confirmed the company's undertaking to call into the office any employee leaving the TGWU and to recommend rejoining, in addition to the old undertaking to point out to new employees the advantages of membership.[12]

Despite the improvements there was a rash of local disputes in early 1925 over schedules – at Seven Kings, Hendon and 'one or two other cases'.[13] By this time negotiations had begun for a revision of the main agreement.

The proposals put to a London Bus Conference in April 1925 represented a slight retreat on the interim arrangements regarding spreadover-length and time on duty. Not surprisingly the Conference rejected them. Draft proposals were then sent to the branches, along with amendment sheets. On 25 May Conference again rejected the proposals. Further negotiation with the Company led to a Conference in July recommending acceptance.

Embarrassingly, the membership rejected the agreement by 7,401 votes to 6,968. This was 'not considered a satisfactory result'(!) by the union, and so a pamphlet was issued explaining the terms of the agreement clause by clause. The provisions of the agreement were much the same as the interim arrangements; the agreement was not finally signed until March 1926.

* * *

Shortly after the signing of the 1926 agreement the London Bus Section made an honourable contribution to the General Strike.

In 1925 the mineowners had come forward with new proposals for wage-cuts. In rejecting them, the Miners' Federation of Great Britain received the support of the TUC General Council. A TUC Special Committee laid plans for a complete embargo of all coal transport, and on 30 July, the day before the mine-owners' notices were due to expire, a conference of trade union executives gave unanimous approval to detailed instructions which had been issued to all unions affected by the planned embargo. The Tory government quickly arranged for a nine-month subsidy for the industry, during which time a Royal Commission would investigate the industry. The day the employers withdrew their notices became known as Red Friday; the miners' reply to the Black Friday of 1921.

Winston Churchill, the Chancellor of the Exchequer, made it clear that the nine-month subsidy for the coal industry and the Royal Commission represented a truce only. The unions also realised that a further attack would come. But while the government set about recruiting blacklegs and giving official support to the creation of an Organisation for the Maintenance of Supplies, the TUC leaders made no preparations.

In March 1926 the Royal Commission recommended that the miners accept lower wages or longer hours. The TUC General Council accepted this on condition that the industry be reorganised. The miners, on the other hand, responded with the slogan 'Not a penny off the pay, not a second on the day'. However, when the mineowners announced that they would negotiate on a District basis only, posting lock-out notices for 20 April, TUC support became firmer. On 1 May the executives of the trade unions voted in favour of a general strike. Two days later the British working class went into action.

On the first day of the strike Lord Ashfield, the LGOC Chairman, posted the following notice:

> The regrettable dispute which has arisen with regard to the terms and conditions of employment in the coal mines cannot justify the stoppage of these services which are essential to the public welfare. While it is recognised that the loyalty which has been shown by all classes of workers to the miners is admirable, it should not be forgotten that there is a wider and greater loyalty which should be shown to the nation at large.
>
> In this crisis each man must decide for himself but we hope that we can rely upon the staff remaining at work. There is no difference between the Companies and their staff, but both have a duty to the public which they should discharge. The Companies are bound to discharge to the best of their ability and resources their duty in providing public passenger services. Those members of the staff who do likewise are assured of their positions.

Despite the implied threat in that final sentence, the LGOC was forced the next day to post a notice calling for volunteers from the public. The company moved 3,300 buses into Regent's Park, 'there to await any volunteer crews who might be brave or foolish enough to chance the unpredictable hazards of angry strikers and chaotic roads'.[14] As far as is known no such volunteers emerged from the ranks of the London Bus Section. Those buses which did take to the roads in London were either pirates or crewed by 'civilians', mainly students. Windows were boarded and many had police escorts. Phillips estimates that by these methods 'one in four of the normal quota of buses were running by 12 May'.[15] That may well have been so, but this should not be taken to mean that numbers increased daily, for Farman says that while 300 were manned by volunteer crews on the first Tuesday, this was down to 40 by Friday.[16]

All buses, whether pirate or blackleg, were of course liable to be attacked. Jack Dash recalls an incident at the Elephant and Castle:

> All eyes were turned in one direction. Coming in from the direction of Westminster were car loads of Special Reserves, all steel-helmeted with truncheons at the ready, the trucks protected by a kind of wire cage over the top to protect them from missiles aimed by the strikers. They were followed by Mounted Police, escorting a General omnibus with passengers, driven by a university student. Stones began to rain down from the tops of the adjacent tenement buildings ... The mounted reserves and police were unseated from their horses. Running fights took place with the foot police. The bus was halted, the passengers were dragged out, a great crowd of men overturned the vehicle, which caught fire and began to blaze away. There were casualties everywhere. Eventually reinforcements arrived and the police, Special Constables and Army Reserve men regained control.[17]

Attfield and Lee reveal that the government, having failed in its attempts to get the trams underway due to the vulnerability of these vehicles, concentrated on trying to get the buses moving. Lord Ashfield, according to this account, was nervous of allowing his buses to brave both strikers and volunteer crews, and so released only the older models. By 5 May 47 General buses had been put out of action, and the government was 'never able to extend the routes much beyond the safe areas into the wilds of the working-class regions'.[18]

Bill Jones, later Chairman on the Central Bus Committee and a member of the TGWU's General Executive Council, was then in his twenties, having joined the LGOC in the previous year:

> Blacklegs rode with police escorts including the man who later became Operating Manager, the bastard. He was an undergraduate. The blacklegs

were in the main students. Of course, we turned the bastards over when we could – turfed 'em off when the police weren't around. I lived at that time just off Kingsland Road, and we used to turn 'em over like nobody's business down there. Because they didn't all have policemen riding with them – there weren't enough policemen for that. And if they didn't have a policeman, that was their lot! One of the lads would get on the bus and drive it anywhere – any side-turning out of the way – so it would sometimes take 'em an hour to find the bus.[19]

The strike lasted for nine days. By the end of the first week the TUC General Council, at war without wanting to be, had no way of winning without calling into question the continuation of the capitalist system. Sir Herbert Samuel, who had led the Royal Commission, rewrote the conclusions to his report in the form of a memorandum. The General Council leapt at the opportunity and even though the miners were violently opposed to a settlement on these terms, virtually the same as the Commission's recommendations, brought the General Strike to an end.

London's passenger workers did not all return to work immediately. The London County Council at first refused full reinstatement for their regular tramways staff, and on 13 and 14 May they attempted to run trams from New Cross with volunteers.

Once again, huge crowds assembled outside the yard. Police battled with pickets to clear a way, but the tram was halted after a journey of just twenty yards; the police ordered the work to stop, to prevent riots. The LCC Tramways Department settled with its employees on Friday 14 May.[20]

Some Tillings busworkers, on hearing over the radio that the strike was over, returned to work and found themselves working alongside blacklegs; they were swiftly called out by colleagues who marched on Catford Garage, staying out until terms for a return to work were arranged. The LGOC also settled on 14 May on terms which guaranteed no victimisation.[21]

The issue of the *Record* which appeared after the strike noted that members of the TGWU's Passenger Group had 'responded magnificently to the call from the General Council. From every area the reports indicated a wonderful display of solidarity and enthusiasm.' The article asserted that as far as passenger workers were concerned there 'was no thought in their mind of any attack upon the constitution ...' Those same members were now asking questions 'regarding the negotiations immediately preceding the calling off of the strike and the reason why the strike was terminated at the time it was and the manner of its termination'.[22]

The miners stayed out on their own until December, by which time they were forced into an acceptance of wage-cuts and the loss of the seven-hour day. In September the subject was banned from the TUC Congress. It soon became apparent that the movement, due to the timidity of the TUC General Council, had suffered a defeat of major proportions. It is probable that militant London busworkers, due to their previous skirmishes with Ernest Bevin and his leading position on the TUC General Council, would have associated him with what was widely perceived as the betrayal of the miners. It is reasonable to assume, therefore, that the experience of the General Strike would have served to sharpen the contradictions between the London Bus Section and the leadership of the TGWU.

* * *

Two years after the signing of the 1926 agreement the Section was becoming restive once more. At a Conference early in 1928 the Bus Committee advised that the present agreement be continued. Some delegates, however, were of the opinion that it should be renewed for a specific term only, while others argued for its immediate termination. Bevin put feelers out to the company and, following a new petrol tax introduced in the Budget, advised caution, hinting that the LGOC might seek to worsen conditions if the agreement were terminated.

Later in the year the membership voted for termination in a ballot and negotiations commenced on 31 October. The Section's demands were for a wage-increase, more holidays, an increase in the minimum meal relief to 30 minutes, and that hardy perennial, the abolition of spreadover duties. Frank Pick argued for the LGOC that this package, costed at between £1 million and £1.5 million, could not possibly be agreed. He further argued that certain of the proposals paid no regard to the 'facts of traffic operation'. The company had been quite prepared to let the agreement run on, but now the union had requested a revision the LGOC itself had 'certain proposals they desired to submit'.[23] In a circular to the branches J.J. Mills gave ample space to the company's case, almost as if the object was to convince the membership that they had been in error to demand termination of the agreement.

In a letter in November Pick suggested that there were two ways of achieving the longer meal relief, 'though enquiry which we have made indicated that the men do not take substantial meals while on duty': to increase the number of spreadovers (which the Section was protesting about in its application), or to intensify the working day. The tone of

Pick's letter is remarkably similar to that of Mills' circular three weeks earlier. Mills had hinted that the company might be considering a worsening of conditions but that it was still prepared to continue the 1926 agreement, while Pick actually spelt out the proposals while, once again, leaving the door open for the continuation of the former agreement. This does not necessarily mean that the union's officers were colluding with the company. Bevin had given the opinion that there were no concessions to be had and it is more likely that attempts were being made to demonstrate that the General Secretary's judgement had been sound.

Another document, produced at the request of the Bus Committee, details the financial difficulties of the LGOC and provides figures which show that, as far as hours of actual work were concerned, the Section led a very aristocratic existence.[24] This demonstrates that, although the average time paid per duty was eight-and-a-half hours (giving drivers and conductors an average of 92s. 6d. and 84s. per week), hours actually worked were, on average, as follows:

Mondays to Friday:	6 hours, 39 minutes
Saturdays:	6 hours, 45 minutes
Sundays:	6 hours, 31 minutes.

On 8 March 1929 the Company announced at a meeting with the union that they were in a much worse situation than when negotiations had commenced. Revenue from the combine's undertakings as a whole had declined by £100,000 comparing the previous two months with the comparable period of 1928, and petrol costs were up by £375,000 that year. The proposals put forward by the union had been costed as follows:

Wage-rise of 3s. 6d. per week:	£190,000
14 days holiday:	£80,000
Schedules proposals:	£185,000
Increase in meal relief:	£83,000

A week later, Pick agreed to increase the minimum meal relief to 30 minutes and to employ the 160 extra crews in order to facilitate this measure. On holidays, the most that the company would offer was an additional two days (making a total of ten) for those crews who took their holidays in the winter period. For very early and very late duties the penalty payments were increased. No offer was made to improve the basic rates.

The Bus Committee agreed to submit these proposals to Conference 'as in the opinion of the Committee they represent the maximum we can obtain at the moment'.[25] The members were balloted on 10 May and the agreement signed on 31 May.

It may seem odd to the present-day reader that the supposedly militant London Bus Section of the TGWU had allowed two years to pass before submitting fresh demands and, even then, settling for a 'zero pay-award'. But it must be remembered that the period was characterised by wage-*cuts*, not wage-rises. Following the betrayal of the General Strike wages had resumed their downward trend. According to the indices used by Routh (who used 1906-10 as his base-line of 100), they fell from 212 points in 1925 to 211 points in 1926, to 210 points in 1927 and thence to 208 points in the following year.[26] However, the cost of living was also falling – from 186 points in 1925 to 175 points in 1928.

So, while the money-wages of London busworkers remained constant throughout these years, their *real* standards rose; moreover, their position relative to most other groups of workers also improved as the latter were being subjected to wage-cuts, thus consolidating the London busworkers' 'aristocratic' position.

Be that as it may, there are clear indications that wage-increases *could* have been achieved in 1925 and 1929, and it was this suspicion which fuelled the Section's discontent.

Whereas in 1920 the buses had carried fewer passengers than the trams or the rail services (surface plus the Underground), they overtook the latter in 1921 and the trams in 1923. There is no doubt that claims by the London Bus Section that the work was being intensified were justified. The K type bus introduced in 1919 was a 46-seater, and from December, 1920 the LGOC began putting the 54-seater S type into service, which cost 'no more to operate than the 34-seater B type' which was being replaced.[27] Between 1924 and 1925 an increase of 24 buses on the road produced an extra seating capacity of 2,422; in the following year a net *decrease* of six buses increased seating capacity by 6,718 and, perhaps more importantly, generated 60 million extra passenger journeys;[28] if each of these journeys had been the shortest possible, each passenger paying a penny, this would have brought £250,000 into the LGOC's coffers.

The authors of London Transport's official history are silent on the question of where this left the LGOC's finances, except to note that:

> The buses – that is, the General's fleet – sustained the unsatisfactory results of the Underground railways and the company tramways, and their earnings

would be required to bear the main burden of revenue profitability of the new London Passenger Transport Board after 1933.[29]

Similarly, it seems likely that the Section could have achieved a better result from the 1928-29 negotiations. As we saw, the LGOC pleaded 'financial difficulties', partly due to the new petrol tax and loss of revenue. The following table shows, however, that passenger-usage was still enjoying a healthy upward tendency:

Date	*Buses owned*	*Seating capacity*	*Passengers carried (millions per year)*
31 December 1926	4,552	221,322	1,543
31 December 1927	4, 678	232,777	1,671
31 December 1928	4,907	243,587	1,834
31 December 1929	5,002	245,035	1,830
31 December 1930	4,945	245,914	1,874

Source: Barker and Robbins, op. cit, Vol. II, p. 215.

We see from the above that the constant upward trend in passenger journeys was interrupted in 1929 by a marginal fall of 4 million. The company claimed at its meeting with the union in March that bad weather over the past months had led to a decrease of £100,000 in the combine's revenue. If this were true, receipts must have improved dramatically (or rationalisation must have been pursued ruthlessly) in the latter months of the year, for total traffic receipts for the LGOC in that year were £9,696,00 – an *increase* of £104,000 over 1928. Even though profits for 1929 fell by £5,000 they were still at the comfortable level of £671,000, allowing the company to declare a dividend of 8 per cent. In 1930, moreover, profits were to soar to £740,000.[30]

Thus even on the basis of the company's own figures for the period, a wage increase of 3s. 6d. per week would only have reduced its profits to slightly below their 1926 level – and this leaves out of consideration the possibility of a compensatory fares-increase.

We must now ask what might have been behind Bevin's obstinate refusal to lead London busworkers into a wages struggle.

It may be objected that Bevin's name has been cropping up too frequently and that conspicuous individuals are not the sole – or even the major – moving force in history. This is true enough, but in the early stages of the TGWU the objective circumstances were such that Bevin's personality *was* a major force. It is doubtful whether the General

Executive Council – a body composed of individuals from the various Areas and trade groups – would have yet entirely freed itself from the sectional interests represented on it. It was Bevin more than any other individual who had pulled the founding unions together, and in the situation following the amalgamation it was he who became the custodian of the union's *global* interests.

Of course, Bevin could have given the London Bus Section its head; but a host of factors stood against such a course being adopted. First there is the tendency noted by Ross and others:

> As an institution expands in strength and status, it outgrows its formal purpose – it experiences its own needs, develops its own ambitions, and faces its own problems. These become differentiated from the needs, ambitions and problems of its rank and file. The trade union is no exception ... This becomes more true as the union becomes better established and more 'responsible'.[31]

One of the TGWU's 'own needs' in this period has already been identified: the need to become a cohesive force rather than a loose collection of trade groups all pulling in different directions. Moreover, as we have seen, at the 1921 Anderton's Hotel Conference Bevin had spoken of the need to build 'a real coalition, so that a combined effort might be brought into being, not to drag down the busmen to the trams, but to raise the trams up to the busmen's level'. Bevin could see that even *within* a trade group two sections appeared to be pulling in diferent directions – or, rather, that the busworkers appeared unwilling to slow down in order that their colleagues on the trams might catch up. This dilemma persisted into the 1930s, and it cannot have led Bevin to look fondly upon the London Bus Section's position. This would appear to be the only reasonable explanation for Bevin's refusal to demand a wage-increase for the busworkers when, just months earlier, he had led the tramworkers to a quite astonishing victory.

Then, too, it was certainly Bevin's philosophy that wage demands should be foregone in favour of protecting conditions in times of economic difficulty. In the winter of 1921-22, when the national tramways employers were demanding a revision of the national agreement negotiated in 1919, he told a national delegate conference:

> You established in 1919 a principle which is, I think, the greatest principle ever achieved in the industrial world. The great thing in this fight is the guaranteed week ...
>
> To get the 48-hour week established it took 30 years of effort. You can recover wages – the money side is not so difficult. When trade revives, then is

> the chance to recover wages. But it is the conditions. Conditions take years to recover ... and you must fight to keep them.[32]

Thus it was in 1924 that the GEC warned that the London Bus Section's application would 'resolve itself into bartering conditions of work for wage increases' and Bevin advised the Section to 'grapple with the whole problem of duties and spreadover, and bend all our energies to securing a satisfactory settlement of the question'.

Nevertheless it must be frankly admitted that Bevin was a collaborationist. He gave no hint of wishing to see the capitalist system replaced. According to Hutt, after the General Strike Bevin identified himself as one who 'feared even more that the strikers, the working class, might win in a revolutionary fashion'.[33] This being the case, he would have viewed the London Bus Section and its 'red union' past with some caution, and would have been keen to reduce its influence – or, at least, to change its political complexion. The outspokenness of Sanders, and his thinly-veiled attack on Bevin's fraternisation with the employers in the January 1921 issue of the *UVW Record* would have made their mark and this may well have played a part in the decision to wind up the journals of the amalgamating unions in June 1921. Just as it would be mistaken to speak of Bevin in purely individual terms, the same is true of Sanders: he was merely the leading spokesman for an influential socialist trend within the London Bus Section. Bevin would have been aware that such leaders would have real influence only if they could show that they were able to win material benefits for the membership. It is in this light that we must view the elevation of the old AAT officers and the minimising of LPU influence, and also the refusal to press for wage increases. If the London Bus Section could be shown to be marking time on wages this would also have reduced the influence of the Section within the TGWU as a whole. This may seem somewhat speculative, but it is curious that the TGWU could 'agree to set on foot a national wages movement'[34] for dockers in 1923 and refuse to lead the busworkers in 1924 – a time when, as we have seen already the LGOC probably could have afforded to pay a wage-increase!

After the trauma of the General Strike the overwhelmingly right-wing General Council of the TUC were anxious to regain 'respectability', and it was this drive which led to the infamous Mond-Turner talks of 1928. In January of that year a group of twenty leading industrialists, led by Sir Alfred Mond of ICI, met the TUC General Council to discuss ways in which the two sides of industry could 'co-operate'. Ernest Bevin was no stranger to this kind of forum. The report which resulted from these talks argued that rationalisation and trustification 'should be welcomed and encouraged' and that a National Industrial Council should be established under which a system of compulsory arbitration would operate. In return employers would take a sympathetic view of trade union recognition. According to Emmanuel Shinwell MP, this would be a system whereby 'the trade union keeps the men in order; the employer in return agrees to employ union men only.[35]

It would be foolish to argue that Bevin's participation in these talks had no influence on his conduct of the 1928-29 negotiations with the LGOC – especially as Lord Ashfield attended the talks on the employers' side! Also, bearing in mind Shinwell's characterisation of the 'deal', it can hardly have been a coincidence that in 1929 the LGOC issued the statement on trade union membership referred to above.

Bevin's attitude and actions inflamed the militants and a large section of the membership in the London Bus Section in two ways: first, his refusal to lead a wages struggle threatened the Section's aristocratic status; secondly, there was his refusal to have anything to do with the kind of socialist vision which had been kindled in the old 'red union' and which, from the early 1920s onward, had been kept alive by a new generation of socialist – and more especially Communists – within the Section. The response of the militants was predictable: they resorted to unofficial forms of organisation, the kind of activity which Bevin had been most anxious to avoid. (Bevin was not averse to using the 'red' spectre in negotiations, however. 'We are conscious,' he told George Shave in 1924, 'that an absolute overhaul is necessary [i.e. of the agreement] ... We do not want unofficial movements to develop and to have our hands forced, to have disturbance and the rest of it ...').

However, the marriage between industrial militancy and political radicalism which had been established under the leadership of men like Sanders in the LPU was never effectively achieved by the leaders of the 1920s, and it was not until 1932 that a manner of unofficial organisation was evolved which mobilised a mass following based on a fusion of both tendencies.

Notes

1. Corfield, op.cit., November 1963.
2. TGWU Cyclo 1639, 14 May 1924.
3. TGWU Cyclo 1701, 16 June 1924.
4. Ibid.
5. Ibid.

6. Ibid.
7. Ibid.
8. E. Bevin, Circular to Branches, London Bus Section, 17 June 1924.
9. *London Omnibus Negotiations, June, July and August, 1924*; transcript of the shorthand notes by Ernest L. Humphries. All quotations from these negotiations are taken from this source.
10. General Executive Council Minutes, 25 August 1927.
11. Clegg, op.cit., p.15.
12. Ibid.
13. *The Record*, February 1925.
14. C. Farman, *The General Strike*, London 1972, p.117.
15. G.A. Phillips, *The General Strike*, London 1976, p.333.
16. Op.cit., p.117.
17. In J. Skelley (ed.), *The General Strike 1926*, London 1976, p.274.
18. Ibid., pp.273-4.
19. Interviewed in *Busworker Monthly*, May 1983.
20. Attfield and Lee in Skelley (ed.), op.cit., p.274.
21. Ibid., pp.275-6.
22. *The Record*, May-July, 1926.
23. J.J. Mills, Circular to Branch Secretaries and Delegates, 7 November 1928.
24. The Emile Burns Papers, Labour Research Department.
25. *Report of the Final Stages of Negotiations* ..., TGWU, 28 March 1929.
26. Routh, op.cit., p.134.
27. Barker and Robbins, op.cit., Vol.II, p.217.
28. Ibid., p.215.
29. Ibid., p.232.
30. Labour Research Department, *The London Traffic Combine*, probably 1932.
31. A.M. Ross, *Trade Union Wage Policy*, Berkeley 1948, p.22.
32. Bullock, op.cit., pp.218-9.
33. Hutt, op.cit., p.110.
34. Ibid., pp.97-8.
35. Ibid., p.116.

CHAPTER NINE

The Roots of The Rank and File Movement

In the last chapter we saw that a major reason for discontent in the London Bus Section was the failure of the official leadership to fight for the improvements in wages and conditions which many members felt were both justified and realisable. The other major factor which must be considered in any attempt to explain the rise of the London Busmen's Rank and File Movement in 1932 resides in the history of previous unofficial activity within the Section.

After the Bolshevik Revolution in 1917 Communist busworkers (some of whom would, presumably, have been part of the syndicalist trend within the London and Provincial Union) played a leading role in such activity. This group was certainly active in its criticism of the Second International after the formation in Moscow of a Third (Communist) International in 1919.

Following the Second Congress of the Comintern in 1920 a Provisional International Council of Trade and Industrial Unions (PICTIU) was established. The National Administrative Council of Shop Stewards' and Workers' Committees (which had grown up in the course of the industrial unrest in the latter stages of the war) agreed upon the

> necessity for acting in close contact with the Communist Party and to assist in furthering the interests of the revolutionary movement as a whole ... The Shop Stewards and Workers' Committees and the Communist Party should devise some convenient arrangement to ensure perfect harmony in the activities of the two organisations.[1]

In December 1920 a British Bureau of PICTIU was established. The following month representatives of the Shop Stewards and Workers' Committees met at the headquarters of the Communist Party, resolving that

> the need for a national unofficial industrial movement is urgent and that every effort should be made to secure that the control of this movement should be in the hands of the Communist Party of Great Britain.

The meeting saw the duty of such an unofficial movement as working 'within the existing trade union movement with the object of recreating that movement along industrial lines', to 'seize such opportunities as arise that tend towards Revolution' and 'to work for the allegiance of the trade union movement being transferred from the Amsterdam [the new International established by the right wing of the old Second International] to the Red International'.

In mid-1921 PICTIU gave way to the permanent Red International of Labour Unions (RILU). The policy of the RILU as determined by its founding Congress was

> to establish the closest possible contact with the Third (Communist) International, as the vanguard of the revolutionary movement in all parts of the world, on the basis of joint representation at both executive committees, joint conferences, etc ... It is imperative for every country to strive ... for the establishment of close everyday contact between the Red Trade Unions and the Communist Party.[2]

It is probably no coincidence that on 16 March 1921 – two months after the meeting at King Street, the Communist Party headquarters – F.W. Johnson was denouncing the Second International in the *UVW Record* as 'but a makeshift, an International of social patriots and would-be Ministers of capitalist governments ...' and calling upon members to

> get to their lodge meetings and get resolutions passed instructing the EC to sever its affiliation to the 'Second' and to link up with the 'Red' International of Trade Unions and Industrial Unions.

The Second International came in for further criticism a fortnight later, this time from Charles Carter:

> Its supporters are advocates of reform and revolution by evolution. They seek to bring about a new order of society as a result of educating the masses to a realisation of their class position and then by industrial and political effort to wrench the power from the capitalist class. I wish them luck, and feel constrained to add 'poor ignorant fools'.[3]

In April the *UVW Record* announced as a straight news item that PICTIU would be holding a Conference at the Socialist Club in City Road, North London, on 7 May. The meeting would be chaired by Tom Mann and the UVW's George Sanders would be among the speakers. Of the 217 trade union branches represented at the meeting, 15 were from the UVW. A motion was passed calling for support of the British Bureau in its attempts to secure affiliation to the Red International. (Emile Burns, of whom the London Bus Section was to see a great deal more after 1932, was involved in the establishment of the British Bureau's London District Committee.) Seconding the motion, George Sanders, who was elected to the London District Committee of the British Bureau,

> warned the delegates against the oily persuasion of Labour leaders who only looked upon the movement as a sort of profession. They would, he said, shortly be coming along and very eloquently declaring that, although they had been defeated, the workers, Phoenix-like from the ashes would rise again. He warned them against that sort of rubbish. There had been talk enough, what we wanted was action.[4]

Considered in this light, Sanders' strong misgivings concerning the UVW's pending amalgamation into the TGWU become even more coherent. The establishment of the Comintern and the RILU had been brought about by social-democratic and labourist support for the war, and it was this very fact which Sanders stressed in his remarks to readers of the *UVW Record* in January 1921. Then again, the 'essential aim' of the British Bureau, in the words of William Gallacher, was

> not to organise independent revolutionary trade unions, or to split the revolutionary elements away from the existing organisations affiliated to the TUC ... but to convert the revolutionary minority into a revolutionary majority.[5]

The UVW, with its militant core of London busworkers, must have seemed to Sanders and his comrades a much better candidate for such an exercise than the TGWU where, in Sanders' own words, the busworkers would be rubbing shoulders with officials who 'went over to the side of the capitalist class while the late war was in progress'.[6]

In Britain difficulties were experienced in implementing the RILU decision to set up a national unofficial organisation. The RILU had been formed at a time when the militant post-war upsurge had receded and, with the economy in crisis, the employers were already staging a determined counter-attack; also, the Communist Party was quite small. Thus, despite pressure from the parent body and the Comintern, the National Minority Movement (NMM or MM) was not inaugurated until August 1924. After the miners (who had gone ahead to form their own Minority Movement in January 1924) and the engineers, transport workers formed the largest section of the NMM. At its foundation, the

Movement boasted 271 affiliates; a year later it had 443, the peak of 547 being reached in March 1926.[7] According to Martin the Movement was strongest in London, where there was 'extensive support in the engineering, railway, dock and bus industries'.[8]

Given the absence of hard documentary evidence it is difficult to chart the activity of the MM in the London Bus Section, but Barrett thinks that the strength of the Movement in North-East London, especially in the Holloway garage, may have been responsible for the threatened strike by nine garages over schedules on New Year's Day 1925. Later in the month there was a threatened strike over schedules at Seven Kings, a strike took place at Plumstead and Sidcup, and another action threatened at Hendon.

Martin points out that after the General Strike the gap between the MM and the official trade union movement widened. By 1927 this had reached the point where William Payne, later a leader of the London Busmen's Rank and File Movement (and, even more ironically, of the breakaway National Passenger Workers' Union) was criticising the MM at that year's Biennial Delegate Conference for attempting to organise a breakaway among London's bus and tram workers.[9]

Unofficial actions continued. During one week in October 1928 there were no less than eight threats of such action. Easter 1929 saw a work-to-rule at Cricklewood over the running time of route 46. This action, according to Barrett, seems to have been led by Communist busmen, 'although the branch officials were also involved'.[10] Upon hearing of the plans for unofficial action, Bevin called a special meeting of the GEC and through the fulltime officials, issued a warning that 'on no account would the Union support any members who took part in unofficial action ...'[11] When the work to rule commenced on Good Friday, J.J. Mills, the London District Secretary, following a meeting with the LGOC, visited one of the route 46's termini and warned several members that the dispute was unofficial and that they must 'be prepared to accept the consequences of such action'.[12] The following day Bevin instructed him to repeat this action. Nineteen members were then suspended by the LGOC. After two Cricklewood deputations to Bevin the union entered negotiations with the LGOC, securing the reinstatement of the suspended men. The GEC decided that a Special Committee should be established to inquire into both the Cricklewood dispute itself and, more ominously, 'the position of the London Bus Section having regard to the existence of unofficial movements'.[13] As a result of this inquiry, C.A. Drabwell, the Branch Secretary of Cricklewood, was removed from office and debarred until 1933.

According to *The Times* the dispute at Cricklewood was an 'open revolt against the leadership of the union by the Communists.[14] That may well have been the case, but Barrett goes too far when he suggests that the co-ordination of unofficial industrial action 'may be attributable to the Minority Movement':[15] the very nature of buswork in London, with so many garages within easy reach of each other and the easy contacts between crews from different garages on the road, lends itself to this kind of co-ordination, and as Barrett himself admits, there is evidence of similar activity in the LPU and the UVW. Ernest Bevin himself seems to have had some difficulty in distinguishing between Minority Movement activity and 'traditional' unofficial action, for having promptly dubbed a strike at Barking (the 'Barking Clock' dispute) in 1929 an MM 'stunt', he quickly found a delegation from the branch on his doorstep, as a result of which he withdrew the allegation. Even so, this did not mean that the Barking men displayed any great loyalty to the leadership, for the very men who insisted that the Strike Committee had no links with the MM pointed out that the busworkers were 'out to fight Mondism' and that they had to fight against both union and company.

The MM was unable to effectively mobilise and co-ordinate the widespread opposition to the Mondist policies of Bevin *vis à vis* the LGOC. To a large extent this is explained by the fact that in 1928 the Sixth Congress of the Comintern propounded its 'class against class' line, according to which social democracy was branded as 'social fascism' and reformist trade union leaders were equated with the employers. The emphasis in the RILU and its affiliates was therefore shifted from working *within* the existing trade unions to the formation of 'red' alternatives.

While the Communist Party of Great Britain accepted the policy with regard to the Labour Party (which was characterised as a 'third capitalist party'), the trade-union component of the line was applied with great reluctance.[16] The fact that it was accepted by British Communists at all was, according to Noreen Branson, conditioned by the fact that since the General Strike the Labour leaders had sought to 'outlaw' Communists in both the Labour Party and the trade union movement.[17] The trade union line involved the concept of 'independent leadership', with the formation of factory committees which were to result in the eventual establishment of new, revolutionary trade unions.

In the London Bus Section the MM now called for the establishment of garage committees 'under the leadership of the MM and entirely independent of the union apparatus'.[18] Even the branch machinery 'with its threatening, lying and confusing instructions from Union HQ cannot possibly supply a lead to us in our struggles to defend conditions except when used UNCONSTITUTIONALLY'.[19] The MM attacked not only Bevin and the LGOC during this phase, but also rank and file militants like Papworth and Payne, later leaders of the London Busmen's Rank and File Movement.

At this juncture a Rank and File Committee (which should not be confused with the Rank & File Committees of 1919 and 1932, although there were obvious connections with the latter), was launched quite independently of the MM. It would seem plausible that this was a response, conscious or otherwise, to the sectarian developments within the MM.. In May 1929, 700 busworkers attended a mass meeting chaired by Bert Papworth which condemned Bevin's role in the Cricklewood dispute and called for the resignation of Mills, the London District Secretary.

Throughout the mid-1920s members appear to have been dropping out of the union. In 1927 the GEC turned down a request for official sanction for strike action over non-unionism, and a similar request was denied in 1931. The actions of the MM during its sectarian phase probably contributed to non-union membership, for while the Rank and File Committee called for 100 per cent membership and called unofficial stoppages on the issue,[20] the MM sneeringly replied that 'the call for 100 per cent membership of the TGWU is nothing but a call for 100 per cent company unionism'.[21]

To the extent that the 'class against class' line was implemented in Britain it proved disastrous. The Fifth RILU Congress in 1930 noted that the MM, then reduced to 700 active members,[22] was 'practically isolated from the masses'.[23] In September that year William Rust wrote in the *Communist International* of 'the most glaring example of the disastrous results of "Left" sectarianism'.[24] Given the behaviour of the TGWU leadership, it is possible that the 'class against class' line had more appeal to Communist busworkers in London than to other sections of the trade union movement; but here, too, it had negative results. In a letter to *The Worker*, the MM journal, in December 1929, one busman warned that 'the more we attack the present policy of the union at this juncture, the more we drive the men into the breakaway union which numbers approximately six hundred members.'[25] (This small breakaway, which according to Barrett was independent of the MM, was formed in the wake of the Barking Clock dispute in 1929.) In the same issue, another busworker complained that:

> ... the MM is in bad favour with busmen, even the most sensible proposition coming from one associated with the MM is received with distrust, and there is a tendency for sympathisers to hide their identity with the MM.

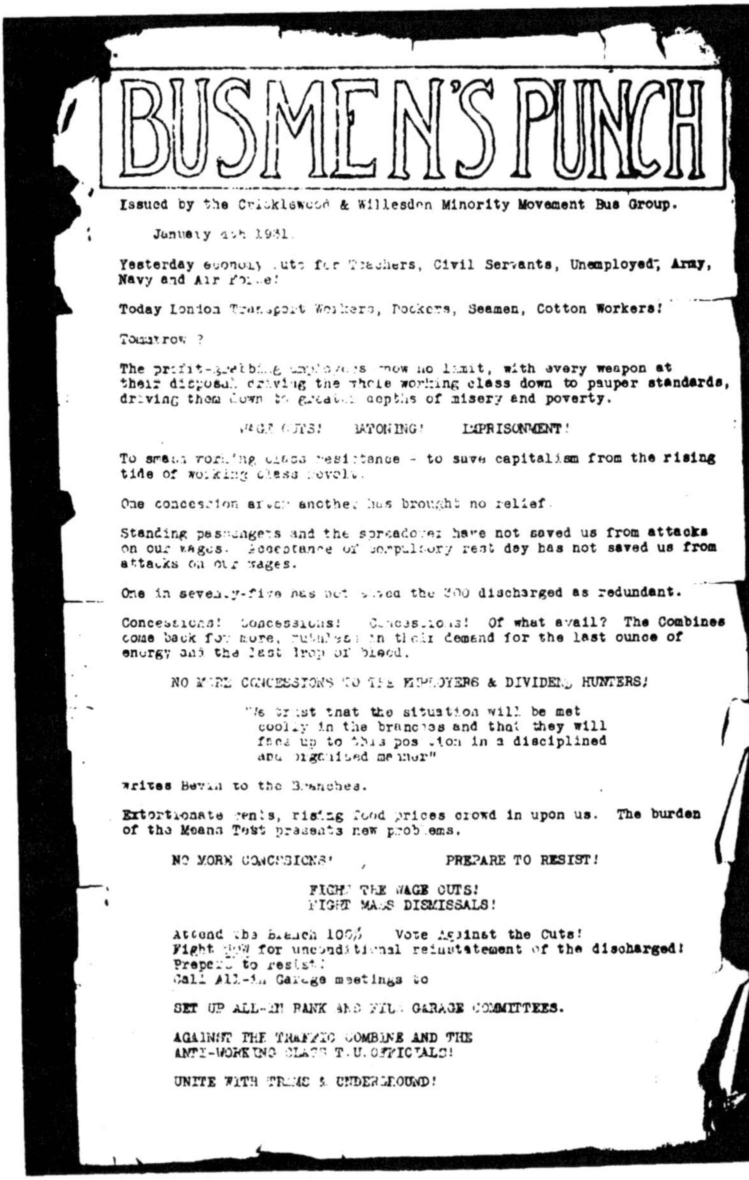

BUSMEN'S PUNCH

Issued by the Cricklewood & Willesden Minority Movement Bus Group.

January 4th 1931.

Yesterday economy cuts for Teachers, Civil Servants, Unemployed, Army, Navy and Air Force!

Today London Transport Workers, Dockers, Seamen, Cotton Workers!

Tomorrow ?

The profit-grabbing employers know no limit, with every weapon at their disposal driving the whole working class down to pauper standards, driving them down to greater depths of misery and poverty.

WAGE CUTS! BATONING! IMPRISONMENT!

To smash working class resistance - to save capitalism from the rising tide of working class revolt.

One concession after another has brought no relief.

Standing passengers and the spreadover have not saved us from attacks on our wages. Acceptance of compulsory rest day has not saved us from attacks on our wages.

One in seventy-five has not saved the 300 discharged as redundant.

Concessions! Concessions! Concessions! Of what avail? The Combines come back for more, ruthless in their demand for the last ounce of energy and the last drop of blood.

NO MORE CONCESSIONS TO THE EMPLOYERS & DIVIDEND HUNTERS!

"We trust that the situation will be met coolly in the branches and that they will face up to this position in a disciplined and organised manner"

writes Bevin to the Branches.

Extortionate rents, rising food prices crowd in upon us. The burden of the Means Test presents new problems.

NO MORE CONCESSIONS! PREPARE TO RESIST!

FIGHT THE WAGE CUTS!
FIGHT MASS DISMISSALS!

Attend the Branch 100% Vote Against the Cuts!
Fight NOW for unconditional reinstatement of the discharged!
Prepare to resist!
Call All-in Garage meetings to

SET UP ALL-IN RANK AND FILE GARAGE COMMITTEES.

AGAINST THE TRAFFIC COMBINE AND THE ANTI-WORKING CLASS T.U. OFFICIALS!

UNITE WITH TRAMS & UNDERGROUND!

The first issue of *Busmen's Punch*, which began life as a Minority Movement sheet edited (and probably written) by George Renshaw, the Communist Party's London industrial organiser.

No. 1. JULY 1931

NUMBER ONE!

The "BUSMENS' PUNCH" has landed home, first time of asking. Its aim is to ventilate grievances at North West London garages, also to show up what is going on in other parts, and to bring together all bus workers who did'nt go to sleep some years ago.

The Company is not asleep. It is now preparing the ground for a bigger speed up and more dismissals than even those it has carried out already.

Your fight is the same as the fight of the engineers, miners, and textile workers. Don't think you are in a safe position. It is a class fight against your class enemies, who are cutting wages and conditions all round, cutting employment benefits, and preparing for war to maintain their rent, interest and profits.

Wake up brothers! Put your strength behind the "PUNCH"! Give it your support by buying a copy regularly, and by sending in letters and notes for publication. Address for correspondence is given on another page.

TRADE UNION AGENDA AND WAR.

At a Trade Union Branch in Cricklewood, one of the items on the Agenda was "The Flying Club". This is rather an interesting development in the way of Trade Union Agendas, and certainly a change from "WAGES" Why a Flying Club for busworkers?

Why is someone so keen on bus workers knowing something about aeroplanes? So that they can fill up the gaps in the Air Force when the time comes?

At the Albert Hall the other day, when employers and parsons and cabinet ministers got together to talk about "disarmament" Baldwin said that the Air Forces were the "spear-head" of invasion. The Labour Government, which sends MacDonald to the Albert Hall and to Geneva to talk about "disarmament" is spending more than one hundred million pounds a year keeping up its armed forces, and is particularly building up the Air Force. At London the other day some of the Labour Government's new aircraft were on show - bigger and faster and able to fly further than the old types. They are "the spear-head of invasion"

Where are they going to invade? A writer in the "Aeroplane" a week or two ago gave the answer -

"When we have to fight hordes of Eastern barbarians...... The air scouts will radio movies of the Soviet Armies direct from the scene of action"

War against Workers' Russia - that is what the aeroplanes are for - that is why the press is campaigning against Russia.

On AUGUST 1st workers in all countries will show that they stand together against the war-mongers and in defence of Soviet Russia.

LONDON WORKERS WILL MEET AT TRAFALGAR SQUARE.

July 1931 *Busmens' Punch*, revived by a group of Communist busworkers in North-West London.

By this time the MM was publishing (or had published) a number of branch newspapers, centred on Holloway, Hackney, Chalk Farm and Battersea bus garages – see, for example, the Cricklewood news-sheet on p.102. In July 1931 *Busmens' Punch*, the first attempt to reach the whole fleet, was launched, only to fold up after a few months. Although produced by a group at Cricklewood (and not, as claimed by Bullock and Clegg, at Holloway),[26] this version of *Punch* was edited by George Renshaw,[27] a member of the British Bureau of the RILU and London Industrial Organiser of the Communist Party. At the same time Frank Snelling of Merton, soon to be chairman of the London Busmen's Rank and File Movement, was associated with a publication called *The Bus Wheel.*

Most of these journals were soon to disappear for, convinced of the erroneousness of the 'class against class' line in British industrial conditions, in late 1931 Harry Pollitt, General Secretary of the Communist Party of Great Britain, attacked the line at a meeting of the RILU Central Council in Moscow, arguing that the British party needed to mobilise opposition *within* the trade unions, not to form alternatives. As a result of this the CPGB was given dispensation to adopt its own line. Thus, in January 1932 a statement entitled 'The Turn To Mass Work' was presented to the party's Central Committee, putting forward a perspective for concentration on London, Lancashire, Scotland and South Wales, with special emphasis on the formation of work-place groups and the winning of leading positions in trade union branches.[28] It was in these circumstances that the MM journals in the London Bus Section were wound up. *Busmens' Punch* would, however, reappear – first as a straightforward Communist publication and then as the journal of the London Busmen's Rank and File Movement, the most spectacular achievement of the Communist Party's new line and the most effective such organisation of its kind the British trade union movement has ever seen.

Notes

1. R. Martin, *Communism and the British Trade Union Movement*, Oxford 1969, p.18.
2. Ibid., p.13.
3. Barrett, op.cit., p.56.
4. *UVW Record*, 11 May 1921.
5. Martin, op.cit., p.29.
6. *UVW Record*, January 1921.
7. Martin, op.cit., p.182.

8. Ibid., p.58.
9. Bullock, op.cit., p.377.
10. Barrett, op.cit., p.56.
11. GEC minutes, 10 April 1929.
12. Ibid.
13. Ibid.
14. Barrett, op.cit., p.56.
15. Ibid., p.42.
16. N. Branson, *History of the Communist Party of Great Britain, 1927-1941*, London 1985, pp.38-43.
17. Ibid., pp.1-15.
18. *The Worker*, 7 February 1930, quoted in Barrett, op.cit., p.64.
19. *Holloway Bus Worker*, April 1931.
20. Barrett, op.cit., pp.65-6.
21. Ibid., p.67.
22. Martin, op.cit., p.126.
23. Ibid., p.152.
24. Ibid., p.153.
25. Barrett, op.cit., p.17.
26. *Busman's Punch*, 4 November 1932.
27. Noreen Branson in discussion with the author, January 1984.
28. Idris Cox in J. Attfield and S. Williams (eds), *1939: The Communist Party and the War*, London 1984, p.95.

PART THREE

The London Busmen's Rank and File Movement

CHAPTER TEN

The Movement is Established

There has been considerable debate over the role of the Communist Party in the foundation and leadership of the London Busmen's Rank and File Movement. In Barrett's view the suggestion by Henry Pelling that the Movement was 'sponsored by the Communist Party',[1] and Bullock's contention that the Communists, while few in number, exercised a dominant influence, are both mistaken.[2] Instead, Barrett maintains that the 'Party did not lead the busmen's movement' and that 'in some respects, the busmen did more for the Party than it did for them' as the Movement 'came to be a model for Communist militants'.[3] In this Chapter, which deals with the events of 1932, Barrett's contention will be shown to be false and that in fact the Rank and File Movement arose largely out of Communist initiatives and was led by Communists.

In early 1932 the London General Omnibus Company, faced with falling receipts due to the depression, gave notice that it intended to terminate Clause I of the agreement. Wages would be reduced by $2\frac{1}{2}$ per cent in the first £2 and by 5 per cent thereafter. It was also proposed that 400 drivers, conductors and garage engineering staff be discharged in August, to be followed by a further 200 in October after the introduction of speeded schedules.

The negotiations between the company and the TGWU lasted until August. The former's 'final' offer consisted of a reduction of three-eighths of a penny per hour for drivers and a farthing per hour for conductors. In return for this, hours would be shortened so that 80 per cent of all duties would come within a maximum of eight-and-a-half hours, a reduction of half-an-hour. The less drastic wage-reduction was seen, in the words of a union circular, as 'monetary compensation' for the speeded schedules.[4] The company agreed to retain the 'surplus' men on condition that the guaranteed week for spare staff be reduced from 48 hours to 40 hours, and then to 32 hours, with the full 48 hours being restored after Easter 1933. Seasonal reductions in the guaranteed week for spare staff had been commonplace in the 1920s,[5] and, in fact, had been agreed as recently as 1931, when the LGOC had been threatening to discharge 375 men.[6] By agreeing to this reduction, the union was concerned not only to retain members but (at least during the earlier period) to guard against unemployed, trained drivers being recruited by the 'pirates'.

The militants within the Section were concerned by the apparent defeatism of Bevin and the lay leadership and moves were soon afoot to organise unofficial opposition to the cuts. By this time the earlier sectarianism of the Minority Movement had resulted in the effective isolation of the Communist Party within the Section; by early 1932 it was reduced to one cell at Cricklewood and a number of individual members at Willesden (including Bernard Sharkey, an ex-policeman dismissed after the police strike of 1919), Holloway, Edgware, Enfield and a few other garages.[7] Now the Party and the Minority Movement set to work organising the submission of protest resolutions. Particular attention was given to Enfield, where two mass meetings endorsed a resolution calling on all garages to 'prepare rank-and-file machinery for strike action' against the cuts and for reinstatement of the dismissed men. The branch reprinted this resolution at its own expense and distributed 10,000 copies throughout the bus fleet. The outcome was that in the Eastern area about 18 garages endorsed the Minority Movement Resolution. In this area two well-attended mass meetings were called at the Stratford Empire which declared for 'strike action against the cuts'.[8] As a result of this activity eight or nine 'busmen from various garages joined the Communist Party'.[9]

In July *Busmans Punch* was restarted by a group of Communist busmen. The big news story in the first issue was that Upton Park had taken a stand against speeded schedules, forcing their withdrawal by strike action. The second issue sought to allay any lingering fears concerning the former sectarianism of the Party with an article warning of the dangers of a breakaway union.

The misgivings concerning the defeatism of Bevin and the CBC were strengthened by the fact that at the 25 July London Bus Conference no full report of the negotiations with the LGOC was given. 'But enough leaked out to make it clear to the delegates that drastic proposals on wages, conditions and redundancy had been put forward by the company.'[10] The refusal to give a full report was made in spite of an undertaking given by Bevin and the CBC

> on three occasions that the Delegate Conference would be consulted on any matter concerning wages, speed and redundancy, and the undertaking was now broken by the announcement that the stencilled report of the negotiations would reach Branch Secretaries and Delegates by 27 July.[11]

When the report did not arrive as promised, Poplar and other garages called midnight meetings for 30 July. The full-time officials sent around two circulars promising that the report would arrive later and asking that the members resist taking unofficial action. Despite the fact that after the eventual arrival of the report 40 branch meetings rejected the terms by overwhelming majorities, the Central Bus Committee decided that the Section should be balloted. The August issue of the reconstituted *Busmans Punch* gave short shrift to J.J. Mills' claim that this decision had been taken in response to requests from many branches:

> *This is a plain lie.* The branches have already expressed themselves definitely against the cuts, and the ballot is a clever last minute attempt to spread confusion and disunity among us, and to sidetrack the definite move for strike action which is growing up in every branch.

The branch at Chelverton Road circulated the fleet with a resolution opposing the wage cuts and invited all branches to be represented at a mass meeting on 12 August. This meeting, attended by a majority of the branches, saw the birth of the Rank and File Movement. There is some confusion regarding how many branches *did* attend the meeting. In his pamphlet quoted below, Renshaw puts the figure at 27; in his report to the Communist Party's Central Committee in October 1932, he quotes 33. Barrett puts the figure at a more modest 21. Bert Papworth, Branch Secretary of Chelverton Road, was elected Organiser. A powerful speaker, Papworth had joined the LGOC in 1927 after amassing considerable industrial experience. At the age of sixteen he had become Branch Chairman and led his first strike at Morgan Crucible and in the following two years, 1917 and 1918, was active during the strikes at the Woolwich Arsenal. Far from favouring a breakaway, he had been awarded the TGWU's gold medal for recruiting 170 new members shortly before the formation of the Rank and File Movement. A professed Catholic, 'Pappy' did not join the Communist Party until after the 1937 strike. Frank Snelling, cool, intelligent and a member of the anti-Communist Socialist Party of Great Britain, was elected Chairman. The Movement's first Treasurer was Bill Payne of Dalston, who had joined the LGOC as early as 1908 to become a founder-member of the LPU five years later. Although a Labour voter, the available evidence suggests that Payne was never a member of any political party. Bill Jones, also from Dalston Garage, became the Movement's Correspondence Secretary. A gravelly-voiced Cockney given to colourful language, Jones remained a bus driver until his retirement in 1968, by which time he had become a member of the General Executive Council of the

TGWU and the TUC General Council.

That first meeting on 12 August 1932 resolved to establish a Committee of Rank and File Delegates and to conduct a campaign against the threatened wage-cuts and dismissals. Mass meetings were immediately arranged for Penge, Stratford, Holloway, Battersea and other venues.

Bert Papworth is commonly portrayed as the main organiser of the inaugural meeting. Of course, as secretary of the branch convening it his name would have been on the circular. But in his report to the Communist Party's Central Committee in October, George Renshaw (the party's London District Industrial Organiser), described it as having been called by 'a group of delegates led by MMers and contacts'. By this time a Communist Party cell of three members had been established at Chelverton Road and, along with Payne of Dalston and Bill Ware of Enfield (the latter being a Communist), Renshaw described Papworth as one of the 'three Committee members most in touch with' him.[12] Thus it would seem that Papworth, while at this stage not a Communist, had entered into a close co-operation with the party.

When the ballot was held the membership rejected the wage-cuts by 16,593 votes to 4,469 and the dismissals by 13,461 votes to 4,212.[13] It is impossible to determine to what extent this result was due to the activity of the new unofficial body, but there is no doubt that it swiftly acquired a very large following. Its first pamphlet, *The London Busmen's Case*, sold 30,000 copies in a single week. A second pamphlet, *Speed*, sold 20,000 copies in a similar period. By its fourth issue, *Busmans Punch*, which the organisation adopted under the technical editorship of Emile Burns (a leading Communist, although not a busman), was achieving a sale of 8,000 copies per month.

The Rank and File Committee stepped up the agitation, organising a demonstration at the London Bus Conference of 29/30 August to which, 'apparently much against Bro. Bevin's wishes', a Rank and File deputation was admitted by Conference vote.[14] The previous day they had organised a mass demonstration in Hyde Park; the following Sunday another was held in Trafalgar Square; two weeks later 2,000 busworkers marched from Temple Station to Hyde Park in torrential rain, to be met by thousands more in the Park where six platforms were used by busmen speakers.

As a result of the massive resistance throughout the fleet the company was forced to abandon its proposals for wage-reductions. The proposal for dismissals was withdrawn also, although the guaranteed week for spare staff with less than three years' service was to be reduced to 40 hours. The improvements in spreadover and time on duty conceded during the negotiations were retained. However the company would not be budged on the introduction of speeded schedules. Lobbying the London Bus Conference which accepted these terms, a Rank and File spokesman warned that 'it is one thing to secure the acceptance of speeded schedules at this Conference, and quite another to actually operate those speeded schedules.' This remark was to prove prophetic, for during the next three months there was industrial action over the new schedules at seven garages.

'Speed' was central to the Rank and File Committee's case. In its first pamphlet it pointed out that the company was saving seven minutes per hour, or 56 minutes per day. With the average 34 minutes 'build up time' in the current schedules, this would give the LGOC 90 minutes in which to schedule extra journeys, resulting in a saving of £911,000 per year. Both driver and conductor were affected by such schedules, as the former was allowed less time to travel between timing-points while the latter had less time in between stops to collect fares (and, due to increased seating capacity, more fares to collect).

In its second pamphlet, *Speed*, the unofficial body noted that whereas previous new bus-types had raised the average speed from 9.3 mph to 10.1 mph, with an actual speed between stops of 20 mph, the schedules introduced now were based on an average speed of 14.3 mph, necessitating a speed of at least 30 mph between stops. As evidence of this the cases were cited of the Forest Gate driver who was fined £2 for travelling at 43 mph and the Elmers End man who had been fined for doing over 40 mph even though he was still a minute late at the timing-point. The pamphlet noted that

> the public must understand that the purpose of the speeding up is not to help the public, but to enable the company to take buses off the road, thus saving running costs, repair costs, and wages for crews and repair staffs, and increasing the enormous profits of the combine.

By taking ten minutes off of each journey, for example, route 110 had been reduced from 24 duties to 16.

Speeded schedules were linked with the fact that while death benefits from the LGOC Employees' Death Levy, Distress, and Sick Friendly Society had totalled 103 in 1926, by 1931 the annual total had increased to 165. Distress grants for sickness in the same years totalled 1,755 and 2,019.

Ernest Bevin, on the other hand, despite his remarks about

THE BUSMANS PUNCH

No. 5. JANUARY 1932.

TERMINATION

No busmen should be surprised at the action of the L.G.O.C. in terminating the agreement. The events of the last few years and especially since the Mond "Peace in Industry" Conferences were bound to lead to the present position. The success in speeding up, schedule wanglings, bigger buses, and the treachery of the officials in putting across the 1 in 60 compulsory has whetted the appetite of the bosses. They are not content with the pickings and prunings alone. They feel the moment has arrived to make a direct attack on wages, and so the agreement has to be ended and negotiations to be opened on the basis of a cut in wages.

BEVIN'S POLICY

The very first utterance of Bevin should warn us immediately that there is no time to be lost in preparing rank-and-file leadership. He says "No meeting of the E.C. has been called. The only thing I can say is that we must face up to the matter and give it the most careful attention." This statement coming on top of the betrayal of the dockers, shows us just where Bevan & Co stand.

Let us keep in mind that the big and little Bevins of Transport House are definitely pledged to Peace in Industry. This means that if we are to combat the wage cuts, we must set about the task of rank-and-file leadership without delay. Every effort must be made to bring together the organised and unorganised busmen.

FIGHTING SPIRIT SPREADS.

Reports from all over London show that the militant spirit is spreading. Garage after garage is pledging itself to resist any cut and calling for strike action. There is no shadow of doubt that the busmen are determined to resist. They realise that the Company has seized upon the crisis to beat us down still further. The L.G.O.C feel that it is an opportunity too good to be lost. A glance at the figures given on another page will show conclusively that they have made, and are making huge profits.

NEED FOR VIGILANCE.

With the steadily rising cost of living it is imperative that we resist all encroachments, whether direct or indirect, upon our already depleted standard of life.

(contd page 2, col.1)

Retitled *Busmans Punch*, by January 1932 the paper had acquired its punching-fist logo.

intensification in 1925, no longer saw speed as an issue worth fighting. At a meeting with the LGOC on 19 March 1930 he

> stated that he did not object to a change being made in the running times, he would advise the staff that they must accept it, but this must be accompanied by concessions in time and/or in money.[15]

It would seem from this that his belief that conditions should not be traded for wage-increases, apparently deeply-held in 1921, had waned.

The battle against speed opened in January 1933 when the new schedules were introduced at Forest Gate. All 500 busworkers employed there struck from midnight, putting a mass picket of 300 on the gate. In the morning, following an address by Rank and File speakers, all 300 marched to Upton Park, where 1,000 joined the strike. The Rank and File Movement (as the Rank and File Committee had since renamed itself) called mass meetings at Barking, Seven Kings, Romford and Dalston garages, all of which joined the strike. By 21 January 13,000 men at 26 garages (over half the fleet) were on strike despite 'repeated orders of the reformist union officials to remain at work'.[16] Lord Ashfield posted a statement at every garage stating that 'in this strike we stand in the same position as the union leaders.'

On the evening of 23 January representatives of all the garages affected were called together by the Rank and File Movement, and a deputation of between 50 and 60 travelled to Transport House and met with the Finance and General Purposes Committee, the Central Bus Committee and the full-time officials.[17] John Cliff, the union's Assistant General Secretary, gave an assurance that the Forest Gate grievances would receive immediate attention and that an undertaking would be sought from the LGOC that there would be no victimisation. On this basis the strike was called off.

On 26 January the Finance and General Purposes Committee attended a Special Conference of the London Bus Section comprising three delegates from each branch. Here Cliff pointed out the facilities which existed within the Section for resolving grievances and that, therefore, it should be understood that

> those members who accept any of the offices of a Branch, membership of the Central Bus Committee, or the office of Branch Representative to the Delegate Conferences, are not entitled and would not be allowed to serve on unofficial Committees formed for the purpose of determining the trade policy of this Union.[18]

At Forest Gate, meanwhile, new schedules were issued which, according to Renshaw, led the members to claim that it 'would have been worth a three-months' strike to win such schedules'.[19] At other garages where disagreements over schedules had been outstanding there were speedy improvements.[20] Over the next few years there were a number of schedules disputes but, although victories were gained in certain cases, the LGOC and, after 1933, the London Passenger Transport Board, succeeded in their attempts to introduce speeded schedules. The following table tells the story.

Thus, although the average time on bus showed a reduction of almost 25 minutes per day between January 1930 and January 1936, miles per crew increased by an average of 2.6 miles per day. It was on the basis of this increased exploitation that the Rank and File Movement developed its arguments relating to the health of busworkers, which were to play an important part in the campaign for the seven-hour day.

On 5 October 1932 the Rank and File Committee met and set itself on a permanant footing, renaming it the London Busmen's Rank and File Movement (RFM). It was here that *Busmans Punch* was adopted as the 'official' organ of the Movement. Membership was to be on the basis of branch affiliations, with each branch entitled to six delegates, including two from the garage engineering staff. An Organising Committee would be responsible for decision-making in between monthly RFM Conference while an Editorial Committee would be elected from the Organising Committee.

This was the 'model for Communist militants'. It should be obvious from the above, however, that the Communists played a major role in the formation of the RFM. But the question remains: was the Movement *led* by Communists? George Renshaw's 1933 pamphlet, *The London Busmen's Victorious Strike*, is instructive in this respect. Before the establishment of the RFM, he says:

> ... the militant forces numbered twelve members spread over the whole Bus Fleet of 25,000 workers. They had no points of contact or roots in the garages. There were no fractions or groups within the Union Branches ...
>
> ... The problem the militant group had to tackle was to bridge the gulf which existed between itself and the busmen, to become *of* the busmen, to cease to be an 'outside' body. This meant dropping the sectarian practice of speaking *at* the busmen, and to speak with them. To cease taking issues *to* the busmen and to find out from the busmen which were the issues with which they were concerned, and on this basis to develop the first elementary forms of an opposition movement of the workers ...
>
> ... Contrary to its previous practice of issuing 'revolutionary' declarations

Comparison of Scheduled Cost and Hours of Labour at Specified Dates

Monday to Friday

Date	*Average time on bus hours minutes*	*Spreadover hours minutes*	*Miles per Crew*	*Wages per car mile per man Driver*	*Conductor* (in pence)
January 1930	6.58	8.30	60.2	2.950	2.714
July 1930	6.55	8.29	59.8	2.967	2.729
January 1931	6.56	8.29	60.0	2.957	2.720
July 1931	6.54	8.28	60.0	2.957	2.720
January 1935	6.35	8.10	63.2	2.789	2.598
July 1935	6.34	8.10	63.1	2.817	2.664
January 1936	6.33	8.09	62.8	2.832	2.679

Source: Emile Burns papers in possession of Labour Research Department.

> and manifestoes, which had little or no effect upon the busmen, the militant group on this occasion set to work in the one trade union branch where it had influence* ...

Renshaw is obviously talking of the Minority Movement/Communist Party when he mentions the 'twelve members' and the 'sectarian practice of speaking *at* the busmen'. Following the agreement of the Communist International to changes in the attitude to trade unions advocated by Pollitt, Renshaw himself, as the party's Industrial Organiser for London, would have been directing the Communist busmen to work along the very lines he describes. By working in this way the party overcame its isolation and by October 1932 had about 40 members in the London Bus Section.[21] Indeed, this isolation was overcome to such an extent that from its inception the RFM was able to associate closely with the Labour Research Department (in which members of the Communist Party played a very active part, and thus was frowned upon by the TGWU leadership) and suffer no ill-effects.

However, the Movement *was* broad-based and the Communists were obviously in a minority. There can be no quarrel with Barrett's characterisation of the Movement as a 'united front' of trade union militants. But this can hardly preclude the notion of Communist *leadership* of such a movement. Leadership surely means the ability to mobilise large numbers of people, of varying political outlooks, behind a given policy – something which will only be possible if that policy reflects the interests of the rank and file. By 'speaking with the busmen', and finding out 'which were the issues with which they were concerned', the leaders of the RFM were able, stepping into the vacuum created by Bevin's right-wing policies, to mobilise a mass movement on 'bread and butter' issues and then to proceed to offer leadership on a host of other questions – peace, the nature of the capitalist system, the role of the Soviet Union, etc. If the leadership on such questions reflected the policy and ideology of the Communist Party it can hardly have been coincidental.

In this way the London Busmen's Rank and File Movement succeeded in re-establishing within the Section the link between industrial militancy and politically progressive policies which had been the hallmark of the 'red button' union.

* It is clear, from a careful reading of Renshaw's pamphlet, that Enfield is the branch to which he refers.

Notes

1. H. Pelling, *A History of British Trade Unionism*, London 1963, p.205.
2. Barrett, op.cit., p.85.
3. Ibid., p.86.
4. TGWU circular to Members of the London Bus Section, 15 August 1932.
5. See *The Record*, November 1922, December 1924 and p.72 above.
6. Minutes, General Executive Council, 21 September 1931.
7. Report by George Renshaw to the Central Committee of the Communist Party of Great Britain, probably October, 1932, now in the possession of Noreen Branson.
8. George Renshaw, report to the London District Committee of the Communist Party of Great Britain, 22 April 1932 now in the possession of Noreen Branson.
9. Ibid.
10. Rank and File Delegates' Committee, *Speed*, 1932.
11. Ibid.
12. Renshaw's report to the Central Committee.
13. *Speed.*
14. Ibid.
15. Minutes of meeting between the LGOC and the Central Bus Committee, 19 March 1931.
16. George Renshaw, *The London Busmen's Victorious Strike*, Red International of Labour Unions, 1933.
17. Minutes, Finance and General Purposes Committee, 23 January 1933.
18. Ibid., 26 January 1933.
19. Renshaw, *The London Busmen's Victorious Strike.*
20. Ibid.
21. Renshaw's report to the Central Committee.

CHAPTER ELEVEN

The Role of the RFM

By the beginning of 1935 *Busman's Punch* was still selling between 7,000 and 8,000 copies per month among the 5,000 tramworkers and 22,000 busworkers. Creditable though this achievement may have been, the call was made to increase the circulation to 14,000 – a figure at which the journal (which was now professionally printed) would become self-financing. It was agreed that two members would be paid by the Organising Committee to travel around the fleet, visiting local coffee-shops and newsagents in an attempt to place orders 'where we have no other method of selling'.[1] By June that year 13,000 copies were printed each month, and William Payne, the Movement's Treasurer, expressed the hope that this would increase to 20,000; the financial situation of the Movement was the 'best ever'.[2]

The fact that the RFM, through its monthly journal, reached such a high proportion of the membership of the London Bus Section can leave little doubt that it cóntributed significantly to the level of militancy and political awareness within the Section. In one sense the Movement was in direct line of descent from the 'red button' union and its Vigilance Committee, but this is only true to a point. The RFM certainly did not harbour any secessionist sentiments, for example. Even before the *Busmans Punch* had been adopted by the RFM, the Communists then controlling it stated quite clearly:

> Nothing could be more against the interests of Busmen at the present time than a breakaway from the TGWU, and nothing could suit the combine better.
>
> How would a breakaway affect us? First it would divide the ranks of busmen and leave us easy prey for the combine. Secondly it would give the union officials just the opportunity they need to negotiate cuts on the plea of 'lack of 100 per cent organisation'.[3]

Indeed, the Movement ensured that the London Bus Section became fully involved in the machinery of the union. First, it consolidated its own influence in the London Bus Section by sweeping to victory in the 1933 election for the Central Bus Committee (CBC) electing Sharkey (who had previously won a seat in a by-election), Papworth, Snelling (who became the committee's chairman), Hayward and Ware. This was repeated two years later, with increased majorities. Secondly, the RFM ensured that its members formed the majority of the No.1 Area Passenger Group's delegation to the Biennial Delegate Conference (BDC – the TGWU's national conference) in 1933 and 1935.

At the 1933 BDC Papworth moved a motion, against opposition from the platform, calling for a united front against fascism. Snelling attacked Bevin's plan to reduce unemployment, demanding: 'What the hell do the boss's problems matter to us? We should be doing everything in our power to help the day when capitalism will be overthrown.'[4] Bevin, meanwhile, obviously judging that the time was not yet ripe for a showdown with the RFM, contented himself with carrying an amendment to the rules committing any member taking office to acceptance of the constitution of the Union and working through its machinery'.[5]

Two years later the RFM was once again present in strength. Reporting back to an RFM Conference in July, Ware said:

> It must be understood that the composition of the London delegation of the bus and tram men, if that part of the conference had not been there, it would have been easy to have understood that the conference would have been asleep one hour after it started ... We were fighting the standing orders committee for all we were worth the whole of the time. We were sabotaged by the conference itself. Everybody speaks in favour of a certain line but when the General Secretary speaks the vote goes against us and in accordance with his wishes. The difference between us and the people who follow Bevin is that the composition of the London delegation in the main was that of class consciousness and the others were of a very low character from that aspect.

As an example Ware explained that not one speaker had opposed the motion calling for affiliation to the Labour Research Department.

> People from the north, the south and the west of England had actually benefited from the work put in by the Department and said so, but when it came to the question of the Chairman calling upon the General Secretary and he had spoken, many of them voted against it.[6]

Also defeated at the 1935 BDC was one of the key demands of the old LPU, and of the Bus Section itself – the election of full-time officials; and while, four years earlier, that motion had attracted 119 votes, now it received less than half that number. Ware concluded his report calling for the RFM to

> make contact with our members up and down the country so that we have the solidarity required for the purpose of being able to sweep aside the reactionary executive policy.

The fact that Papworth was elected to the General Executive Council in 1935 is another indication that the RFM saw the London Bus Section as an integral part of the TGWU. There were really two processes at work in this activity. On the one hand the RFM was attempting to win control of the TGWU by the rank and file. On the other, it must surely have occured to the RFM leaders that the TGWU, due to its size, played a crucial role in the policy-formation of the TUC and the Labour Party. Seen in this light the activity of the RFM can be understood as part of the wider struggle by the progressive movement to win the TUC and the Labour Party to more combative, class-oriented policies.

Of course, the RFM was very much in the LPU-Vigilance Committee tradition in that it was brought into existence to mobilise the membership to fight against attacks by the employer in the face of an apparent reluctance by the official leadership of the union to do so.

In this respect it is surprising that there were so few disputes during the lifetime of the RFM. There was in fact no really major dispute between the Forest Gate strike of January 1933 and the Coronation Strike of May 1937. The wage-cuts made in 1921 were fully restored in January 1934, followed by increases of 1s. for drivers and 2s. for conductors in April 1935 and 1s. 6d. and 6d. respectively after the Coronation Strike. As will be seen from the chart on page 123, all but two of the disputes recorded by the LGOC and the London Passenger Transport Board during this period concerned schedules. Moreover, the smaller Trams Section had rather more than their fair share. Clegg notes of the RFM that as 'soon as its leaders became the official leaders of the section they saw problems from a different angle'.[7]

There is some evidence to support this. For example, during the course of a Country Service dispute at Slough in 1935, Papworth and Snelling were asked by the men concerned to visit the branch. Meanwhile Bill Jones, by then the Secretary of the RFM, called by telegram an emergency meeting of the Organising committee. When Papworth and Snelling returned from their meeting at Slough a discussion ensued during which it was announced that they had advised the Slough men to return to work. The Green Line and Country Services men held a meeting and decided to follow this advice. After the Organising

Records of Disputes, 1933-37 Involving LPTB Staff

Date		Location	Duration	Cause
1933				
18 to 23	January	LGOC Garages	Six Days	Objection to new schedules
22 to 23	January	Hanwell Trams	Two days	Sympathy with LGOC crews
22 to 24	January	Stonebridge Park trams	Three Days	Objection to new schedules
1934				
9	May	Hanwell and Acton Trams	One Day	Alteration to arrangements for inspection of new schedules
1	October	Bromley	One Day	Non-fitment of self-starters to '6' type engines
1935				
29 June and 2 July		11 Garages	Two Days	Disciplinary action against two members (the 'Nunhead Dispute')
1936				
10	March	Clapham and Streatham Trams	One Day	Schedules (meal times)
11	March	Wood Green Trams	One Day	Objection to new schedules
8	April	Fulwell and		
9	April	Hounslow Trams	Two Days	Objection to new schedules
5	August	Norwood	Until 7.28 a.m.	Objection to new schedules
7	October	Nine Garages	One day	Objection to new schedules
10	October	Hammersmith and Putney Bridge	One Day	Objection to new schedules
1937				
11	March	Bexley Heath Trams and Trollies	One Day	Objection to new schedules
26	March	Hornchurch	One Day	Objection to revised schedules
1	May	All Central Bus Garages	27 Days	Claim for $7\frac{1}{2}$ hour-day.

Source: 'Record of Industrial Disputes In Which Staff Have Taken Action Since 1 January 1933', London Transport Board.

Committee left, however, the Green Line and Country Service members held a further meeting and reversed their previous decision, but the strike ended the following day.

Shortly afterwards a meeting of the Organising Committee was called to discuss the policy of the Movement arising out of the Slough dispute. The moment the meeting opened, Papworth and Snelling, who had obviously been the target of considerable criticism for their actions, announced that they were resigning their positions in the Movement.

The Organising Committee met next on 13 August. That evening they reported to a full conference of the RFM that only affiliated branches would be able to have members on the Organising or Editorial Committees, with no co-options allowed; ordinary branch members who were not delegated by their branches would be welcome to attend RFM conferences, but as observers only. It later transpired that Snelling had laid down a number of conditions to the Organising Committee: he would return if Communist influence was curtailed and as long as it was made clear that the Movement was for busmen only. It would seem likely, then, that the move to exclude members of unaffiliated branches from positions in the Movement was aimed at Sharkey, whose Willesden branch had at that time declined to affiliate. The amendment to restrict election to affiliated members had been moved by a man called Arlotte who, during his speech, remarked that 'we cannot have any political party creeping into the rank and file movement.' It was Sharkey himself who retorted that: 'No political party pulls this movement one way or another, and we do not receive any instructions from any party at all.'[8] It further emerged that Snelling had remarked to the Organising Committee that 'this movement is becoming an electoral machine, that it was tending to become a breakaway union ...'[9]

On the specific issue of the Slough dispute Papworth and Snelling were exonerated – a Slough man named Kane explained:

> Papworth and Snelling did advise the men to go back to work, but the men at Slough attached no blame to either Papworth or Snelling for this. They came down and spoke to us as two men.[10]

With regard to Snelling's charge of Communist infiltration, Jones remarked testily that:

> Snelling as Chairman has had a better opportunity than anybody else of seeing since the inception of the Movement whether Communism was creeping in, and he has never noticed it until now.[11]

The Organising Committee later endorsed the two men's action over Slough and soon after they re-occupied their old positions in the Movement.

This episode illustrates not only Clegg's point, but the political divisions which were coming into the open at this stage; it is quite possible, of course, that Snelling, the SPGB man, had made an ill-timed bid to increase his own political influence in the Movement. A few months earlier, in June, a similar case had cropped up at Nunhead, where a crew had been placed into discipline for failing to report an accident in which they had allegedly been involved some time previously.

Later in the month the CBC, noting that Nunhead had made no approach to them, decided that no action by them was needed. Two days later the Committee was told that a Nunhead deputation 'desired to wait upon' them.[12] Having heard the case the CBC invited the Nunhead men to elect a sub-committee of three to accompany them to a meeting with the LPTB where it was decided that a special Disciplinary Board would review the case the following morning. This was later postponed for a week as most members of the CBC were travelling to the Isle of Man for the Biennial Delegate Conference. Nunhead undertook to take no action in the meantime.

On the Saturday night a delegate to the Isle of Man Conference brought in a London evening newspaper which made reference to the fact that Nunhead and several other garages were on strike. Bevin and Harold Clay, the National Passenger Secretary, agreed that an aircraft be chartered to take Papworth, Snelling and Sharkey back to London, followed by a meeting with the LPTB, where the latter agreed to suspend disciplinary action against the Nunhead crew, pending a review of the disciplinary machinery. Payment for all time lost was agreed.

When the RFM came to discuss the dispute at its next conference it was suggested that Brockwell, a Nunhead man and candidate for the General Executive Council, had engineered the dispute, in effect telling his members: 'This is what your RFM does for you. The CBC are away in the Isle of Man enjoying themselves and that's what you get out of the RFM.'[13] A delegate named Rance asked whether

> the policy of the RFM had changed from the early days? If a garage after four-and-a-half months of using the machinery cannot get a decision, and it then takes action it must help the CBC to get a decision on that particular point.

Metzger agreed, charging that the RFM was adopting the wrong attitude; the Board had no case, and so the dispute had not been engineered; there was practically unanimous support for Nunhead across the fleet.[14]

Sharkey replied that Nunhead had *not* used the machinery and that: 'If we give a decision we think and claim is a correct decision ... we expect some discipline to be maintained as far as our membership is concerned ...'[15]

Of course, there was not necessarily a contradiction in the RFM heading off a dispute if the aim was to harness all the forces of the Section behind a single set of demands, or to instil a disciplined approach in the membership. In fact, the slogan of the Movement at this time was 'Keep Your Powder Dry', as it was felt that the Section's strength, rather than being dissipated in local disputes, should be conserved for the struggle for the seven-hour day. But in July 1935, precisely the period we have just referred to, Sharkey was complaining at an RFM conference that

> I am wondering when the time will arrive when the RFM can start again on the question of the seven-hour day which was a prominent factor in the inception of this movement.[16]

The demand was renewed after this but, following the tortuously slow negotiations Payne and Jones were, by February 1937, echoing Sharkey:

> The Movement, in our opinion, is losing a grip of the seven-hour day position, and as an agitational and propaganda body failing in its objects.
>
> ... We feel sure there is no lack of support for the Movement providing it gives a clear and concise lead to the membership. At the moment it is not giving that lead.[17]

Thus while there is certainly much truth in Barrett's suggestion that, rather than becoming more moderate in their role as members of the Central Bus Committee, the RFM leaders were 'operating on a higher level of political consciousness than rank and file busmen', [18] the record suggests that the decision to discourage action in preparation for the fight over hours had the effect of demobilising the membership. This is a question we will return to later.

Having gained the support of vast numbers of the Section's membership through its efforts on 'bread and butter' issues, the RFM was able to offer leadership on those issues which, had the TGWU leadership been of a more progressive stamp, would have been pursued through the normal trade union channels. Indeed, one way of viewing this period is to see the RFM as pursuing the progressive traditions of

London busworkers while the Bevinite leadership took the TGWU as a whole on a Mondist bifurcation.

For example the Movement organised support for workers outside their own industry and union (with the organisation of garage collections for striking aircraft workers in 1935 and their call upon the GEC to levy the membership in support of an impending miners' strike), and championed a number of causes which the official movement either ignored or adopted tardily. While the TUC and the Labour Party dragged their heels on aid to the Republican side in the Spanish Civil War, the issue was taken up vigorously by the RFM. Sharkey attacked both the TUC and the Labour Party for their original support of 'non-intervention', calling upon all branches in the London Bus Section to flood the National Council of Labour with resolutions. In January 1937 Bill Jones reported that Bill Brisky, a member of the Dalston branch, had joined the International Brigade:

> Should the Nazis take him prisoner they will not find Bill Brisky's [trade union] card; we have that, keeping our promise ... to keep it clear.
>
> ... It seems only a few days ago that Bill was marching in a London anti-fascist demonstration, was selling anti-fascist literature, was in the branch room as a member of the committee, and now he is fighting for his life, and the life of his class, in the front line in Madrid, practising what he preached – Down with Fascism![19]

Bill Brisky, in fact, died in the defence of Madrid as a Company Commander. Jones used Brisky's obituary to launch a stinging attack on Bevin:

> Bill's death has many lessons for us all – for none more than his General Secretary with his fat well-fed belly (made possible by the Bill Brisky's of the working class), afraid of Fascism, as he is afraid of the whole boss class, knowing only two words: *Unofficial* and *Reds*, who refuses to publish a speech he made at the International Conference recently held in London, a speech which sent the Spanish Trade Union Leaders back home convinced that they can expect no real help from the Citrines and Bevins, knowing that they must depend on the Bill Briskys who only have their lives to offer.[20]

Early in 1937 Papworth went on a tour of Spain, visiting Barcelona, Alicante, Valencia and Madrid. Obviously deeply affected by what he saw there, he concluded his report in the *Busman's Punch* with the words:

> I beg you to do something to help the people of Spain. Create such an agitation that the National Government shall either fall beneath it or be

> forced to render justice to a friendly country and a friendly democratic government. Please help the people of Spain.[21]

The Movement gave prominence to the fight against fascism wherever it appeared. As early as Easter 1933 Payne and Snelling had attended an anti-fascist conference in Copenhagen, where they

> received a wonderful reception because of their association with the London Busmen's Rank and File Movement, which was looked up to by trade unionists even in other countries because of the stand they had made against attacks on their wages and conditions.[22]

In 1934 the RFM made contact with militant transport workers in Berlin, whose newspaper, *The Red Signal*, reported that contrary to the promises made by the Nazis before they came to power, wages had been cut and 3,000 jobs lost in their industry.[23] Later that year *Busman's Punch* carried a five-page Anti-Fascist Supplement 'issued by the London Transport Workers Anti-Fascist Movement'.[24]

In October 1935 the RFM was calling for support of Abyssinia against Italian agression. In January 1936 it called for the release of Ernst Thälmann, the German Communist leader imprisoned by the Nazis, urging that 'fifty thousand postcards and letters from the London bus and tram workers ... be poured into the office of the German government ...' In April the same year *Busman's Punch* published a letter from the Vienna Tram and Bus Workers' Group of the illegal Trade Union of Municipal and Transport Workers of Austria. This related a story similar to that of the Berlin workers, but 265 tramworkers and busworkers had been imprisoned by the fascists in February 1934, with another 650 arrested in November 1935, so 'maintaining the families of our imprisoned and victimised comrades is one of our most urgent and difficult tasks. Sixty per cent of our dues ... are used for this purpose.'

In Britain, of course, the Movement was active in combating the activities of Mosley's fascists. A large contingent of London busmen participated in the famous march to Hyde Park on 9 September 1934, when 100,000 people turned up to demonstrate their opposition to Mosley. In March 1936 Papworth reported to the RFM conference on the 'Albert Hall incidents' when the police had attacked the crowds demonstrating against Mosley. This conference also discussed the embarrassing problem of drivers of private-hire buses hired by fascists. Papworth pointed out that the LPTB did not tell drivers who was hiring the vehicles, and individuals were, at the very last moment, faced with the dilemma of whether to carry them or to refuse and risk disciplinary action by the Board.[25]

On the related issue of peace the RFM was also active. Jones, Payne, Snelling, Sharkey, Papworth and four others travelled to the International Peace Conference in Brussels in September 1936. However, although the Conference may have been for peace, it was certainly not for pacifism, as the 6,000 delegates were addressed by Dolores Ibarruri, *La Pasionaria*, and two members of the workers' militia 'straight from their struggle against the Spanish agents of the war lords of Europe, Hitler and Mussolini'. Reporting the Congress in *Busman's Punch* of the same month, Payne and Jones asked 'why are our leaders not playing their part in the National Peace Movement in this country, in order to preserve the workers from another 1914?'

It may be thought that the support for the Soviet Union displayed by the RFM was due to the influence of the Communists. But this explanation is less than adequate. The Russian Revolution, which had occurred less than a generation earlier, had generated considerable support in the British labour movement. Many class-conscious trade unionists, whether members of the Communist Party or not, had set their sights on a socialist society for Britain, and it was Socialism the Soviet Union was building. Then again, Britain and the other capitalist nations were in deep economic crisis and, before the age of 'consumerism', the Soviet Union had obvious attractions.

For London passenger workers, however, there were quite concrete attractions – the conditions enjoyed by their counterparts in Moscow. In August 1933 *Busman's Punch* reported that Moscow tramworkers worked:

> seven hours, with one day in five free and a month's holiday with pay each year. The only spreadover allowed is two hours, but this does not occur more than once or twice a month for each man.
>
> The number of inspectors is much less than in London and the conductor is not blamed for not collecting any fares if there are people standing on the tram. The onus is on the passenger to pay. The amount of bonus paid to each worker is decided by a committee of the trade union, with a member of the administration present, and any complaints made by inspectors or passengers come before this committee.

In May 1934 the journal reported that the working day on Moscow's trolley-buses was seven hours for conductors and six hours for drivers.

Members of the RFM appear to have visited the Soviet Union with some frequency. In October 1933 Nunhead garage elected a delegate to attend the anniversary of the revolution in Moscow, and the following year the RFM itself agreed to send a delegation to the celebrations and to 'co-operate with other sections of London transport workers to secure leave of absence for the delegation'. Plans for a similar delegation the following year went badly wrong, for all the Central Bus Committee members were refused leave by the LPTB, and only Brown of Dalston went. In his report in the July 1935 issue of the journal, Brown informed his readers that busworkers in Russia worked similar hours as tram and trolleybus-workers: only seven hours a day, and six on the larger vehicles. Brown wrote that:

> Wherever I went I was acclaimed with much credit when they heard that I was a member of the London Busmen's Rank and File Movement. They much appreciate our Movement, and they let me know all about it!

It may be seen from the above that Clegg's claim that the Movement was in its origin a syndicalist movement has validity only if by 'syndicalism' he means militant trade unionism: the fight to defend jobs, wages and conditions came first.[26] But very early in its life the RFM also became a *political* movement, mobilising the membership of the London Bus Section on the crucial issues of the day.

Notes

1. Minutes of RFM Conference, 21 January 1935.
2. Ibid., 24 June 1935.
3. *Busman's Punch*, August 1932.
4. Bullock, op.cit., p.521.
5. Ibid., p.524.
6. RFM Conference Minutes, July 1935.
7. Clegg, op.cit., p.106.
8. Minutes of RFM Conference, 13 August 1935.
9. Ibid.
10. Ibid.
11. Minutes of RFM Conference, 16 September 1935.
12. Ibid., 15 July 1935.
13. Ibid.
14. Ibid.
15. Ibid.
16. Ibid.
17. *Busman's Punch*, February 1937.
18. Barrett, op.cit., p.102.
19. *Busman's Punch*, January 1937.
20. Ibid., March 1937.
21. Ibid., February 1937.
22. Ibid., May 1933.

23. Ibid., May 1934.
24. Ibid., September 1934.
25. Handwritten minutes, Emile Burns Papers, dated 23 March 1936.
26. Clegg, op.cit., p.103.

CHAPTER TWELVE

The Quest For Unity

In attempting to forge links with workers in the road passenger transport industry in other parts of the country, the London Busmen's Rank and File Movement had two aims: the straightforward trade union aim of mobilising solidarity with other workers in struggle; and, perhaps more importantly, to build that network of contacts which, as Bill Ware had said in his report of the 1935 Biennial Delegate Conference, was necessary 'for the purpose of being able to sweep aside the reactionary executive policy'.

Busman's Punch regularly published news and views from elsewhere in the bus and tram world. As early as March 1933, a 'Lancashire Rank and Filer' was writing of the intolerable conditions which busworkers endured in that part of the world, vowing that:

> We, the active element, intend to spare no efforts in organising the Rank and File within the TGWU to make a united effort against the existing conditions.

In May the same year busworkers from Salford, Coventry and Leicester all wrote asking for regular supplies of the journal. In the same issue a Birmingham conductor reported on the wage-cuts and speed-up in the city, following which 'many men left the TGWU and formed a new Union, which was the wrong policy'; the correct policy, the writer declared, would be to

> work for a better Rank and File expression, and, instead of leaving the Transport and General Workers' Union, all must get into it for the purpose of fighting for the restoration of the 2s. cut, and raising our general standards to a higher level ...'

This does not seem to have been achieved, for a year later 'Brumbus' was writing that 'we want to get a Rank and File Movement going'.[1]

In June 1935 a Scottish correspondent was asking awkward questions concerning the ballot of members employed by Scottish Motor Traction for strike action on a wage-demand. Why had the members not been informed of the result? Why had no propaganda meetings been held?

Three months later ***Busman's Punch*** reported on the strike of over 2,000 busworkers and tramworkers in South Wales, calling for contributions to the strike fund. Following the strike, two members were suspended from branch office by the union and asked, during the subsequent inquiry: 'Did you attend a Communist meeting and have you been in touch with the London Busmen's Rank and File Movement?' When the two members concerned were debarred from office for two years, a local Rank and File Movement was formed which issued a South Wales edition of the ***Busman's Punch*** for several months. In 1936 Bill Jones and William Payne accepted an invitation to visit Swansea. Interestingly, the local Rank and File leaders asked Jones and Payne to give special emphasis in their speeches to the dangers of seceding from the TGWU.[2]

The South Wales dispute was followed by a strike by staff employed by United Counties. Again, this was given full coverage in the RFM journal and a deputation from the Movement visited the area.[3] In 1936 busworkers in East Yorkshire and the Thames Valley were in dispute, and it was at this juncture that the RFM issued a provincial edition of the *Busman's Punch*, although this survived for only a few months.

It has been suggested by Glatter that members of the Rank and File Movement 'were isolated, even within their own industry ... They won the bus section for the election of full-time officials but they did not lead a union-wide fight for it.'[4] Such charges are unjustified. The Movement certainly attempted to build up national support for its policies within the road passenger transport industry. In fact, we will see later that this very fact would be used against the Movement during the union's inquiry into its activities in the wake of the Coronation Strike. In this work it must have faced massive difficulties. On the one hand, it was an unofficial movement composed of men in full-time employment as busworkers; on the other hand stood Ernest Bevin, with all his undoubted abilities as an organiser and with the entire machinery of the union at his disposal. It was not altogether surprising that, in the end, it was Bevin who emerged victorious.

As we have seen, the TGWU had campaigned almost from its foundation, for a single transport authority for London. Such a course had been recommended by a Royal Commission in 1905 and by a Parliamentary Select Committee in 1919. In the early 1930s serious attempts were made to form such a body. The London Passenger Transport Bill was introduced by the second Labour government in

1931, piloted by Herbert Morrison, the Transport Minister. With the formation of the National Government the Bill was picked up and enacted.

The London Passenger Transport Board (LPTB) began its life in July 1933, taking over the operations of the 19 companies in the traffic combine (including, of course, the LGOC), several small bus companies, the Metropolitan Railway Company and the tramway undertakings run by 14 local authorities. The Rank and File Movement saw obvious advantages here, arguing that

> every opportunity should be taken to keep all sections of London Passenger Transport – buses, trams, railways and coaches – in close touch with each other, so that the employers' old policy of 'Divide and Conquer' can be defeated.[5]

While the *Daily Telegraph* complained that the formation of the Board was 'nationalisation in disguise, the RFM took a consistently hostile view of the Board itself. Discussing the Bill in its issue of December 1932, the *Busman's Punch* predicted that the Chairman and the four other board members would be grossly overpaid, and noted that the Bill made no mention of any requirement to pay a decent wage to the Board's employees. In the event, the generous salaries of the LPTB members surprised even the RFM, for while the *Busman's Punch* had used the £5,000 annual salary received by the Chairman of the Tariff Commissioners as an example of overpayment, Lord Ashfield was retained as Chairman at the price of £12,500 a year; Frank Pick, as vice-Chairman and chief executive officer, received £10,000. Moreover, John Cliff, former official in the Amalgamated Association of Tramway and Vehicle Workers and now Assistant General Secretary of the TGWU, was to 'resign his office ... and ... cease all participation in the business and activities of the Union' in order to join the Board.[6] Curiously, the RFM's reaction to the news of Cliff's defection to the employer's side appears to have been muted. Bill Jones later recalled that Cliff

> was very much his own man and never saw eye-to-eye with Bevin. The story goes ... that Cliff got the chance of a job with the Board and that Bevin urged him to take it because he wanted to get rid of him ... He was as right-wing as Bevin, but a capable man.[7]

Under the terms of the Bill the LGOC would receive 4½ per cent 'A' stock to the tune of £2,240,429; £3,350,000-worth of 5 per cent 'B' stock and £5,087,000-worth of 'C' stock yielding interest of 5 per cent for the first two years and 5½ per cent thereafter, with a limit of 6 per cent. Although a statutory Board, the LPTB would receive no public subsidy and was expected to provide profits to satisfy the stock-holders.

There was therefore nothing socialist in the formation of the Board. The RFM looked upon the new body as a means by which the industry would rationalise itself in the face of the Depression:

> Every industry is carrying out rationalisation and speeding up. Capitalism is trying to make the workers bear the brunt of the crisis, and at each step it is making the crisis worse by cutting down wages and employment. In these circumstances a fall in traffic receipts is inevitable. But the purpose of the London Passenger Transport Bill is to secure and even increase the profits of the rich bankers and industrial magnates who hold immense sums invested in London transport. In view of the falling traffic, this result can only be attained by new vicious attacks on the workers' wages and conditions, and by reducing staff, at the same time intensifying the work done by those kept on. It is rumoured that 1,500 trams and buses are to be taken off the streets, leading to reductions in staff up to 6,000 to 7,000 men. This will undoubtedly be carried through, and all our conditions will be thrown into the melting pot, if we do not organise for defence. The issues of the seven-hour day, no spread-overs, and the definite limitation of speed (with compensation for speed) – these are practical issues which the coming position makes it imperative to raise and to fight for.[8]

In its first financial year the LPTB made a profit of £4,778,782. However, the RFM's fears regarding the slimming of the bus and tram-fleets were unjustified for (if we take account of the new trolleybuses in the tram total) both fleets were expanded between 1934 and 1939.

It is, though, the unifying aspects of the LPTB which chiefly concerns us here. From the very outset, even before the formation of the Board, the declared policy of the RFM was for the maximum unity of London passenger transport workers. The second issue of the *Busman's Punch* argued that in order to fight the Combine's attack, a 'united TOT (Trams, Omnibuses and Trains) stand' was required. 'OUR FIGHT CANNOT BE SEPARATED FROM THAT OF THE UNDERGROUND AND TRAMWAYMEN. UNITED STRIKE ACTION IS THE WAY FORWARD IN DEFENCE OF OUR CONDITIONS.'[9]

When the journal was adopted by the RFM, this policy, in theory at least, was continued although we will see that very real problems were to develop. A TOT Conference called by the Movement in July 1934 attracted delegates from 31 bus and tram branches and five rail branches. The demands voiced here were for the seven-hour day, the abolition of spreadovers, busmen's rates for tramworkers, improved holidays and better rest-day arrangements. A joint campaign was planned and a TOT Anti-Fascist Movement launched. Even before this Conference a Trams Rank and File Committee appears to have been formed, and an unofficial journal, *The Call Note*, had been welcomed by the ***Busman's Punch*** as early as March 1933.

The goal of unity with the tramworkers was complicated by the London Passenger Transport Board's introduction of trolleybuses in the mid-1930s. The Central Bus Committee attempted to persuade the TGWU's Trams Council to recognise the latter as buses and to press for bus rates of pay. 'You can imagine,' Haywood told the RFM conference in April 1935; 'that it would have been far easier to have done this while there were a few to negotiate for than when there will be a great many.' However, the Trams Council had refused to come to such an agreement. Fulwell depot, meanwhile, refused to be represented by the Trams Council. Burr, the RFM delegate from that depot, pointed out:

> Our conditions are different, our uniforms are different, and we do one-and-a-half days more work a week than they do. The conductor takes approximately an average of £10 a week more than he did on a tramcar. The intensification has increased from 10 to 15 per cent compared with the trams ...

Later in the year a Western Divisional Trolley Bus Vigilance Committee was established, and the RFM immediately saw the danger of sectionalism developing, despite the fact that the Central Bus Committee had adopted a policy of central bus rates for trolleybus workers earlier in the year. It would appear, however, that the formation of a separate unofficial group by trolleybus workers was prompted by the fact that, like the busworkers, they did not trust Bevin to put this policy into effect: he had, after all, refused to meet the Trams Council to discuss the demand, even though he was in the process of negotiating with the LPTB. Sheehan, giving the trams report at the 16 September conference of the RFM, feared that Bevin 'is coming back with an offer of a hybrid grade. We must resist this'. According to Sheehan, the trolley workers had set up their own group because 'only five out of 35 branches are affiliated to the RFM and some of the other branches are scared of the term "rank and file" movement'.[10]

The bus-dominated RFM had reason enough to wish to control the trolleybus section, for as another RFM delegate pointed out:

> 248 miles of trolleybuses are to come into operation in October, and this will revolutionise transport and eliminate not only trams but buses. If we allow them to come on without bringing them up to our standard, we shall become the weaker section numerically and we know what that means.[11]

To complicate matters further, a Justice for Tram and Trolley Bus Committee was set up in September 1935. This followed the same organisational principles as the RFM. There appears to have been no political differences with the RFM: *The Lever*, the Justice Committee's journal which appeared in June 1936, while giving adequate space to industrial questions, contained a full-page report of a visit to the Soviet Union by an Australian tramworker and a review, almost as long, of a Communist Party pamphlet entitled *The London Transport Scandal.* An earlier Justice Committee publication, a pamphlet entitled *Justice On The Trams*, paid tribute to the support received from both the Central Bus Committee and the RFM for the levelling-up of tram and trolleybus wages to the bus level, and called for unity with the busworkers. It is likely, therefore, that the Justice Committee had been set up because progressive tramworkers suspected that support of busworkers for the levelling-up principle might prove rather less sincere as time went by. This possibility is certainly borne out by later events.

All three unofficial organisations took part in a joint conference in October 1935. Here Papworth called for one Rank and File Movement. Tramworkers, he said, saw in trolleybuses their opportunity to raise their wages to the bus rate, but they had never been prepared to accept bus conditions, preferring, for example, to take their meal reliefs on the car rather then in a canteen. Although the conference voted to support a united front on wages, there were dissenting voices. E.C. Firminger, Secretary of the Justice Committee, voiced the demand for 'the same back and front' for the trams which, even though busworkers were sympathetic to abolishing the differential between drivers and conductors, would have further complicated matters. Forge of Hackney went so far as to doubt the sincerity of the bus delegates:

> They agree to support our demands one day, and the next day they go to the Board asking for a seven-hour day. Let them support one body of men first of all to get what they want and then go ahead with what they want for themselves.[12]

This contradiction was not resolved. The demand for the seven-hour day preceded the formation of the RFM. It was a demand which flowed naturally from the speeded schedules which had been introduced over the past three or four years. It would obviously have been suicidal for the RFM to now abandon that demand, even for the cause of greater unity with the tram and trolleybus workers.

At the end of November 1935 Bevin met the Trams Council and promised that an immediate start would be made to bring up tram wages, step by step, to those of the central busworkers. He then asked the Central Bus Committee if they intended to remain stationery during this period. The CBC replied that this most certainly was not the case. 'It means,' Snelling told an RFM conference that evening, 'that the programme of the trams has to be accelerated ...' The conference, having heard Snelling's report, went on to unanimously adopt the following resolution:

> That in our considered opinion the ultimate object is to press for an all-in-bus and tram agreement as outlined at the TOT rank and file conference, and we pledge ourselves to use our utmost endeavours to enlarge the representation of these joint committees under the auspices of the rank and file movement to achieve that object.[13]

One of the steps taken as a part of this effort was to publish *Tram & Bus Punch*, but this venture was short-lived.

As far as the tramworkers themselves were concerned, Bevin's efforts to level-up their wages, and the way the negotiations were conducted, left much to be desired. Their demand had been for an increase of 7s. 6d. The negotiations yielded only 4s. An angry Firminger informed the RFM conference in December

> quite definitely that no member of the London Trams Council, no member of the Joint Divisional Committee and no member of the negotiating committee was aware of this settlement or that it had been signed by the Executive Committee prior to the Tuesday of the week it was posted in all depots by the Board.[14]

Despite Firminger's prediction that an unofficial tram strike would result from the signing of this agreement, this did not happen. Early in 1936 fourteen tram branches lobbied the Trams Council with the demand that they meet the Board the following day and press for the full claim. Although negotiations were re-opened, however, the demand was not met. The increase of November 1935 brought the top rate for tram drivers and conductors up to 78s., compared to 88s. 6d. for a bus driver and 83s. 6d. for a bus conductor; a year later, the tram rate was improved to 80s. per week, but it was not until December 1939 that the

TRAM & BUS PUNCH

Tram Edition of the *Busman's Punch*. Official Paper of the London Busmen's Rank and File Movement

No. 38 (New Series) SPECIAL NUMBER, DECEMBER, 1935 TWOPENCE

ISSUES TO BE FACED

OVERLAP

Not satisfied with the many concessions already agreed to by the Union in return for the extra days' holiday, the Board have again made further demands, the chief of which is that 1935 holiday be allowed to overlap one week into 1936 and so save a considerable number of crews. The offer of conference was as you know turned down by the Board. They want concessions but are not prepared to pay on the grounds that they have given enough. verb sap.

SATURDAY RESTDAYS

The Saturdey rest position has again come up for review, or should we say, the Board are asking for the Status Quo, in view of the unsatisfactory state of affairs in connection with their difficulties in obtaining rest-day workers. Further, the Industry is developing towards the total abolition of Saturday rest. We know London Busmen are prepared to resist this attempt to further worsen their lot.

INSIDE STAFF HOLIDAYS

The long delayed extra holidays have at last been granted. Not only for Bus inside staff, the Tram inside staff also are to enjoy the extra holidays.

The inside staff wage demand is the next step that must be forced.

NON-UNIONISM

This question of "Nons" is one of paramount importance. While it is true that most of the garages are now 100 per cent. there are still a few men who will not fall into line with their fellow workers. The time is long past when we can tolerate this. The C.B.C. have by resolution asked for plenary powers from the G.E.C. to enable the Fleet to withdraw their labour rather than work with nons.

DISCIPLINARY MACHINERY

The Union's proposals in this connection we understand are now before the Board for their consideration, and an early meeting may be expected.

NEW AGREEMENT

We understand branches have submitted their suggestions for a new agreement and one has been prepared ready for submission to the G.E.C. The main features being:

Seven-hour day with increases in pay (Sunday included).
Limitation of Speed.
Equal pay for driver and conductor.
No rest-day working.

TRAM SETTLEMENT

A serious position has arisen through the acceptance by the G.E.C. of a tram settlement which is against the declared wishes of the membership. Full details are given in the report from the Justice for Tramwaymen's Committee printed on a later page.

(Continued on page 2).

Tram & Bus Punch, produced by the Rank and File Movement in its efforts to unite different passenger-transport workers in London.

tramworkers achieved parity with central bus conductors, although even then their conditions of work were more onerous.[15]

The failure to win unity between the busworkers, tramworkers and trolleybus workers can be attributed to a number of factors, first and foremost to the fact that the militant tradition in the London Bus Section was not present to the same degree in the other two sections. In these circumstances unity could only have been achieved by reducing the demands of the busworkers. Had this been done it is doubtful whether the RFM would have retained the phenomenal support it enjoyed, for that support had only been won by the RFM putting forward those slogans (principally for the seven-hour day) which represented the real interests of busworkers. Bound up with this is the fact that the differential between busworkers and tramworkers was the most immediately identifiable token of the former's aristocratic status. It is entirely possible that some busworkers (including Snelling, to judge from his remarks quoted in Chapter 11) *wanted* a differential between themselves and their colleagues on the trams. Moreover, for the busworkers to stand still while the tramworkers caught up with them would have meant that, meanwhile, their status *vis à vis* other sections of the working class would have been lowered. At this time, London bus drivers were still second in the earnings league for semi-skilled workers, and they would not have abandoned this position lightly.[16]

There can be little doubt that this dilemma, real as it was, and the busworkers' decision to push on with their own demands rather than waiting for the other two sections to be levelled up, had dire consequences for the 1937 Coronation Strike, when the busworkers found themselves alone.

Notes

1. *Busman's Punch*, May 1934.
2. Ibid., October 1936.
3. Ibid., February 1936.
4. P. Glatter, 'London Busmen: rise and fall of a rank and file movement', *International Socialism*, January 1975. With Glatter's more specific charge, Bill Jones replies that: 'We did lead a Union-wide fight for the election of full-time paid officials at BDC after BDC, but never succeeded.' (Letter to the author, 11 April 1983.)
5. *Busman's Punch*, 12 August 1932.
6. June 1933, quoting from *Hansard*.
7. Interviewed in *Busworker*, May 1983.
8. *Busman's Punch*, March 1933.
9. Ibid., 12 August 1932.

10. Minutes of RFM Conference, 16 September 1935.
11. Ibid.
12. Minutes of TOT Conference, 14 October 1935.
13. Minutes of RFM Conference, 26 November 1935.
14. Ibid., 9 December 1935.
15. Clegg, op.cit., p.71.
16. Routh, op.cit., p.107.

CHAPTER THIRTEEN

The Seven-Hour Day

The demand for the seven-hour day can be traced back as far as June 1931, when it appeared in the *Holloway Bus Worker*, a Minority Movement publication. As we have seen, the London Busmen's Rank and File Movement immediately adopted the slogan. The slow progress made on the demand produced frustration and led to Sharkey's impatient outburst.

In July 1935 Merton garage successfully put forward a motion at a special Bus Conference held at Transport House, calling for the termination of the agreement. Subsequent events were strongly reminiscent of 1925. The General Executive Council 'declined to accede to the request' as the Conference had proposed no amendments to the agreement.[1] Accordingly, the Section formulated proposals for a wage-increase and the seven-hour day. 'On examination,' Bevin told the Section's leaders, 'we found that the proposals as a whole were impossible of realisation, representing as they did a colossal sum.'[2] This conflicted with the estimation made by the RFM over a year earlier that in its first year of operations the London Passenger Transport Board would achieve a surplus from speeded schedules of 'not less than £600,000 on buses alone', a sum identical to that needed for the reduction to seven hours a day without loss of pay.[3]

The Section's patience began to wear thin. In February 1936 Bromley carried a resolution demanding a ballot of all London busworkers with a view to seceding from the TGWU. A week later the motion was again put to the branch and, due to the efforts of the branch officers, defeated. A further motion was put demanding that effect be given to the Section's July resolution, failing which the branch would withhold contributions.[4] *Busman's Punch* noted that

> while under no circumstances can this movement support the line taken by Bromley, we do suggest to the EC that the Bromley meetings are an indication of the dangers of dallying with the position any longer.[5]

The Central Bus Committee met Bevin at the end of March and agreed with his contention that the full demands were unrealisable. Bevin raised the question of the undertakings already given to the tramworkers. The CBC, faced with the tramworkers decision to proceed on their own for a levelling-up of wages, decided that they, too, would go their own way.

In April a Delegate Conference unanimously demanded the implementation of the seven-hour day by Whitsun, the calling of special branch meetings to discuss the question, and for an emergency Bus Conference to be held 'immediately following the negotiations with the Board... for the purpose of discussing the progress made in the negotiations and to decide policy arising therefrom'.[6] The RFM leaders appear to have taken a more moderate line, arguing against the Whitsun deadline. As Papworth put it, 'it is a totally irresponsible position to get it by Whitsun – or August – it might take even nine months."[7]

Bevin and Clay met the Vice-Chairman of the Board in early May, when it was agreed that a Joint Committee be established to investigate the possibility of implementing the seven-hour day. Meeting on 11 May, the General Executive Council formally agreed that the Bus and Tram sections should negotiate their wages and conditions separately, thus freeing them from the undertakings on levelling up made in 1934. Whilst it was not prepared to be bound by the deadline set by the Bus Conference, it authorised Bevin's approach to the Board. Even so, the GEC refused to commit itself to 'the seven-hour day or any other proposals'.[8]

The management-union Joint Committee held its first meeting on 27 May, followed by meetings on 4 and 15 June. At the second meeting the Board announced that specimen schedules based on the union's proposals were being compiled which would be available for inspection the following week; a statement with regard to the cost of the proposals would also be supplied.

Upon receipt of this information the Central Bus Committee appointed a sub-committee consisting of Papworth and Snelling to approach the General Secretary to seek the assistance of the union's Statistical Department. Bevin agreed to this, and also authorised the employment of a firm of accountants. The accountants took longer than anticipated and their written report was not produced until August. After a meeting with them at the end of August Bevin concluded that the Board would be unable to meet the full claim and, at a meeting of the Joint Committee the following day, a number of demands were withdrawn, amounting to a third of the cost of the claim.[9]

The August edition of *Busman's Punch* reported:

> On or about 27 August a Full Delegate Conference will assemble to hear a report from the CBC on the position regarding the Seven-Hour Day. At that Conference we expect some plain speaking from both the delegates and the platform.
>
> Without presuming to anticipate the trend of the debate which will follow the report, we know from the Branch resolutions which have come in that the Section has reached the limit of its patience.

By the time the September issue appeared the promised Conference had still not materialised, and it finally took place on 10 September.

During the Conference Papworth was at pains to stress the fact that the officers of the Section had 'given unlimited assistance', and that when Bevin had been approached he 'went out of his way to give every possible assistance without hesitation'.[10] It is likely that Papworth was trying to do two things here: retain Bevin's support for the claim and, somewhat more subtly, ensure that those who were beginning to revive secession within the Section were left in no doubt that the official leadership *was* behind the application. As a result of this Conference it was decided to drop all other demands (a maximum spreadover of ten hours, increased holidays and the restriction of speeded schedules) in order to concentrate on the seven-hour day.

In mid-November the CBC and the Section's fulltime officials met Bevin and Clay at Transport House before attending a meeting with the Board. It was at this point that Bevin revealed his support for the application to be lukewarm and stated that on examining the notes of their last meeting two weeks earlier he had come to the conclusion that the seven-hour day really meant a six-hour day, as the average time on duty would work out to between six and six-and-a-half hours. To this Papworth replied: 'If you have not made up your mind that the busmen are entitled to a seven-hour day we will be in the position of our General Secretary not believing in the case.'[11]

The meeting with the Board proved abortive. Lord Ashfield dismissed the demand, claiming that the shorter working day could only be brought about by a national movement, not by a single industry.

> If we gave favourable consideration to your proposal it would bring disaster ^ our undertaking ... The Board has its responsibility to those who provide ^oney and also to the travelling public.

[illegible]l, he had 'no knowledge that would lead him to believe that [illegible]uffer more than other sections of the Board', a somewhat [illegible] statement.[12] Snelling appears to have shown signs of willingness to compromise, as he is recorded as having said: 'This slogan of the seven-hour day is a basis. Even if you do not talk of hours, give us easement.'[13]

This, indeed, was the line agreed by the CBC when they next met Bevin at the end of November, for it was decided that the Board be approached on the questions of speed, hours, meal reliefs, stand time and weekend work. Meeting Bevin on 3 December, Ashfield indicated that the Board would be willing to discuss these items, although he could not hold out any hope for a reduction in hours as the average time currently worked was 6 hours 33 minutes at the wheel and 7 hours 13 minutes overall. He agreed that if a new agreement had not been concluded by the first week in February 1937, he would meet Bevin to discuss a compensatory payment payable from that date.

At a Special Delegate Conference on 16 December it was decided that all branches hold special meetings to discuss whether the negotiations should be continued, or a month's notice to terminate be given. The January 1937 issue of *Busman's Punch* reported that by 32 to 18 the branches had decided to continue negotiations. The report hinted strongly that the demand for the seven-hour day was very much in the balance:

> The *form* which the negotiations will now take is hours, speed, meal reliefs, stand time, Saturday and Sunday operations, etc. The *substance* must be easements equal to those which the seven-hour day would have brought us.

The negotiations made little progress, even after the Section, in line with the GEC, reduced the demand to a seven-and-a-half hour day. Bevin argued that the Board could pay, but the Board merely replied that the profits of the Central Buses were needed both to meet interest-payments and to balance the losses of the Board's other sections.[14] On 31 March, after negotiations had dragged on for two months beyond the February deadline, the union gave a month's notice to terminate the agreement. Despite talks at the Ministry of Labour no settlement was in sight, and thus the General Executive Council granted plenary powers to the London Bus Section from midnight on 30 April.

The view is widely held that Bevin utilised the Coronation Strike to crush the Rank and File Movement and there is considerable evidence to support this.

Prior to 1937 the official leadership had met with little success in its attempts to curb the Movement. In 1933 Sharkey was the subject of a motion from the Mortlake branch calling upon him to resign because of his association with the RFM. The GEC invited him to attend a meeting to answer the charge. Sharkey, in replying to Bevin's letter, pointed out that

> Mortlake Branch officials (with your apparent concurrence) have taken no obvious steps to afford me the courtesy of addressing their members. Permit me to suggest that this course is still open to you, and failure on your part to do so will be interpreted by me as a contradiction of your own expressed opinions on the subject of democracy.

Sharkey's own branch, Willesden, then placed on record its own confidence in him, protesting at the GEC's action over the complaint of one branch when Sharkey had been elected to the CBC by a majority vote of the whole Western Division.

After he had attended an interview with the Finance and General Purposes Committee in June, the GEC resolved a month later that unless Sharkey furnished them with evidence of his complete dissociation from the RFM within seven days, his seat on the CBC would be declared vacant. Sharkey replied that this 'would not only be most humiliating to me, but could only be regarded as an act of gross cowardice by even the most apathetic member of our organisation' and gave notice of his intention to appeal. After the appeal the FGP finally resolved on 3 November that it

> does not consider that any good purpose will be served by taking any further steps to enforce the decision of the General Executive Council arising out of the complaint.[15]

During the same period the GEC also considered disciplinary action against Papworth and Payne for appending their names to an RFM leaflet convening a meeting of members of the Bus and Tram Sections. At the end of the day a secret memorandum containing the conclusions reached by the Finance and General Purposes Committee, and endorsed by the GEC, was communicated to both men.[16] Two days after their interview by the Finance and General Purposes Committee, the Area Secretary, Scoulding, called them to an informal meeting. When this proved to be abortive, he invited the whole Organising Committee of the RFM, less the two tram delegates. This time, Papworth outlined the ...vement's complaints and Scoulding promised to mount an inquiry.

...lding's purpose, however, was clear. According to Ware he ...ed the names of Wal Hannington and Harry Pollitt (both leading ...ists, the latter the party's General Secretary), alleging that there ...tain understandings' between the Communist Party and the ... File Movement.[17]

> His method of dealing with me personally and with Duhigg was one that he had a very good idea of where we stood ... If we are prepared to wind up the rank and file movement Scoulding will give us everything. Furthermore, they are prepared to have a bundle with anybody who will raise an objection to this.

Ware counselled against anybody thinking that Scoulding was 'a good chap'; as he understood it, Scoulding's strategy was to introduce political divisions into the Movement. Metzger agreed with this.

> Everyone will admit that there are different complexions and views inside the rank and file movement and there are certain views and tendencies that they [the TGWU leadership] would like to get at ... Bevin is as bitter and as foul as can be that this movement is communist and as bad and as rotten as it can be, and that it must be smashed, and that Scoulding had to fetch the members in to see where he could find weaknesses.[18]

For several years after this, however, Bevin appears to have bided his time, aware that any attempt to smash the Movement would be difficult, in view of the support it obviously enjoyed within the London Bus Section, and perhaps because he recognised that any attempt to destroy the Movement would have inflicted damage upon the Section and the union as well. Thus while the Movement quite openly intervened in disputes elsewhere in the union, Bevin merely sat and watched – and waited.

On 14 April 1937, just a fortnight before the London Bus Section's agreement was to terminate, a strike by busworkers flared up in Maidstone, quickly spreading through Kent. Over the next few days the strike was joined by busworkers in East Yorkshire, Northampton, Bedford, Norwich, Oxford, Cambridge, Essex and Sussex. It looked as if, by 1 May, there would be a national strike of busworkers. The GEC, however, adamantly refused to recognise the provincial stoppages. Gradually support for the strike weakened and, following the union's assurance that it would prevent victimisation and commence negotiations immediately, it collapsed completely. By 10 May all provincial busworkers were back at work and the London strikers were isolated.[19] They were soon to discover that they would not be able to rely on support from the tramworkers either. Ernest Bevin would then have the chance for which he had waited so patiently.

Notes

1. Bevin, circular to London District Secretary, Central Bus Committee and Delegates, 13 May 1936.
2. Ibid.
3. *Busman's Punch*, May 1934.
4. Ibid., March 1936.
5. Ibid.
6. Ibid., May 1936.
7. Handwritten notes taken at meeting, author unknown.
8. Bevin's circular, 13 May 1936.
9. J.J. Mills, circular to Delegates, 9 September 1936.
10. Handwritten notes taken at Conference, author unknown, in possession of London District Secretary, London Bus Section, TGWU.
11. Handwritten notes taken at meeting, author unknown, in possession of London District Secretary, London Bus Section, TGWU.
12. Ibid.
13. Ibid.
14. Bullock, op.cit., pp.606-14.
15. Minutes, Finance and General Purposes Committee, 3 November 1933.
16. Minutes, General Executive Council, 20 November 1933.
17. Rank and File Movement conference minutes, 16 October 1933.
18. Ibid.
19. Barrett, op.cit., pp.126-7.

CHAPTER FOURTEEN

The Demise of The RFM

In early May 1937 London was flooded with visitors, as George VI was due to be crowned on 12 May. The May issue of *Busman's Punch* accused the LPTB of

> deliberately engineering a deadlock, creating a strike position, at this period of the Coronation, in an attempt to alienate public opinion from the busmen, and to confuse the issue ... The strike is due to take place on 1 May. May this May Day, 1937, be the most memorable May Day in the history not only of the London busmen, but of the whole of the international working class of the world.

The strike went ahead, starting on Cup Final day. Initial reports were not promising: despite the strike, fans had little difficulty in reaching Wembley with the three other methods of public transport – Underground, trams and trolleys – all working. This pattern was to be repeated during the working week, and although *The Times* wrote of 'extraordinary scenes of traffic congestion in the streets, on the railways, both above and below ground, and on the tramways', employers reported that workers had little difficulty in getting to work and that timekeeping was hardly affected. The strike was unable to have any significant effect on the movement of travellers into and around the capital. The prospects for victory were not good.

The government appointed a Court of Inquiry whose first hearing was held on Monday 3 May. Bevin spoke for four hours. Medical evidence in support of the claim was given by Doctors S.J. Woodall and H.B.W. Morgan and by Professor Millais Culpin. Mills and Cassomini gave evidence in respect of time schedules. Both parties agreed that demands for a modification of the agreement could have been accomodated, with the exception of the seven-and-a-half hour day. The Court found that the evidence of injury to health was inconclusive, but that a *prima facie* case had been made for further investigation

THE BUSMAN'S PUNCH

The Official Paper of the
LONDON BUSMEN'S
RANK AND FILE MOVEMENT

SPECIAL FEATURES

London Busmen to Fight for Rights — By A. F. Papworth

Schedules. — By W. Payne.

Facts and Fancies. By Hugh Cares.

SPECIAL CARTOON.

No 55 (New Series) — MAY, 1937 — ONE PENNY

Editorial View

SOLIDARITY AND UNITY

THE crisis is upon us. The Delegate Conference has met. The C.B.C.'s recommendation has been adopted. In the words of Bro. Bevin: "This appears to be the end of the chapter. So far as I can see at present a stoppage will take place."

IN our opinion a correct line has been taken. Very late in the day, but from our angle this was unavoidable. We believe the L.P.T.B. have never taken the busmen's application seriously. We believe that they have been inconsiderate in relation to the conditions of health that have resulted from their policy. We believe that their persistent "No" to the section's original and amended applications, plus their own proposals, have been both unreasonable and provocative. We deplore the departure of the section from a 7-hour day; we feel that in consenting to a change to 7½ hours, while not giving the easement that is so much needed by the busmen, will at least show the public what lengths the Negotiating Committee and the full Delegate Conference have been prepared to go in trying to effect a settlement.

THE next move is with the members. We are convinced that the Board, backed by the City interests are prepared to fight. We even believe that moves will be made for Government intervention. The members must resist at all costs. Remember the Government were asked to intervene in the Maidstone and District dispute, but refused. What they refuse to do in one case we will refuse to tolerate in another. The busmen themselves are the decisive factor. They know whether or no their conditions are bad, good or indifferent. They know that procrastination on the part of the L.P.T.B. has deliberately taken place to rob the busmen of fair and decent conditions. We accuse the London Passenger Transport Board of deliberately engineering a deadlock, creating a strike position, at this period of the Coronation, in an attempt to alienate public opinion from the busmen, and to confuse the issue. We are

(*Continued on page 2*)

Busman's Punch on the eve of the Coronation Strike.

by a properly qualified body ... Should such a body find that the complaints ... are substantiated ... immediate and appropriate steps should be taken, either by reduction of hours and/or by other such measures as may be agreed ...'[1]

On the night of 8 May, with the strike a week old, the General Executive Council reported to the Central Bus Committee and the Bus Conference on the terms offered by the Board following the Court of Inquiry. The delegates returned to their branches and placed the terms before the membership the following day. The LPTB's intelligence service faithfully collated and recorded the results. Thus we learn, for example, that at Chelverton Road 377 members out of a possible 441 attended the meeting and that, by a vote of 374 to three, it was decided to continue the strike. At Leyton, a phenomenal 900 out of a possible 947 attended, voting by 898 to two to continue the strike (the Board's report also noted that one of the speakers – Harman – was currently on the sick list). Only three garages – Old Kent Road, Palmers Green and Harrow Weald – voted to resume work. 15,684 out of a total staff of 25,050 had attended meetings and voted to continue the strike.[2]

On 13 and 14 May a second round of branch voting took place. This time, again according to the Board's intelligence (compiled from reports submitted from each garage), the vote was 15,596 to 1,927 for a continuation of the strike. The three branches which had voted for resumption previously were joined by Tottenham.

On 5 May, meanwhile, the Tramway and Trolleybus Delegate Conference had requested that they be joined to the claim and that they, too, be granted plenary powers. However they were bound by an agreement which could only be terminated with six months' notice; moreover, this notice could not be given before mid-1938. This agreement was, of course, the one signed in November, 1936. If the allegations made about the way in which it was concluded (see Chapter 12) were true, it is surprising that Bevin was not accused by the RFM of deliberately inserting the six-months clause for this very purpose. The GEC believed, said Bevin later,

> that the breaking of the agreement would create an impossible situation and make matters worse for the busmen in dispute, and in the light of the agreement existing it was in fact impossible to join the tram and trolley bus members with the claim.[3]

Papworth and Snelling paid an official visit (i.e. as Central Bus Committee members, with Bevin's blessing) to a meeting of the London

Trams Council on 18 May. The LTC decided to refer the busworkers' request for solidarity action to a full conference of the Trams and Trolley Bus Section. Now, without the possibility of being joined to the claim, that conference voted by 31 to nine against a sympathy strike. However, the delegates then unanimously pledged to 'assist in carrying out any action that the Executive Council desires'.[4]

Bevin called the CBC together, pointing out that in his view the dispute would not be won even if the trams *had* decided to lend support. Nevertheless, the CBC requested that the GEC approach the Trams and Trolley Bus Section as the tramworkers

> by continuing to run and carry passengers normally carried by the bus workers who are now officially in dispute, are jeopardising the interests of the busmen and injuring the future of our Union. Furthermore, the GEC's very decision of plenary powers for the Bus Section is being nullified by the trams continuing to operate.[5]

The GEC were called to a meeting on 23 May to discuss this request. They argued that since the Court of Inquiry had recommended further investigation of the working day any involvement of the tramworkers would be meaningless.

The logic of such a position implied, of course, that there was little point in continuing the dispute anyway. Sure enough, two days later Bevin urged the CBC and the London Bus Conference to consider ending the dispute on the basis of the Court of Inquiry's Interim Report and the undertakings subsequently given by the Board. Conference expressed its

> indignation of the Executive Council's action in reaffirming the decision not to extend the dispute to the Trams Section. In our considered opinion, such decision is contrary to the recognised principles of trade unionism and the spirit of amalgamation upon which this Union is founded, and will be harmful to the Passenger Carrying Section of this Union and to the whole trade union movement of this country.[6]

In a desperate last-ditch attempt to gain support, the delegates called on the GEC to issue an appeal to all branches, to convene an Area Conference, to instruct tram and trolleybus branches to picket their depots to ensure that cars were not overloaded and that extra journeys were not run – given the undertaking made by the Trams and Trolley Bus Delegate Conference to 'assist in carrying out any action that the Executive Council desires' it is likely that the latter would have agreed to this modest request, at least. They also called on the GEC to approach the NUR and ASLEF with a view to securing similar action by railwaymen, and to organise central demonstrations.

It was all in vain.

Plenary powers were withdrawn by the GEC and the executive officers were instructed to commence negotiations with the Ministry of Labour for a settlement of the dispute.

Bevin met the Board on 26 May. Ashfield was reluctant to issue any further documents, taking the view that the LPTB had already made a firm offer on 8 May. He stressed the fact that the Interim Report had been accepted by the Board and that discussions would be resumed on that basis. It was agreed that work be resumed at the old rates and conditions and that negotiations for a new agreement be commenced immediately after this. Joint machinery would be established to investigate the consequences of proposed modifications and the effects of working conditions upon health, following which there would be 'immediate and appropriate steps as may be required either by reduction of hours, and/or by such other measures as may be agreed, to meet the position'.[7] The new agreement would be backdated to the date of resumption.

Meeting to discuss the results of the negotiations, the full GEC decided to instruct the members to return to work on Friday 28 May. The day before, a dispirited RFM conference surveyed the position and concluded that most branches, while incensed at the GEC's action in withdrawing plenary powers, could see no alternative but to return to work.

Defiant to the last, the June issue of *Busman's Punch* appeared with the headline 'The Fight Goes On'.

The fight, however, did not go on. The resulting agreement, signed on 15 June, made no concessions on pay other than to consolidate an accident bonus of 1s. 6d. for drivers and 6d. for conductors into the basic rate; moreover, the period of time before the top rate was achieved was lengthened from six to eighteen months, although for new entrants only. On hours, the main cause of the dispute, the maximum time on duty was reduced from eight-and-a-half to eight hours. Holidays were increased from eight to twelve days.

The health question was pursued through a series of conferences between the Board and the union under the chairmanship of Sir John Forster. The Report did not surface until August 1939 (at which time another health hazard appeared on the horizon, as we shall see in Chapter 16). It found 'no evidence in the figures of sickness incidence that the busmen's occupation has become less healthy' between 1931 and 1938. The figures for 1933-35 disclosed, however, 'some evidence of a slight excess of gastric illnesses ...' Certain spells of duty appeared to be too long before a meal relief; the importance of adequate time at termini was recognised 'both in respect of the break which they permit and of the opportunity they provide, on occasions, for taking more frequent refreshment'.[8]

The most important outcome of the Coronation Strike was the destruction of the London Busmen's Rank and File Movement.

When the GEC met on 4 June, just days after the strike had terminated, it charged the Finance and General Purposes Committee with the task of investigating the RFM and making recommendations, with a further brief to examine the rule book with a view to suggesting amendments 'for the purpose of protecting the Union against unofficial action and movements'.[9]

The Inquiry, led by the Assistant General Secretary, Arthur Deakin, occupied ten days. Many of its findings had been common knowledge for five years: that 'the London Busmen's Rank and File Movement is a distinct organism, with elected officers and committees and its own journal ...'; that the RFM had maintained contacts in the provinces; that the RFM had 'induced' branches to affiliate to the Labour Research Department, an organisation looked upon with disfavour by the union.

The assertion was made earlier that Bevin had merely been waiting for an opportune moment to attack the RFM. This is borne out by the fact that most of the charges could have been brought much earlier. Leading members of the RFM were also of the view, after the strike, that Bevin

> knew we were going to be beaten and he worked that way ... he wasn't averse to the timing of the strike because he thought that the popular feeling against us – being on strike while the Coronation was on – plus the fact that he felt capable of sewing up all the other sections, would sink us.[10]

Frank Pick's biographer suggests a tacit collaboration between Ashfield and Bevin:

> Many years later Herbert Morrison recalled how Ashfield, if he had decided for peace, 'would be prepared to pay any price to avoid trouble'. But there were other occasions when he would judge a strike to be desirable and then would order his managers to stand firm; if necessary he might even arrange for a strike to be deliberately provoked. Here clearly was one of those occasions. Suppose he did want a strike; what could be its purpose this time? London Transport and the Underground Group before it had had a lot to put up with from this red busmen's committee. Perhaps the moment had come when it would be possible to secure that the power of the committees should be broken. Only one person was capable of doing the breaking, Ernest Bevin, the architect of the Transport and General Workers' Union and still its

> general secretary. Ashfield the superlative card player knew that there are certain hands that tell you at once that your best chance of winning is to enlist the help of your opponent. Bevin in this present game was an opponent indeed: he had spoken long and passionately in support of the busmen's claim. Ashfield, however, was one of the few intimates who were aware that beneath that great show of loyalty there lay a sense of cold disapproval – more than once in the past ten or twelve years the Central Area committee had been warned by Bevin that it must moderate its rapacity. If London Transport continued to stand firm, was it not possible that Bevin might decide that his union, like London Transport, had had enough? And that is precisely what did happen.[11]

There is also the possibility that Bevin prolonged the strike unnecessarily. If the GEC felt that the Court of Inquiry's recommendations were sufficient to end the dispute in the fourth week of May, why had they not withdrawn plenary powers during the second week, after the publication of the Interim Report? It surely must have entered the minds of Bevin and the GEC that the membership would be more dispirited, more disenchanted with the RFM and the CBC, after being on strike for a month.

The Finance and General Purposes Committee recommended that Papworth, Payne and Jones be expelled immediately and that Hayward, Sharkey and Ware be debarred from office until 1942; Mark Cravitz of Leyton was debarred until 1940. It further recommended that the constitutional machinery of the London Bus Section, already suspended, be withdrawn pending the introduction of a new machinery which would 'form an integral part of the constitutional machinery of the Union ...'[12] At the Biennial Delegate Conference at Torquay in July standing orders were suspended in order that the GEC's report and recommendations could be heard, with no restrictions on the length of speeches. The report was adopted by 291 votes to 51.

After an absence of two months, *Busman's Punch* reappeared in September, 'certain' that it would 'enjoy an even larger circulation than hitherto', although this was to be its final issue. Following the suspension of the Section's machinery, the GEC convened a series of District meetings and, overriding the demands that a new CBC be elected by the branches, insisted that the meetings themselves elect the committee. 'It was,' wrote one of the new CBC's members, 'very evident that this new CBC were expected to do just what they were told without any regard to the desires of the members.' Not surprisingly, the whole committee resigned after just three meetings.

The branches continued to press for the reinstatement of the expelled and debarred members. A delegate conference in November was informed by the GEC that individual applications for reinstatement might be considered once a new constitution was agreed and a new CBC elected.[13] In April 1938 the GEC announced that those debarred from office would be eligible for office at the next elections and that, providing they promised to work within the constitution, Jones and Papworth would be allowed back into the union, although debarred from office for four years.[14] Jones and Papworth, now both members of the Communist Party, applied for re-admission and after serving their four years, regained their old positions. Jones joined Papworth on the GEC and both, in time, were elected to the TUC General Council. By January 1940 at least three ex-members of the RFM – Duhigg, David and Harman – were sitting on the CBC. Two years later there were five such members – Jones, Papworth, Sharkey, Ware and David.

For some months the LPTB continued to collect intelligence concerning the activities of the RFM members. Thus, a Depot Superintendant named Morley reported in late June that Duhigg, although on holiday, was actively collecting signatures on a petition to be presented at the BDC, protesting at the actions of the GEC. The Divisional Superintendent of 'C' Division sent a memo to the Operating Manager on 17 July 1937 to the effect that a meeting of the Willesden branch had attracted only twenty members; Sharkey had spent 50 minutes explaining his activities in the RFM and Communist Party, during which a Conductor Batstone 'appealed to the Chairman against allowing Sharkey to occupy the whole of the time available with what was termed "tripe" '. Two months later, Sharkey was still having trouble with attendances at his meetings: called by the North-West Communist Party Busmen's Group, a meeting on 20 September drew only twelve; the 'only matter discussed was the relationship of the Spanish war to British trade unionism. No busmen in uniform attended.'

After this, the Board seems to have ceased its intelligence-gathering activity, secure in the knowledge that the London Busmen's Rank and File Movement was dead.

An interesting footnote to the Coronation Strike was provided by Unity Theatre which had opened in 1936 and represented a major cultural intervention by the Communist Party. In the early months of 1938 Unity staged a 'living newspaper' entitled *Busmen*. A drama-documentary using cinematic techniques, the play chronicled the struggle from the speed-up of 1931 to the defeat of the strike of 1937 and the subsequent expulsions, using both fictional and real characters; among the latter were Bevin, Cassomini, Mills, Papworth, Jones and

Sharkey, were made to voice extracts from real speeches. *Busmen* was written by a small group of Unity members along with Herbert Hodge, a London taxi driver, and the left-wing writer Montagu Slater; Alan Bush provided music. The play was a great success and was seen by many busworkers, as a result of which several TGWU bus branches affiliated to Unity.[15]

It is difficult to assess the achievements of the RFM. Its claims to have achieved improvements in working conditions and to have staved off attacks by the LGOC and the LPTB were contested by the General Executive Council in its Report on the Internal Inquiry, saying that those achievements had been made by the union. In a sense, both claims are justified, because while the RFM *was* unofficial and *did* have its own machinery, it was very much a product of the London Bus Section of the TGWU; moreover, it was loyal to the union in that it was a fierce opponent of secessionist tendencies and fought vigorously to achieve 100 per cent membership. Inheritor of the 'red-button' tradition, it kept alive the industrial militancy and political radicalism of the Section during a period when those qualities were distinctly unwelcome in the official trade union movement – and especially in the TGWU.

As we have seen, though, the Communist Party played a leading role in the Movement. By April 1937 there were 98 Communist Party members in 29 garages. Most were in Party groups organised around their particular garages, although some 15 were individual members in scattered garages who had 'never done more than sign the form of application'.[16] Eight of the organised groups were linked up with the Party branches in their localities, and had been allocated instructors to provide them with political education. To opponents of the RFM in general and of the Communist Party in particular, such activity was tantamount to 'infiltration'. Such a charge was groundless, however. An internal Communist Party document (undated, although clearly from this period) makes the call for 500 members within the LPTB's employ; thus, rather than 'infiltrating' its members into the TGWU London Bus Section, it was calling upon its members already there to recruit.

At the same time the London bus 'fraction' would have been called together from time to time to discuss the tactics to be followed within the London Bus Section. There can be no doubt that such activity was unconstitutional. It might be thought that in this sense, Ernest Bevin's worst fears were justified, but this overlooks the fact that other political persuasions also organised into 'fractions' and attended unconstitutional meetings.

Communists within the London Bus Section would not have judged their actions in terms of the constitution of the union but by what they perceived to be the needs of their class. Their predecessors, the syndicalists and socialists in the LPU, had done much the same thing with impunity; but the Vigilance Committee had enjoyed immediate access to a membership concentrated in London and LPU officials had all been elected. It is pointless to discuss such problems in ethical terms. The relative success enjoyed by Communists in the London Bus Section was made possible by the objective circumstances: an economy which was in deep crisis, a labour movement which was largely on the retreat, a Union leadership which, largely because of the objective problems *it* faced in the years following amalgamation, centralised control, and a strong militant Section whose members wished to preserve their aristocratic status. Once all these factors came together, there developed a struggle for rank and file control of the union's affairs. Indeed it might be said that a further contribution made by the members of the RFM – Communists and others – was the raising of this struggle to an unprecedented level. Almost twenty years later this struggle bore fruit with the election of Frank Cousins to the post of General Secretary. From that moment on the TGWU's policies would move to the left, and control of the organisation would shift back to the members.

Ironically, though, the London Bus Section would have by then lost all claim to aristocratic status.

Notes

1. Interim Report by a Court of Inquiry Concerning the Stoppage of the Central London Omnibus Services, 1937, Cmnd. 5454.
2. These 'intelligence reports' were submitted by observers at local level and collated at 55, Broadway, the Board's headquarters. They are still in the possession of London Transport, and have been studied by the author.
3. E. Bevin, 'To the Members of the London Bus Section, Central Area', 29 May 1937.
4. Ibid.
5. Ibid.
6. Ibid.
7. Bevin, circular to Branch Secretaries and Delegates, 26 May 1937.
8. 'The Health of London Busmen; Report of Conferences Between Representatives of the LPTB, the TGWU and the Medical Research Council Under the Chairmanship of Sir John Forster', 1939.
9. 'Interim Report Of The General Executive Council On Unofficial Actions And Movements Within The Union', TGWU, 1937.
10. Bill Jones, *Busworker Monthly*, May 1983.
11. C. Barman, *The Man Who Built London Transport*, Newton Abbot 1979, pp.158-9.
12. 'Interim Report Of The General Executive Council ...'

13. Clegg, op.cit., p.128.
14. Ibid.
15. For the information on Unity Theatre, the author is indebted to Colin Chambers, author of a forthcoming study tentatively entitled, *A History of Unity Theatre.*
16. Record of Communist Party Bus Fraction meeting, 6 April 1937. Emile Burns Papers, in possession of Labour Research Department.

CHAPTER FIFTEEN

Aftermath: The NPWU

On 21 December 1936 the Central Bus Committee discussed, during the course of its regular meeting with representatives of the London Passenger Transport Board, a problem which had arisen at Merton, Snelling's garage. The committee complained that an organisation calling itself the Merton Protection Society was

> publicly criticising the Union in the various messrooms and places where the staff congregated ... The Society collected from their members, paid any fines incurred and had a share-out at the end of the year. They were not able to take any action on behalf of their members, but criticised the Union without carrying any responsibility. The men at the garage were very incensed, and it had been necessary to take action to avoid the staff coming out on strike.[1]

The CBC requested that the offending staff be transferred.

There were other instances of such activity. Early in 1937 there were complaints that staff at Palmers Green and Old Kent Road were causing 'disaffection', and again the CBC requested, without success, that the men be transferred to other garages.[2] Bevin himself thought this case to be sufficiently serious to enquire whether a particular driver had been suspended by the Board for abusing the union.[3] We have already seen that Bromley branch had threatened to secede from the TGWU as a result of the slow progress towards realisation of the seven-hour day. It is possible, then, that moves were afoot to form a breakaway union even before the Coronation Strike. It is equally possible that Frank Snelling of Merton was involved at this early stage, for it is inconceivable that the Chairman of the Central Bus Committee would have allowed the Protection Society to develop within his own garage without taking firm action – unless, of course, he was sympathetic to it. The flame of secession had burned brightest at Merton in 1921 so this garage would not have been chosen at random by the instigators of an incipient breakaway.

After the failure of the Coronation Strike some members withheld their contributions, pending appeals by the expelled or debarred members. The Board's intelligence-gatherers revealed that contributions were either not being paid or had dropped off at Leyton, Forest Gate and Dalston. Such a motion was moved at Willesden, however, and Sharkey himself asked that it be not seconded. By late July it was clear that a breakaway union was in the process of being formed. A 'TOT Protection Society', with an address in Theobalds Road, was circulating literature and appealing for members. This organisation claimed to be 'non-political, non-fascist, non-communist'[4] but that it was 'purely an expression of resentment with past Trade Union representation and an attempt to organise ourselves with a view to better representation in the future'.[5] A report to the Board's Operating Manager on 15 September 1937 claimed that 'ex-Conductor Peters is the main organiser' of the Society and that it had the support of 600 members of staff. The members of the 'provisional committee' named in this report are all obscure and thus it would seem unlikely that the Society had grown out of the ruins of the Rank and File Movement.

Throughout this period the Communists in the RFM argued against the formation of a breakaway union. Rumours of such a possibility must have been rife shortly after the strike, for Papworth and Sharkey 'strongly recommended members not to break away from the Union' at a meeting in the Memorial Hall on 23 June.[6] Similarly, the Norwood Bus Group of the Communist Party issued a leaflet which, whilst agreeing with criticisms of Ernest Bevin, argued:

> But our answer to this should not be to form a new Union or to withhold our cons. We must, now more than ever, make up our minds to carry on the fight *within* the TGWU and this we can do by:
> 1. *attending our Branch meetings*, in order that a really militant policy shall be stated
> 2. *paying our cons* without which we have no right to vote in Union matters.
>
> By forming a new Union we would split even the Bus Section itself, and a good many brothers would probably not be in either Union. But disunity on our part means strength for the Board, and they will soon take advantage of our weakness even more than hitherto.[7]

Such exhortations failed to have the desired effect. After a motion calling for the formation of a breakaway was narrowly defeated at the last meeting of the Rank and File Movement, Payne, Hayward and Snelling joined forces with W.J. Brown, General Secretary of the Civil

Service Clerical Association, and launched the National Passenger Workers' Union (NPWU) in February 1938.[8]

Having been a Labour MP between 1929 and 1931, W.J. Brown had resigned from the Labour Party and joined Oswald Mosley's New Party.[9] Later, in his trade union activities he assumed an anti-political stance, and re-entered Parliament as an Independent in 1942. Given the proudly anti-political tone which the NPWU was to adopt, it seems likely that those in the TOT Protection Society (which, as we have seen, also bore the anti-political label with some pride) were persuaded to abandon their efforts and join their forces to an attempt to create a new *national* union. Earlier, Snelling had been trying to form an organisation called the Garage Alliance'[10] it is not known whether Hayward and Payne were also involved in this. One thing is clear: the only factor uniting the founders of the breakaway appears to have been hostility to the TGWU.

A week after the formation of the NPWU, Bevin circulated all London bus branches with a copy of a pamphlet issued by the Union of Post Office Workers in which W.J. Brown's attempts to interfere in the affairs of that union were exposed.[11] 'As you will know,' said Bevin,

> Mr Brown 'ratted' on the Labour Party and caused the loss of a good Labour seat. We are told, too, that this same gentleman is interfering in other Civil Service Unions in a similar way that he is with us and so it seems to be a kind of disease with him.[12]

Bevin later announced that he himself had been approached by members of the Civil Service Clerical Association, Brown's union, with the request that he organise a breakaway.

In one of its earliest pamphlets – *A Real Union For Passenger Workers* – the NPWU charged that 'the Transport and General Workers' Union must bear a large share of responsibility for the actual worsening of conditions in the Passenger Transport Industry' and that the latter could no longer be made 'an effective instrument of struggle'. The organisers of the new union made no bones, however, about their readiness to shield behind the Tory Trade Union Act of 1927 when faced with what they called 'victimisation' by members of the TGWU.

The Central Bus Committee responded with their own pamphlet, entitled *The TGWU Is The Real Union For Passenger Workers*. Although the CBC opened by promising that 'we have no intention of entering into a printed warfare', these two pamphlets represented the first exchange of fire in just such a war. At times, the exchanges were vitriolic:

an NPWU pamphlet issued in 1944 dubbed the TGWU the 'Tired and Generally Worthless Union'. For its part, the TGWU issued a series of pamphlets outlining the benefits of membership and the record of struggle of the London Bus Section. In fact, the inter-union conflict seems to have aroused the Bus Section at official level to a degree of agitational and educational activity which would otherwise have probably not been attempted. Individual branches also produced material. A pamphlet issued by the Upton Park Branch Committee (*Substance Or Shadow?*) found it strange that tramworkers, previously denigrated by Brown and Hayward, were now being asked to join the NPWU; the pamphlet concluded with an appeal to 'all men employed at Upton Park Garage to remain a member, *or re-join* the Transport and General Workers' Union' (thus intimating that the NPWU had enjoyed some success there). A similar pamphlet was produced by the Barking branch in August 1938. In early 1939 the Mortlake branch produced a leaflet (*How the Breakaway Union Manufactures Its Facts*) exposing how, following a schedules strike at Mortlake on 7 January, Snelling had asked the three NPWU members involved to issue a statement to the effect that they had refused payment from the breakaway when they had, in fact, been paid from the Mortlake Incidental Fund.

In its very first pamphlet the NPWU had sought to calm fears that the NPWU would not achieve recognition from the employers by claiming that

> no body of employers can afford to conclude agreements with a Union which does not represent the workers concerned. If it does, the agreement is valueless ... There will be no difficulty in winning recognition as soon as we can show, as we shall show, that our Union represents the bulk of Passenger Workers.[13]

But the breakaway was never able to make good that promise and it was never recognised by the LPTB. In 1939 the NPWU decided to test the legality of the Board's position by taking to court the case of a Driver Moscrop, whom the Board had denied the right to be represented by his NPWU spokesman – Payne – at a Disciplinary Hearing. After failing in the High Court, the breakaway went to the Appeal Court, where it met with more success. The Board responded by withdrawing the rights of *all* staff to be represented at Disciplinary Hearings, causing the NPWU to bleat:

> on all matters, other than the question of representation before Disciplinary Boards, [the Board] maintains the privileges given to the TGWU representatives and denies them to our representatives.[14]

The Board, having suspended the disciplinary machinery, took the case to the House of Lords and secured the reversal of the Appeal Court ruling.

National membership of the NPWU – to quote its own figures – reached a peak of 14,000 in 1943. Corfield argues that the real figure (i.e. *dues-paying* membership) was less than half this, although it is probably also true that the breakaway enjoyed some growth on London buses and trams during the war due to the concessions which (as we shall see in the next chapter) were granted to the employer in order to aid the war effort. Even so, Corfield maintains that it was only at Leyton and Forest Gate that the NPWU enjoyed membership equal to the TGWU, although there were substantial minorities at Merton, Tottenham, Elmers End and Sutton.[15] At no time did the breakaway come near to achieving the boast, made in *A Real Union For Passenger Workers*, that it would have 150,000 members within its first year.

Allen claims that the effect of the breakaway 'was to submerge the grievances many busmen had against the Union and unite them behind the Union officials.[16] Although, as we shall see later, this perception is at least, partly inaccurate, it is true that Jones and Papworth were allowed to rejoin the TGWU on the understanding that they play a leading role in combatting the activities of the NPWU.[17] In fact, however, both *willingly* took on this role, as they obviously viewed the NPWU as divisive, and on occasion levelled harsh criticism at the Central Bus Committee for not combatting the activities as forthrightly as they would have liked.[18] According to Papworth, in early 1943 the NPWU were advertising meetings, using the names of Central Bus Committee members and then attacking the latter when they failed to appear.[19] When Chalk Farm asked the CBC to send speakers to two open meetings and to confront Snelling and Hayward on the platform, this was agreed. At the first meeting, despite personal invitations, neither Snelling nor Hayward appeared. Despite the fact that the meetings were convened for the employees of Chalk Farm and Holloway, NPWU members from all over the fleet attended the second one.

> The bill was read pointing out the meeting was for Chalk Farm and Holloway employees only, and they were told that would be strictly adhered to. Snelling arrived with Hayward. I took the opportunity of pointing out to him the breach he had made. His answer was that it was an open meeting. We refuted this, produced the bill, and he then said: 'What about it? Our people demand the right to come in; they are here and you try and keep them out.' I protested at this attitude and he then said he would speak to his people. He went outside, told his people they were not to be admitted because they

> were not members of Chalk Farm or Holloway. But in an aside, said, 'I can't help it if you force your way in.' He came back to me and said his people would not stand for it – they would come in even by force. Under such a threat, I said if such a thing happened the meeting would be cancelled. I was not going to be intimidated. He said this was a pity because at 7.20 p.m. a ceremonial entry would be made into the meeting by W.J. Brown. This put me in the position of saying that we would not allow Brown in. The answer was 'You stop him.'
>
> Then, although we had 12 stewards on the door the crowd after an incident of fisticuffs overpowered the organisation of the stewards, and marched in. I then cancelled the meeting amid catcalls whilst awaiting for the people to go from the hall and the Minister, whose hall we were in, had appealed for order, and then Snelling from the body said he would organise another meeting and in a few minutes announced a meeting in another hall to hear W.J. Brown.[20]

There is hardly any sense in which the NPWU can be said to have been the bearer of the 'red-button' tradition, for that tradition, as we have seen, always had a strong socialist colouration. Indeed, in that the breakaway was *anti*-political, it might be true to say that, in part, Clegg's claim that the RFM had been 'syndicalist in origin' might be more accurately applied to the NPWU. The 'red button' had displayed a fierce devotion to the whole working class, and there exists little evidence of any interest within the NPWU other than the desire to recruit and poach as many members from the TGWU as possible. It is no exaggeration to say that the breakaway represented little more than the interests of the handful of opportunists who formed its leadership. Payne and Snelling had earlier (the latter less than three years before the formation of the NPWU) been critical of breakaway movements; why should their views have changed in 1938? A letter from William Jenkinson,[21] himself an organiser of the TOT Protection Society,[22] suggests that within two years of the foundation of the NPWU leading members were thoroughly disenchanted by the whole exercise; he characterises Payne and Snelling as

> a couple of low bred tricksters and the only useful purpose of the union was to keep them in a job and provide cars for them to run about, creating further expense ... I do not stand alone in my segregation here are some more EC members who are 'out' Opie, West Ham Trolley, Smart of Holloway Trams, Evans of New Cross trams, Saunders of Swansea, Langdon of Neath, Sheekey of Bromley Kent and ordinary members galore.

In Snelling's case, his own party's anti-Communism possibly played a part in his decision to form the breakaway, although at a public meeting called to discuss the new union by the Socialist Party of Great Britain in July 1938 he was opposed by W.E. Waters, also of the SPGB.[23] This is hardly surprising, for Snelling would have found it necessary to turn his back on his socialist beliefs in order to go along with W.J. Brown's conception of the apolitical trade union.

The NPWU, rather than a continuation of 'red-button' tradition, was the last gasp of the secessionist sentiment which had been a component of that tradition at an earlier stage. By attempting to rob that sentiment of all its political content and then adapt it to the completely different circumstances of 1938, the NPWU was doomed to failure.

By 1945 the breakaway was claiming 8,000 members nationally,[24] and between 4,000 and 5,000 in London, although the Board put the figure closer to 2,000.[25] In the TGWU, meanwhile, agitation for 100 per cent membership was building up. At a Joint Delegate Conference of the Central Buses, Trams and Trolleybuses and Country Services on 20 June 1946, it was resolved that plenary powers be sought from the General Executive Council from 1 September because, the resolution read, 'it is our opinion that all who share in present agreements between the TGWU and LPTB shall be members of the TGWU.' Thus the demand put to the Board, as explained by Bill Jones in a pamphlet issued by the Dalston branch, was that

> once a man enters your employment he will have to pay the cost of maintaining and improving the wages and conditions obtained from you. If he wishes to continue to enjoy them but refuses to pay, then we shall put into operation our right to refuse to work with him. Put another way, it means that we shall fight parasites of the working class as we fight parasites of the boss class.[26]

Previously, the Board had been hamstrung by the 1927 Trade Union Act which forbade the imposition of any condition 'whereby employees who are not members of a trade union are liable to be placed in any respect either directly or indirectly under any disability or disadvantage as compared with other employees'. In May 1946 the Act was repealed. Unashamedly, W.J. Brown admitted that he had voted against the repeal of this clause.

Following the Joint Delegate Conference in June, the TGWU launched a recruitment drive and within a month the number of non-members (including members of the NPWU) had been reduced from 3,264 to little more than a thousand.[27] In the meantime, twelve tramworkers at New Cross, Wandsworth and Clapham had been suspended on full wages because the TGWU members refused to work with them. The Board finally agreed that all non-TGWU members be dismissed from 31 August. When that date arrived 176 busworkers were sacked. The NPWU attempted to secure an injunction against some of the dismissals, but this failed.

Allen stresses that throughout, 'the impulse for action came ... from the lay members', while Deakin, who led the negotiations with the Board, 'followed the instructions they laid down through their delegates'. Thus the drive to exclude the NPWU had come not from a central bureaucracy wishing to safeguard its own power and influence but from ordinary members who, in Jones's words, were seeking to 'fight parasites of the working class'.

By June 1947 the NPWU could boast six members who paid regularly, and a bank balance of £4 13s.[28] A chapter in the history of the London Bus Section had been closed.

Notes

1. Minutes of meeting between Central Bus Committee and London Passenger Transport Board, 21 December 1936.
2. Minutes of meeting between CBC and LPTB, 10 February 1937.
3. Ibid., 1 March 1937.
4. Circular letter, TOT Protection Society, 1937.
5. Ibid.
6. Report of meeting in possession of London Transport.
7. Norwood Bus Group of the Communist Party, 'To Our Brothers in the Norwood Bus Garage', 1937.
8. Barrett, op.cit., p.134.
9. Corfield, op.cit., June 1964.
10. Memo from Depot Superintendent, Merton Garage, to Operating Manager.
11. TGWU Cyclo. 10313/A.
12. TGWU Cyclo. 10312.
13. *A Real Union For Passenger Workers*, NPWU, 1938.
14. *Correspondence Between the NPWU and LPTB*, NPWU, 1941.
15. Corfield, op.cit., June 1964.
16. Allen, op.cit., p.73.
17. *Busworker Monthly*, May 1983.
18. Barrett, op.cit., p.136.
19. Typed Report (to Central Bus Committee?), A.F. Papworth, 4 March 1943.
20. Ibid.
21. W. Jenkinson in a letter dated 28 April 1940. It is not clear to whom this letter was addressed. A copy is at the TGWU Regional Office, Green Lanes, London.
22. Memo from Staff Superintendent, Central Buses to H.S.F. Lansdown, Operating Manager, 15 September 1937.
23. *Lewisham Borough News*, 26 July 1938.

24. Barrett, op.cit., p.135.
25. Clegg, op.cit., pp.129-30.
26. *What Is The Difference Between Closed Shop and 100% Trade Unionism?*, TGWU Branch 1/498, 1946.
27. Allen, op.cit., p.163.
28. Ibid., p.164.

PART FOUR

The Decline Of An Aristocracy

CHAPTER SIXTEEN

The Second World War: The Beginning of Decline

V.L. Allen claims that the formation of the National Passenger Workers' Union had the effect of submerging the grievances of 'many London busmen ... against the Union and uniting them behind the Union officials'.[1] In fact, the 'unofficial' leaders of the Section from April 1940 regrouped around the rank-and-file publication *The Transporter*, continued their criticism of the official leadership and their agitation for improved wages and conditions, and it was not until the Soviet Union's entry into the war in June 1941 that these differences were submerged. *The Transporter* differed from *Busman's Punch* in that from its inception it was aimed at *all* LPTB employees, and therefore could not be considered an unofficial TGWU publication; even so, the journal was dominated by contributions from the Bus Section. Even then, however, this was so only because the rank-and-file leaders were agreeable to the granting of certain concessions to the *employer*. This had the *appearance* of a truce between the TGWU leadership and the militant rank and file of the London Bus Section because the battles of the 1920s and 1930s had been fought over the former's reluctance to press for improvements.

In the first months of the war the TUC declared an 'industrial truce'. In July 1940 strikes were banned and a system of compulsory arbitration introduced. In the first three months of the war, however, there were 40 local strikes throughout the country, and 1940 saw the highest number of strikes for a decade. Experience in the London Bus and Trams and Trolleybus Sections of the TGWU reflected these developments. Hanwell depot struck for three days in late November 1939; Edmonton crews were out for two days in May 1940, and Victoria struck in December 1940. In each case schedule alterations were the issue. From a very early date conditions were made more onerous by the withdrawal of buses to save fuel. This not only intensified the work-load of those remaining on the road, but necessitated the transfer and loaning of staff from their home garages. By early 1941 J.J. Mills, the London District Secretary, was complaining that the lightest duties were being cut, leading to an increase in the average time on duty.[2]

During the war wage increases were made on the basis of War Wage Advances, which were added to the basic rates for the purpose of calculating overtime. The first such award, payable from December 1939, was 4s. per week, a sum which compared badly with the union's claim for 10s. Meeting the Board on 5 January 1940, the union's National Passenger Secretary, Harold Clay, complained that the union side 'found themselves in a difficulty because there was no difference between the terms Mr Pick had outlined for London Transport workers and the provincial settlements'. For the Board, Frank Pick replied that

> there was no case for granting a higher increase in London than in the provinces; indeed, he thought there might be an arguable case for a lower differential in London than in the provinces ...[3]

It was an early indication that the London Bus Section's aristocratic position might be in jeopardy.

Most of the former leaders of the London Busmen's Rank and File Movement were still debarred from office at this time. They were kept from office for a further two years by the General Executive Council's decision, early in the war, to suspend all elections for the 1940-41 electoral period. In January 1940 Bill Jones wrote to Bevin on behalf of 21 members (including Sharkey and Papworth) requesting that the General Secretary receive a deputation to discuss the matter. Bevin noted in his reply that

> you are not writing on behalf of your branch and it seems to me that the tactics which you are employing are for the purpose of creating a situation very similar to that which existed in the days of the Rank and File and other unofficial movements which cost the Union so much money and led to so much disruption.[4]

Jones then circulated each of the 21 members with a form letter to Bevin which repeated the request for an interview. In acting upon this, J.H. Bailey, Chairman of the 1/363 branch, informed Bevin that he was concerned by the growth of the NPWU in his garage, and that one of the arguments used by the breakaway was the TGWU's suspension of elections.[5] Nevertheless, the deputation was not received.

It was shortly after this that the first issue of *The Transporter* appeared. The fact that the journal was printed on the Communist Party press in Cayton Street points to clear involvement by the party. The line adopted regarding the nature of the war was also that of the Communist Party:

> Sheer and urgent necessity in this most difficult period for the trade union and the working-class movement has compelled us to make our position and the policy we intend to follow unmistakeably clear. Only struggle and the preparedness to struggle will rid us of war conditions and wages. We must, every single one of us, take an intelligent interest in the fate of our organisations and the policy of the present leadership.[6]

'Whitesea', in his 'Transport Review', asked whether the war was really

> for the defence of democracy, freedom, and the total destruction of fascism? Or is it specially for the benefit of LPTB and the other monopolies to establish their power in the country?

In the same issue, 'Chalky' urged readers to attend their branch meetings in order to force action on the accumulating grievances – standing passengers, black-out conditions, compulsory transfers and the ineffective lighting of vehicles. 'Whitesea' returned to the attack in the June 1940 issue, congratulating the members at Edmonton, Grays and Northfleet (the latter two being Green Line garages) on their strike actions:

> We cannot defend out interests by giving them away. Freedom cannot be defended by surrender. Trade union conditions and wages cannot be maintained by allowing them to go ... We must maintain the independence and freedom of our movements. We must develop our unions to their fullest possible strength and maintain their activity; it is more vital now than ever before.

Following a War Wage Award of 3s. per week in June 1940, the Editorial Committee of *The Transporter* compared the situation with that which had existed during the first World War:

> Then, as now, it is profits, war profits that count ... When our leaders, who apparently are afraid of the industrial struggle (the refusal to refer the wage increase back to the branches shows this) and are incapable of understanding the political struggle (their attitude to Russia, three months ago and now, shows that) begin to understand that our 'love of country' and 'capitalistic patriotism' are two completely different opposites, we shall be on the road that will lead to real working-class freedom and democracy.[7]

One of the major issues tackled by *The Transporter* during this phase of the war was, however, not wages, conditions, or trade union rights, but the right to live. During the period of the Blitz, which ended in mid-1941, London was the target of 50,000 high-explosive bombs and millions of incendiaries. The policy of the Board was clear: if stopped by the police or an Air Raid Warden when the raid was not in the immediate vicinity, the driver should protest and, if forbidden from continuing, take the policeman's or Warden's name and report him.[8] When the first casualties began to occur this policy generated considerable anger. Such anger was directed at the Board, and also at the Central Bus Committee, for a London Bus Conference, having decided that all work should stop as soon as the air raid warning sounded, was faced with the fact that the CBC called a second conference, apparently in the hope of securing the reversal of that decision. In the meantime J.J. Mills had refused to issue a leaflet on behalf of the CBC setting out conference policy. When the second conference refused to budge on the issue, the CBC succumbed to pressure from the full-time officials and disregarded the agreed policy. The October 1940 issue of *The Transporter* carried the headline: 'SACK THE CBC!' For the first time the tone of the journal recalled that of *Busman's Punch* as pent-up grievances were given expression:

> The mishandling of the new union position quite early in their office, the upsetting and abrogation of the agreement permitted by them, their mess-up of negotiations, all these are as nothing compared to their decision to go back on two overwhelming conference decisions.
>
> ...Then the CBC goes back on its own decision and upon the delegate conference.
>
> Why? Because they have not got the qualities of leadership to back up their decision.
>
> They were afraid of a scrap, a scrap against officialdom.
>
> They probably had visions of members being debarred from holding office for 2 to 5 years, or being expelled for doing what the members wished and wanted.
>
> These members got there by the efforts of the real militant leaders. They never could have got there on merits of leadership, hence the reason why they supported no elections in 1940-41.

At this stage, therefore, the militant rank and file leaders were arguing that, notwithstanding the need to defeat fascism, 'patriotic' calls to withhold demands for improvements should be resisted; moreover, the traditional means of industrial struggle – the strike – should continue to be used when considered necessary. Indeed, following the banning of strikes in 1940, *The Transporter* reminded readers that this had been the first action of Hitler and Mussolini.[9] In 1941, when seven shop stewards at an engineering factory in London were arrested for striking, several branches of the London Bus Section were represented on the Defence Council formed to defend them. 'The prosecution,' reported *The Transporter*, 'is at the insistence of the Minister of Labour. The Minister of Labour is Mr Bevin, General Secretary of the TGWU'.[10] It is clear from this, as in their criticism of the handling of the NPWU and the air-raid questions, that Allen's claim that the militants had united behind the official leadership, submerging their differences, is far from the truth.

All this changed after the Nazi attack on the Soviet Union in June 1941. *The Transporter* declared:

> Nothing about this war is the same as it was before Germany's attack on Soviet Russia. Not only has a *bigger* force than ever before been drawn into the struggle, but a force *of an entirely different kind.* Hitler is now fighting the only people in the world without capitalists. He is fighting the largest body of organised Trade Unionists in the world – Trade Unionists who run and own the industries they work in ...
>
> ...In our own interests we have to fight against everything that holds up aid to Russia now. And by that we mean against profiteering, corruption, monopoly interests, inefficiency, attempts to destroy working-class standards and rights and organisation. We have plenty to do in that fight right here in the ranks of the LPTB.[11]

The 9th Biennial Delegate Conference at Llandudno provided a clear indication of the change that was taking place. Of the thirteen-strong delegation from the London Bus Section, at least seven were former members of the RFM. And yet the only real point of disagreement at the conference was over the ban which had been placed on the *Daily Worker* following its support of the People's Convention which in January 1941 had put forward a programme for a People's Government. On all other issues – war aims, wages, nationalisation of transport, etc. – there was agreement between right and left.[12]

From this point on *The Transporter* consistently pursued a policy of removing all impediments to war production and, with Jones, Papworth and Sharkey back on the CBC from January 1942 (with Papworth as chairman), this policy was followed by the Section as a whole. As early as September 1941 *The Transporter*, in criticising the cut in petrol supplies to the Board, made its own position clear:

> ... *If this petrol cut, with all the intensified working involved, were essential to the war effort, and if it would help war production, we would not only accept it, we would demand it.* Our Russian comrades are working worse

The **PETROL CUT DANGER (p. 8)**

Transporter

The Paper for all L.P.T.B. Workers

No. 14 July 1941 **Id.**

Editorial Opinion

Now or Never!

NOTHING about this war is the same as it was before Germany's attack on Soviet Russia. Not only has a **bigger** force than ever before been drawn into the struggle, but a force **of an entirely different kind.** Hitler is now fighting the only people in the world without capitalists. He is fighting the largest body of organised Trade Unionists in the world—Trade Unionists who own and run the industries they work in.

Some of the changes we are seeing are laughable. Look at the Press which is so busy sneering at the "political somersaults" of others. Remember four or five years ago—the horrors of the "purges," and the "truth-drugs," and the "torture chambers" in Russia? **Now** they admit that Russia was the first country in Europe to get rid of its Quislings (let **us** add—the **only** country). Remember eighteen months ago, the "dastardly attack" of Russia on the "democratic" Finns? **Now** they thank their stars that the frontier is no longer only ten miles from industrial Leningrad. Remember a few weeks ago, how Stalin was Hitler's boot-boy, and terrified to death of him, and the Red Army was an inefficient rabble, and the Russians would revolt if war broke out? **Now** these slanders are temporarily stored on the shelf.

BUT more serious changes have taken place too. Hundreds of thousands of people have been deeply suspicious of the war aims and the peace aims which have so far been behind this war. But now they say—**the interests of the Soviet people and the British people are one—if they act quickly and together German Fascism can be smashed and the peoples of Europe freed—now it can and must be a people's war, a people's revolt, a people's victory, before we can get a people's peace.**

It is not difficult to state what is needed. We must see that every possible ounce of aid is given to the Soviet Union. Real aid, not just words. Aid in the forms in which the Soviet Union wants it. Aid **now,** not when our military and economic leaders find a spare moment to think about it.

There are plenty of people in high places who will do all they can to prevent such aid being given. They are fundamentally pro-Fascist and profoundly anti-Soviet. They have felt all along that this was the wrong war for the British Empire. They want to see it line up with Germany

1

Transporter in July 1941, now in full support of the war.

schedules than ours in the tanks on the battlefields in the East. They are fighting *our* battle, and it would not only be a 'dirty trick', but it would be a mad and suicidal lack of foresight if we did not help them to the last ounce of our strength.

This dramatic change of tack was not confined to the London Bus Section. In August 1941 the Engineering and Allied Trades Shop Stewards' National Council organised an all-London production conference at which the idea of Joint Production Committees (JPCs) was mooted. Such JPCs would involve the shop-floor workers in eliminating inefficiency and boosting war production. In February 1942 the government announced that such committees would be set up in all its Ordnance Factories. Bevin, as Minister of Labour, opened talks between the TUC and the employers for their establishment in all workplaces covered by the Essential Work Order. By 1944 there were 4,500 JPCs and 82 Joint District Committees.[13] These committees, by introducing workers into a realm of policy-formulation hitherto reserved for management, had varied results. In some cases they helped prepare these workers concerned for the struggle for socialism after the war, building their confidence in their own abilities to take on management tasks. In other cases the employers were able to make use of them to their own advantage.

In October 1941 *The Transporter* organised a Production Conference at Holborn Hall. The 89 delegates from 33 garages and depots

> drew the unanimous conclusion that the LPTB alone cannot be relied upon to give the kind of service that is needed. Speaker after speaker emphasised how essential it is that the workers in the industry, who know its problems and its possibilities from the practical point of view, must have a share in management. Through their representatives, they must be drawn in at every stage of the organisation, from top to bottom, for consultation and for a share in the decisions taken. On the other side of the medal the Conference left no doubt about the readiness of all to make sacrifices, to scrap long-cherished ideas, to make a new approach, in order to improve service.[14]

The Board was approached by the Bus Section on 23 April 1942 with a proposal for a Central Joint Production Committee aimed at increasing the efficiency of the war effort, although it would be excluded from dealing with matters covered by the agreement. Complementary to this, it was suggested that there should be local JPCs in each garage, with one member elected from each route. The LPTB, however, countered this with a proposal for three Divisional Joint Consultative Committees, and these were eventually established in early 1943. Interestingly, their terms of reference were amended so that all reference to the war effort was deleted and the words 'the national interest, having regard to the need for economy in manpower, fuel, rubber and other materials' were inserted.[15] Presumably by this the Board hoped that the Section might be persuaded to continue its sacrifices after the war.

By August 1943 Mills was complaining that the JCCs were not functioning as they should.

> When a reduction of service was suggested, arrangements to implement the suggestion were made quickly, but when the suggestion was to augment a service there was a long period of waiting and they were told there was no case.[16]

Despite continued attempts to get the Board to agree to implement Garage Consultative Committees, these were not achieved until 1946.

Considerable concessions were granted to the Board throughout the war. Perhaps the most important of these was the attitude of the militant rank and file to strikes. This is best exemplified by a piece by 'Nutshell' of Putney Bridge in the December 1941 issue of *The Transporter*:

> I want to see our disputes settled in a different way from such strike action as at Glasgow, which undoubtedly did not assist the production of all the needs for our main struggle ... I say we should take the buses out and carry on in the usual way, but the conductors should leave their ticket boxes, etc. in the garage; why collect fares?

By March 1942 J.J. Mills felt able, with the blessing of the CBC, to approach the Board and suggest that a notice be issued to the effect that the buses must continue in operation after altercations with inspectors. Hitherto on such occasions buses had been withdrawn from service by the crews concerned.[17] It is worth noting that Jones, Sharkey and Papworth were present at this meeting. Two months earlier, along with Mills and Cassomini the Schedules Officer, they had attended a meeting with the Board and indicated that the CBC

> desired to do whatever they could to further the interests of the war. Any proposals, therefore, that were outside the terms of the agreement would be considered, provided that the departures from the agreement were registered and suitable penalties fixed. In such cases they were prepared to take any recommendations to Conference, on the understanding that the Board would not desire to take advantage of any departure from the agreed conditions.[18]

This approach led to a temporary amendment to the agreement whereby 20 per cent of all duties could be regarded as outside that

Date	*Staff Affected*	*Duration*	*Cause*
21 April 1943	106 drivers, 109 conductors, Sutton garage	Half-day	Objections to new schedules following increased spread-overs
10-11 July 1943	224 drivers, 223 conductors, Hanwell and Alperton	Two days	Cuts of three duties
15-16 April 1944	2,301 drivers and conductors, various tram and Trolley depots	Two days	Objections to schedules
19-21 April 1944	2,018 drivers and conductors, 7 bus garages, 2 tram and trolley depots	Three days	Objections to schedules
22 April 1944	111 drivers and conductors, Hounslow tram and trolley depot	Half-day	Objection to schedules
25 October 1944	114 drivers and conductors, Uxbridge bus garage	One Day	Objection to schedules
28 October, 4 November 1944	357 drivers and conductors, Hendon bus garage	Two Days	Objection to schedules
4 November 1944	34 drivers and conductors, Hanwell and Turnham Green bus garages	One Day	Objection to schedules
2-6 May 1945	4,783 drivers and conductors, various tram and trolley depots, 1,434 drivers and conductors, various bus garages	Five Days	Objection to schedules
16 August 1945	182 drivers and conductors, Hendon trams and trolleys	One Day	Protest against Sunday duty schedule during VJ holidays

Source: 'Record of Industrial Disputes in which staff have taken action since 1 January 1933'. London Transport Board.

agreement, with a maximum spreadover of 13 hours. The maximum time on duty would be eight hours and *all* spreadover time in excess of eight-and-a-half hours would be paid.

These proposals were not greeted with universal acclaim. At Sutton (where, as we have seen, there was a significant minority of NPWU members), there was a half-day strike over the new schedules. As the table on the previous page shows, resistance to the wartime conditions grew throughout the latter stages of the war, particularly in 1944. In mid-1943 there were complaints registered over no less than 360 schedules.[19] By September that year the CBC was asking if the Board was making money from the reduced running time which had been introduced. Mills complained that crews were suffering additional strain from the extra speed and requested that the heavy duties not be further increased. In reply, A.F. Andrews, the Board's Schedules Superintendent, promised that the Schedules Office would attempt to comply with this, levelling up the lighter duties.[20] In February 1944 a whole meeting was occupied with the question of running time. Mills, who had pointed out earlier that more running time was needed in central London during the shopping period, accused the Board of a breach of faith when its representatives suggested that this could be achieved at the expense of cutting the running time on the outer sections of the routes concerned. The Board's case was that the CBC had struck a bargain – minimum meal relief increased to 40 minutes and a maximum spell of duty of four-and-a-half hours in return for speeded schedules.[21]

Some critics have accused the Communist Party, of which the lay leaders of the London Bus Section were members, of having participated in a 'sell-out' of the British working class after June 1941, of becoming 'His Majesty's Communist Party'.[22] Any evaluation of the party's industrial policy during the Second World War is conditioned by an assessment of the role played by the Soviet Union and of the primacy or otherwise of the struggle to defeat Hitler and halt the spread of fascism. Any such evaluation must also question whether the results for the trade union movement *were* negative and whether the policy did, in fact, play a crucial role in the London Bus Section's decline.

In the years before 1945 the Soviet Union was, of course, the one country where the working class had deposed capitalism and taken power. Any attack upon the Soviet Union was therefore viewed by Communists and many other socialists as an attack on the most prized possession of the international working class. If such an attack created a situation in which the Soviet workers were fighting alongside the bourgeois-democratic powers, it was argued that the workers in this latter group of countries should spur their rulers on to greater efforts, thus shortening the sacrifices made by the workers' state. In the course of so doing, a certain amount of belt-tightening seemed fitting if this aided the war effort.

The period is often presented as one in which the workers made all the concessions. This is not true: Britain's rulers made important *ideological* concessions. For the duration of the war, anti-Soviet propaganda was replaced by references to the heroism and sacrifices of the Soviet soldiers and people, thus contributing to the creation of an atmosphere in which socialist ideas were disseminated more freely – an atmosphere leading to the shock defeat of Churchill and the Tories and the return to office of a Labour government on its most radical programme to date.

Most importantly for the purposes of our discussion, Ernest Bevin's anti-Communism was also temporarily abandoned:

> Nothing gave me greater joy than when on that day the Cabinet decided to accept the twenty years' treaty with Russia ... Russia had been almost a nation ostracised, recognised it is true in certain respects, but with mutual suspicion on both sides. In our movement we have often experienced those moments when, representing the workpeople, after struggling for recognition, finally achieving it. The day comes when for the first time you have a feeling in your bones, 'The old days have gone. Equality has been established.'[23]

This was not Jones or Papworth speaking, but Ernest Bevin, addressing the Tenth Biennial Delegate Conference of the TGWU at Edinburgh in August 1943.

The London Bus Section was active in supporting the Soviet Union. A branch meeting at Shepherds Bush called for

> a campaign to aid our brother trade unionists in Russia. While it is recognised that the government must implement their promise of FULL military aid immediately, we who have participated in industrial fights, know and appreciate the value of donations to our strike funds from other sections of the working class. It is the concrete example of working-class solidarity.[24]

On 7 August 1941 a joint meeting of the Putney Bridge and Chelverton Road branches adopted a similar resolution, with the additional demand for the removal of all Nazi sympathisers from positions in industry, the civil service and the BBC. The same month, the London Bus Conference issued a call for aid to the Soviet Union. The New Cross tram branch, representing some 1,400 members, pledged itself 'to make every possible effort in an endeavour to assist the USSR in the fight against

Average Earning

Average weekly earnings in last pay week of	*All workers*		*Males*		*Average weekly earnings of LPTB staff in year (ending)*	*All weekly paid staff*		*Central bus drivers*	
Oct. 1938	£2 13s. 3d.	100	£3 9s. 0d	100	June 1938	£4 2s. 9d.	100	£4 14s. 9d.	100
July 1940	£3 9s. 2d.	130	£4 9s. 0d.	129	Dec. 1940	£4 10s. 11d.	110	£5 0s. 9d.	106
July 1941	£3 15s. 10d.	142	£4 19s. 5d.	144	Dec. 1941	£4 14s. 5d.	115	£5 4s. 0d.	110
July 1942	£4 5s. 2d.	160	£5 11s. 5d.	161	Dec. 1942	£4 19s. 4d.	120	£5 11s. 10d.	118
July 1943	£4 13s. 7d.	176	£6 1s. 3d.	176	Dec. 1943	£5 5s. 5d.	127	£5 14s. 3d.	121
July 1944	£4 16s. 8d.	182	£6 4s. 4d.	180	Dec. 1944	£5 11s. 2d.	134	£6 4s. 3d.	131
July 1945	£4 16s. 1d.	180	£6 1s. 4d.	176	Dec. 1945	£5 13s. 10d.	137	£6 6s. 10d.	134
Oct. 1946	£5 1s. 0d.	190	£6 0s. 9d.	175	Dec. 1946	£6 0s. 3d.	145	£6 7s. 6d.	135
Oct. 1947	£5 8s. 2d.	203	£6 8s. 1d.	203	Dec. 1947	£6 5s. 5d.	151	£6 8s. 6d.	136
Oct. 1948	£5 17s. 4d.	220	£6 16s. 11d.	200	Dec. 1948	£6 15s. 10d.	164	£7 1s. 6d.	169

Source: Clegg, op. cit., p. 95.

fascism ...'[25] By January 1942 the London Bus Section had raised just over £1,000 towards the cost of X-ray equipment for the Soviet Union. In the following month Harry Pollitt, General Secretary of the Communist Party, addressed a special meeting of the Hendon trolleybus branch members, their friends and relations on

> not only ... his own work and some of his experiences in this connection, but on many matters besides, including the magnificent achievements of the Soviet Armed Forces, the devotion and sacrifices of the Russian peoples ...[26]

Clearly, such activity aided neither the LPTB nor the capitalist class as a whole. Nationally, the Communist Party's membership rocketed to 60,000, a growth fully reflected in the London Bus Section.

By the end of the war the British trade union movement was far stronger than it had been in 1938, especially in terms of work-place organisation. The working class as a whole was also better off in real terms, as the previous table shows.

We see from this that while by July 1945 the average weekly earnings of Central bus drivers had increased by 34 per cent since October 1938, those of all male workers during the same period had increased by 76 per cent. Clearly, the Section's 'aristocratic' status was threatened as never before. It may be tempting to lay this decline at the door of the policy followed after June 1941, but the above table shows that the decline *vis à vis* other male workers was far more severe *before* June 1941. When compared to retail prices and broken down into two phases, pre-1941 and post-1941, the following picture emerges:

Year	*Retail prices**	*Central bus drivers' earnings*	*Average male earnings*
1938-41	+27 per cent	+10 per cent	+44 per cent
1941-45	+16 per cent	+21 per cent	+22 per cent
1938-45	+48 per cent	+34 per cent	+76 per cent

* Derived from British Economy Key Statistics, London and Cambridge Economic Service.

While it is true that London bus drivers were worse off in real terms by the end of the war, it is also true that this decline took place *wholly* before 1941. This must, then, be explained by the conditions which existed after the defeat of the 1937 Coronation Strike: demoralisation, the loss of an effective lay leadership and the activities of the breakaway union. Equally significantly, the above figures show that between 1941 and the end of the war the London bus driver's wages kept pace with those of other male workers and *out*paced inflation.

There can be no doubt, however, that the post-1941 policy resulted in worsened conditions, and these have been outlined already. As for the Joint Consultative Committees, these came nowhere near the aims set for them by the Production Conference in October 1941. Bill Jones recalls that they were:

> a real waste of time. Very little came out of them. They couldn't interfere with wages and conditions. They were a way of letting off steam and kidding yourself that you were really doing something on the question of productivity. They were a joke.[27]

Indeed the LPTB even refused to alternate the chair between the Board's Divisional Superintendents and the TGWU Divisional Officers. Inroads into the area of managerial prerogative could only have been achieved had the Section maintained its militant stance, for without it the Board would hardly have been inclined to yield its decision-making functions. Although the Committees were supposed to confine themselves to questions of productivity and to refrain from discussing wages, the reverse was not the case, according to Jones:

> In the wages negotiations at that time, we signed more than one agreement, or the lads were kidded to accept more than one agreement, which was supposed to increase productivity, and that was the only reason for getting a wage increase. On one occasion, Deakin came up with: 'The way to do it is to increase standing passengers' in order to get a 4s. wage increase. It was one big fiddle. You gave away conditions in order to increase wages.[28]

Ironically, the rank and file leaders who in the years 1932-37 had been responsible for re-establishing the link between industrial militancy and socialist politics were the very men who, between 1941 and 1945, were primarily responsible for divorcing the two. As far as the London Bus Section is concerned, it is possible that this industrial demobilisation of the rank and file was the most serious drawback of the post-1941 policy. In the post-war years other sections of workers would begin to erode the differential which existed between themselves and the London busworkers. It is possible that, had its militancy been preserved, the London Bus Section could have prolonged its 'aristocratic' status. Even if this had been so, the Section would have confronted overwhelming odds, for the war had provided tens of thousands of working-class men and women with the driving skills which until recently had been a token of the London bus driver's superior status. More seriously, the proliferation of the private car was soon further to devalue that skill and also constitute a new threat to public transport.

An era was passing.

Notes

1. Allen, op.cit., p.73.
2. Minutes of CBC-LPTB meeting, 3 April 1941.
3. Minutes of TGWU Negotiating Committee and LPTB, 5 January 1940.
4. Bevin, letter to J.W. Jones, 29 January 1940.
5. J.H. Bailey, letter to Bevin, 29 January 1940.
6. *The Transporter*, April 1940, p.1.
7. Ibid., July 1940, pp.1-2.
8. Ibid., p.6.
9. Ibid., August 1940, p.1.
10. Ibid., June 1941, p.1.
11. Ibid., July 1941, p.1.
12. Ibid., September 1941, pp.1-2.
13. Hutt, op.cit., pp.152-3.
14. *The Transporter*, November 1941, p.7.
15. Minutes of CBC-LPTB meeting, 7 December 1942.
16. Ibid., 26 August 1943.
17. Ibid., 18 March 1942.
18. Minutes of CBC Sub-Committee/LPTB meeting, 12 January 1942.
19. Minutes of CBC-LPTB meeting, 11 June 1943.
20. Ibid., 3 September 1943.
21. Minutes of Special CBC-LPTB meeting to discuss reduced running time, 14 February 1944.
22. Coates and Topham, *Workers' Control*, London 1970, p.143.
23. E. Bevin, *A Survey of the War Situation and Post-War Problem*, TGWU, 1943, pp.13-4.
24. *The Transporter*, October 1943, p.3.
25. Ibid., September 1941, pp.6-7.
26. Ibid., February/March 1942, p.8.
27. Bill Jones, interviewed by the author, August 1984.
28. Ibid.

CHAPTER SEVENTEEN

A Revival of Militancy?

In mid-1946 the three TGWU sections in the employ of the LPTB – Central Buses, Trams and Trolleybuses and Country Services – elaborated a programme for a Common Agreement which called for a 40-hour week with no loss of pay, the levelling-up of Tram and Trolleybus and Country Services 'wages to the rates enjoyed by Central Buses, time-and-a-half for Saturday afternoons, Sundays and Good Fridays, three weeks' holiday and increased stand-time. This represented 'an objective to be reached in stages' and 'not something to be obtained in a short space of time'.[1] As we shall see in this and succeeding chapters, by the time some of these objectives had been achieved the London Bus Section had fallen from its aristocratic perch and the occupation of the London busworker was looked upon as just another semi-skilled job – and not a very desirable one at that.

In a leaflet written for the Dalston Branch, Bill Jones argued forcefully for a reduction in hours:

> The facts show: a) Today, 15 years after the 1932 settlement, you will still find duties in the London passenger industry which mean that drivers and conductors are called upon to work a bus through the centre of the busiest traffic city in the world for as long as 7 hours 50 minutes. We must also add the fact that both vehicular and passenger traffic have grown enormously since 1932, and that we are operating with vehicles which it is admitted are sub-standard and would have been off the roads years ago, had it not been for the war. b) Today, 10 years after the 1937 settlement, we find ourselves working (if we include excess relief time) an average 42 hours a week and at a speed far in excess of 1932 or 1937.[2]

As an illustration of the intensity of the busworker's job, Jones cited the case of a duty on route 11 which, on 19 March 1947 carried 1,072 passengers in a first spell of four-and-a-half hours. But while the London Bus Section – and especially the militants within it – had always complained of the intensity of the job, Jones struck a new note in this pamphlet by comparing the London busworker's lot unfavourably with other occupations. It marked an early indication that the loss of status was appreciated by the Section.

Passenger Worker	*Factory or Office Worker*
Works seven days running, then one day off.	Works five-and-a-half or five days running then one-and-a-half or two days off.
Has 64 days off a year, viz., one day per pay roll week, plus twelve days annual holiday. One in summer, two in winter.	Has 95 days off per year if five-and-a-half day week, or 121 days if five-day week, viz., 52 Saturdays, 52 Sundays, half or whole day. Six Bank Holidays, eleven days' annual leave – usually in the summer.
Irregular working hours. May leave home as early as 3.30 or 4.00 a.m. No normal transport facilities on first or last duties.	Regular working hours. In the main, leave home between 7.00 and 9.00 a.m. Normal transport facilities.
Meals: no regular or fixed times. In the main, 40 minutes' meal time, which varies from within two to five hours of starting work. No tea breaks.	Meals at regular fixed time and place. Generally one hour in the centre of day. Tea breaks.
While the working day cannot exceed eight hours, duties can be spread over thirteen hours from start to finish.	Duties usually straight through, even if shift work.
Restricted social life. Evenings and weekends worked every other week.	Full social life. Evenings and weekends free.
Public Holidays are extra heavy working days, most of staff at work.	Public Holidays free.

As we saw in the previous Chapter, the decline in the Section's status had begun before the war. It would appear probable that the wartime mood of the Section, which had resulted in the curbing of militancy in the interests of boosting the war effort, extended to the immediate post-war years. In 1944 the TUC had adopted a programme for post-war reconstruction calling for the nationalisation of key industries and the public control of others, price controls on consumer goods, a National

Industrial Council with trade union representation and the formation of a National Investment Board to plan finance and investment. In the atmosphere created by increased understanding of the Soviet achievement, the wartime controls placed on the private sector and the consequent strengthening and growth of the socialist constituency in Britain, many workers were persuaded that the construction of a socialist society would be on the agenda after the war. Thus, when a Labour government was returned after the war (with 390 seats to the Tories' 211), there was considerable pressure to continue the restraints on militancy while Labour implemented its programme. As nationalisation of the transport undertakings formed a part of this programme, the London Bus Section of the TGWU would not have been immune to such pressure.

The government could argue convincingly that such restraint was necessary. The war had transformed Britain from a major international creditor into a debtor; overseas assets worth £1.2 billion had been sold off and exports were down to a third of their pre-war level. The United States stepped in to grant Britain a loan of $3.75 billion on condition that it ratify the Bretton Woods agreement, which included free convertability of currency and the removal of restrictions on foreign trade. The loan itself was intended to help plug Britain's balance of payments' gap with the USA, but when this turned out to be wider than anticipated, leading to a crisis in 1947, the government turned its sights on the restriction of imports, extending rationing to goods – such as bread and potatoes – which had never been rationed in the darkest days of the war. The course adopted by the government had two long-term effects: the British economy was subordinated to American interests and the socialist movement was both demobilised and, in the long run, demoralised.

Just as it had during the war, the LPTB took full advantage of the political situation. The minutes of the regular meetings between the TGWU and the Board during these years reveal that on issue after issue quite modest demands were turned down: that women conductors being discharged be given a month's notice so that they might be trained for other industries; that two men in each garage be given time off to scrutinise new schedules; that Bank Holidays worked be compensated by days in lieu; that the Board assume responsibility for conveying staff to and from work for very early and very late duties when service buses were not available. An indication of how the feathers of the London Bus Section were being ruffled came at a meeting in 1948, shortly after nationalisation, when the union side requested that a member of the London Transport Executive attend such meetings as the TGWU

Passenger Services Group Committee (this comprised representatives from the Central Bus, Tram and Trollybus and Country Services Sections) was of the opinion that 'the present arrangement tended to reduce their status'.[3] This was turned down with little discussion.

It eventually became clear, at least to class-conscious observers, that the Attlee Government was not contemplating the construction of a socialist society. Harry Selmes, then a driver and a Communist Party member, recalls that 'the things that had been promised seemed to be still in the distance'.[4] Instead of socialism, the government followed a pattern which would be repeated by future Labour governments: concessions to sections of the working class, following which it buckled down to the task of managing capitalism. Given the post-war mood of the working class, of course, the concessions had to be substantial. Thus the National Health Service and the abolition of the 1927 Trade Union Act strengthened the workers' position. The true nature of the government became clearer with the nationalisation of coal, transport, gas and electricity, when excessive sums were paid in compensation, involving loans which would burden the industries for years to come. Moreover, the managing élite was drawn from the ranks of the capitalist class. Explaining this, the 'socialist' Stafford Cripps stated that

> ... workers simply did not have the necessary skills to participate in management. In general, managements went as far as they thought necessary to appease and conciliate their workforce; but in essence the line between was as firmly defined as it had ever been.[5]

The British Transport Commission, which entered into the ownership and control of most inland transport undertakings, was established in 1948. The London Transport Executive, one of several separate Executives subordinate to the BTC, took over all the LPTB's undertakings and certain mainline railway sections. The Board's stockholders were compensated to the tune of £3.8 million per annum. This had obvious implications for wages and conditions within the industry. Bill Jones wrote at the time that:

> Every application we make either on wages or conditions will be balanced against that £3,800,000 which is to be the first charge on the 'new pint pot' of the London passenger transport industry.
>
> If this is what nationalisation in its present form means, we ought to express the hope that some of our leaders will indicate to us how we are to get those improvements in conditions and wages which our members are rightly demanding, while these tender, sacred and generous compensation terms remain.[6]

Indeed, being part of a much larger organisation would have further implications for wage-negotiations. Larry Smith, who joined the London Bus Section as a driver at Victoria in 1948, and later became London District Secretary and National Passenger Secretary, explains that the lay members

> weren't too enamoured with the British Transport Commission because they saw themselves being soaked up by a larger organisation and they thought, as they'd always thought, themselves to be independent of anybody else. That's why they didn't go for this co-ordination with the other groups – the Municipal and the Company Bus Sections. Indeed, as time went on they saw it as very much a drag anchor on their own possible progress directly with London Transport.[7]

Clearly, by shelving militancy during and immediately after the war, the struggle for socialism – or, more modestly, even for a more progressive form of nationalisation – had not been strengthened. While more workers than ever before may have been *ideologically* for socialism, in the absence of the *organisational* means with which to carry that struggle through, and the *mobilisation* of the working class on its day-to-day demands, the post-war dream was bound to turn sour. And so it did. Order 1305, the wartime measure banning strikes, had still not been lifted and in February 1948, Attlee presented parliament with the government's 'Statement on Personal Incomes, Costs and Prices', which was subsequently issued as a White Paper. First an exercise in capitalist nationalisation, now wage restraint. The emperor had no socialist clothes.

The first signs of renewed militancy had already begun to flicker in the London Bus Section. In June 1947 agreement on a 44-hour week had been reached with the Board. However, a flexibility clause allowed the employer to schedule up to 46 hours weekly, although the average time on duty for the fleet could not exceed 41 hours 15 minutes. However, no penalty payment was conceded for Saturday afternoons, and payment for Sunday remained at time-and-a-quarter. On Sunday 6 July 18,849 Central drivers and conductors and 3,724 tram and trolleybus drivers and conductors took unofficial strike action in support of the demand for time-and-a-half on Sundays.[8] In November almost 2,600 drivers and conductors struck over new schedules arising from the agreement.[9]

The following year the claim for time-and-a-half on Sundays and Good Fridays was conceded. Additionally, one day's holiday with pay was granted for each Public Bank Holiday worked, giving a possible total of six days' extra holiday. The wages settlement, however, fell well short of the demand of £6 16s. for drivers and conductors in both the Central Bus and Tram and Trolleybus Sections, both grades in the latter Section being awarded £6 5s., the same as Central Bus conductors, while Central Bus drivers received £6 9s.

In October 1948, the union once again submitted a claim for time-and-a-half for Saturday afternoons. By this time the Section was not only disenchanted with the performance of the Labour government but, according to Larry Smith:

> ... it was as much against the current full-time leadership of the Passenger Group in the union and of course the General Secretary, who tended to lean towards a pay policy with the government and, indeed, accepted the Stafford Cripps pay-freeze. They blamed the Passenger Group leadership for the slippage which occurred in the wage-rates for London busmen at that time.[10]

Despite the attitude of the full-time officers, the Area No.1 Passenger Trade Group Committee disowned the GEC's endorsement of the government's wages 'standstill', and it began to look as if the London Bus Section was moving towards confrontation with both London Transport and the union leadership. On 30 December 1948 the Passenger Group Committee, accompanied by A.E. 'Jock' Tiffin, the Assistant General Secretary, and Sam Henderson, the National Passenger Secretary, attended an eleventh-hour meeting with Lord Latham, Chairman of the London Transport Executive, John Cliff, the LTE's vice-Chairman, and other members of the Executive. Once again, the claim was rejected. The Committee decided to recommend to its Conference that the matter now go to arbitration.

The London Bus Conference had already recommended that strike action be taken on Saturday 1 January 1949 if the claim was not met. At midnight on 31 December meetings were held at garage level, with most deciding to go ahead with the strike action. London Transport's own figures show that 13, 532 drivers and 13,602 conductors took part in the action.[11] The original intention was to repeat this action every Saturday until the claim was met, but from this point on considerable pressure was brought to bear upon the membership to abandon this course. Lord Latham posted a notice in all garages which threatened with dismissal all staff who 'did not keep ... good faith and honourable observance of agreements'.[12] This was a reference to a 1940 agreement to arbitration. Pressure was also brought to bear by Arthur Deakin, now General Secretary of the TGWU. According to Allen, it was Cliff who complained of the action to Deakin, following which the latter recalled the London Bus Conference on 5 January.[13]

He told the delegates:

> I want to make it clear that I will not move one finger to seek a discussion with the LTE so long as you have taken your decision, which is flat contradiction to the policy of the Union and the agreement that your Executive had appended its name to on your behalf.

Thus, Conference agreed to lift the strike action and the matter went to arbitration. The Tribunal, chaired by John Cameron, agreed the union's application, as a result of which the enhanced payment for work completed after 1 p.m. on Saturday was introduced on 5 March.

The London Bus Section appeared to be riding the crest of a wave. A new mood of militancy had been established and several demands had been achieved. Just months later, however, the Section was to see its most influential lay leaders deposed from office.

Notes

1. J.T. Barrett, 'To All LPTB Branches ...', TGWU, 10 July 1946.
2. *Divided We Walk, Together We Drive*, J.W. Jones, Dalston Bus Branch, 1947.
3. Minutes of meeting between TGWU Passenger Group Committee and the London Transport Executive, 6 May 1948.
4. Harry Selmes interview.
5. A Marwick, *British Society Since 1945*, London 1982, p.108.
6. J.W. Jones, *What's Yours?* Dalston Bus Branch, 1948.
7. Larry Smith, interviewed by the author, 31 July 1984.
8. London Transport Board, 'Record of Industrial Disputes ...'
9. Ibid.
10. Larry Smith, interviewed by the author 31 July 1984.
11. 'Record of Industrial Disputes ...'
12. *Socialist Standard*, February 1949, p.14.
13. Allen, op.cit., p.169.

CHAPTER EIGHTEEN

Deakinism

In an earlier chapter we saw that Ernest Bevin's style of leadership had been the product of his personal characteristics, and also of a set of specific circumstances – the need to weld the new union into a coherent whole in the face of employers' attacks. Between 1940 and 1955, first as Acting General Secretary (while Bevin was Minister of Labour) and then as General Secretary, the TGWU was led by a man who was every bit as authoritarian as Bevin: Arthur Deakin. His style of leadership, however, was also conditioned by certain influences. Allen points out that:

> ... for eight years Deakin worked in the central office of the Union and for five of these he was Bevin's immediate subordinate. In those years Bevin was Deakin's model of a trade union leader. Deakin was, moreover, trained in Bevin's ways. He would have been a strange man if he had not reflected the influence of those formative years in his subsequent activities.[1]

The same writer draws attention to the fact that Deakin achieved the position of General Secretary at a time when the economy was showing signs of improvement, at least compared to the 1930s, and when there was a Labour government. 'At every move [trade union leaders] were exhorted by the government, by the press and by prominent members of the public to consider the effect of trade union activity on the community.'[2]

The new General Secretary's attitude to unruly elements among the rank and file was, however, largely conditioned by the state of international relations and the anti-Communist hysteria which gripped many capitalist countries in the late 1940s. After the Second World War the capitalist powers looked eastward and saw the Soviet Union as a country which was no longer isolated. En route to Berlin, the Red Army had liberated several East European nations under Nazi occupation. In some of those countries, popular movements had joined with the Soviet forces, facilitating the adoption of a socialist path; in other countries such as Poland, where the socialist movement was weaker, the Soviet Union, with 20 million dead and obviously conscious of the need to protect its borders, decided to attempt the construction of socialism anyway. Not only was the Soviet Union stronger than ever, but its prestige was at its highest – even Churchill was forced to admit that its forces had 'torn the guts out of' the Nazi army. It was in this atmosphere that in October 1945, the World Federation of Trade Unions was formed, uniting 70 million members in 71 countries, including the Soviet Union and Great Britain. The international capitalist class feared for its future.

Something had to be done.

In Fulton, Missouri, Winston Churchill spoke of the need to 'roll back the frontiers of Communism'. The Cold War had begun. Churchill's wartime Cabinet colleague, Ernest Bevin, his words regarding the heroism of the Soviets apparently forgotten, alleged that the Soviet Union was 'coming across the throat of the British Empire'.[3] The USA launched its Marshall Plan, lavishing aid on those Western European countries whose leaders promised to turn their backs on socialism and exclude Communists from their governments. The American Federation of Labour spread money around Europe too, attempting to woo the trade union centres in countries earmarked for Marshall Aid away from the WFTU. Working together, the AFL and the British TUC convened two conferences of such centres in London in March and July 1948.[4]

The President of the WFTU at this time was Arthur Deakin. It is not known whether he was implicated at an early stage in the moves afoot to split the WFTU. Anti-Sovietism had certainly raised its head in the TGWU. In August 1947 Deakin had written to complain of a circular signed by C.J. Van Ryne, J.J. Kane, E.A. David and Bill Jones inviting branches to affiliate to the British-Soviet Society. It was, he wrote,

> impermissible for any Member of the Union to invite our Branches to consider affiliating to the British-Soviet Society, or to take part in any propaganda on behalf of an organisation which is proscribed.[5]

In July 1948 Deakin publicly denied that the WFTU was 'acting as a tool of Soviet imperialism'.[6] Seven weeks later he announced at the Margate TUC that, after all, the organisation of which he was President was 'nothing more than another platform and instrument for the furtherance of Soviet policy'.[7] The following January, the British, US and Dutch representatives walked out of the WFTU Executive meeting, and by December the pro-Western International Confederation of Free Trade Unions had been set up.

The domestic counterpart of the Cold War comprised an anti-Communist witch-hunt to facilitate the imposition of the Labour government's wages 'standstill'. According to Hutt the call for such a witch-hunt came first from Morgan Phillips, secretary of the Labour Party.[8] In October 1948 the TUC General Council threatened to de-register Trade Councils which refused to observe official policy, and attempts were made to revive the aim of banning Communists from union office, a device first attempted in the 1920s and continued in the 1930s. The TGWU had gone on record against the 'Black Circular', as the 1934 TUC document was called; now it was the only major trade union to implement the ban on Communists.

The 1949 Biennial Delegate Conference at Scarborough decided:

> No member of the Communist or Fascist Parties shall be eligible to hold any office within the Union, either as a lay member or as a permanent or full-time officer, this rule to take effect as and from the beginning of the 1950/1951 electoral period.

Thereafter, anyone nominated for a position in the union – from the lowliest Branch Secretary to the General Secretary – would be required to sign a declaration professing his or her political purity. The same Biennial Delegate Conference also decided that changes to the rule book would in future be made at a separate Rules Revision Conference – to be held every six years. Thus, it was not until 1969 that the ban on Communists was rescinded.

While not specifically aimed at the London Bus Section, the ban would obviously have serious consequences for not only was the Section's lay leadership largely Communist, but the party was still strongly organised within the Section. Max Egelnick, then the Communist Party's Area Secretary in North-West London, recalls that the Party was 'very much involved in Hendon, Cricklewood, Middle Row, Willesden and Edgware', with CP branches in all of those garages and that Hendon was probably strongest 'with fifteen or more members'.[9] Interestingly, the Party's decision to wind up its industrial branches in 1944 in order to adopt a more community-based, electoral approach seems not to have been implemented by the London bus branches. 'Although officially we wound up,' says Egelnick, 'we were still issuing stamps at these places, and so we never *really* wound up.' Elsewhere in London, Dalston continued to have a very large branch of between 35 and 40,[10] and Merton and several other garages also had healthy CP branches.

In the years following the ban many branches 'fell away, although individual members remained' here and there.[11] This was not because the Communist Party's organisational framework had been impaired, for a ban on Party members holding office simply could not have had this effect. In Egelnick's view it was in large part due to the fact that Communists were removed from their *leadership* role:

> Dalston had been the leading light. Jones and several others around him had been leading lights. They had set the tone for all London busmen ... And, of course, there was a witch-hunt in the union.

However, if Deakin anticipated that the membership of the London Bus Section would be swayed by the anti-Communist hysteria, he was disappointed. Larry Smith recalls that the lay membership of the Section

> saw themselves being caught up in a policy that they disliked intensely, and it has to be remembered that at that time the Passenger Group supplied something like a third of the officer force in the union and also had about a third of the Executive. It had half of the Finance and General Purposes Committee and it dominated ... the Biennial Delegate Conference. All the major issues that were discussed at those Conferences were mainly through the efforts of the London Bus Section ... Sam Henderson, as the National Secretary of the Passenger Group, was the most popular officer. The lads identified with him and felt that he was the best leader that they had had; he came straight in from being a tram driver to National Secretary. He was highly popular and the members were enraged about the ban and ran a series of meetings in London, especially at Holborn, right up until the time that he got the sack.[12]

According to Harry Selmes the reaction of the rank and file membership to the ban was rather more mixed, with the strongest opposition coming from those branches where Communists had held leading positions.[13]

The ban on fascists was seen for what it was by the militant rank and file – a smokescreen to divert attention from the fact that a Communist witch-hunt was underway. A Committee For Trade Union Democracy was formed to combat the ban, with J. Harding, the non-Communist Branch Secretary of Dalston, playing a leading role. A deputation of 70 was organised to protest at Transport House, and a meeting of 300 was held outside. As the GEC refused to see the deputation it was decided to organise a national deputation to the GEC at its December session. In the circular calling this deputation, the Committee presented the situation thus:

> Workers in all sections are beginning to feel the effects of devaluation in lowering their real wages, and the employers are coming out more and more openly for longer hours, harder work and cuts in the social services. Members

have also noticed Mr Deakin's bodyblow in the October *Record*:

> It is clear that the trade union movement must continue to exert an even greater measure of restraint than that to which we committed ourselves at the Bridlington Conference.

Their eyes are being opened to the fact that the drive against the Communists in the trade unions will weaken the resistance of the unions to the employers' attacks.

Bill Jones of Dalston took no heed of Deakin's instruction, circulated to all branches, to have nothing to do with the Committee, and immersed himself in fund-raising for the nine full-time officials sacked by the GEC after they refused to sign the declaration. As a result of this activity he was instructed to appear before a GEC Committee of Inquiry in May 1950. A week before he was due to appear his branch met and gave

> notice that our patience is exhausted at the continuing purging of militant members at a time when our section is riddled and rotten with dissatisfaction at the present wages and conditions on the job.

The meeting decided to strike on the day of the Inquiry and assemble outside Transport House.

The ban meant, of course, that Jones, Bert Papworth and all other Communists holding office within the London Bus Section were out of office from 1 January 1950. Some indication of Jones's attitude to the declaration is given in a letter he received from A.J. Townsend, J.J. Mills' successor as London District Secretary, in which Townsend drew attention to a form nominating Jones: 'You will note that the declaration has not been signed, and in addition that the last two paragraphs of the declaration have been interfered with ...'[14]

* * *

Some indication of the feeling which continued to exist at branch level almost two years after the ban had been agreed was provided by a debate conducted by the Merton branch in May 1951. The motion read: 'That this meeting is of the opinion that the Transport and General Workers' Union is a democratic organisation.' Speaking for the motion was Jack Barrett, the Regional Passenger Group Secretary; he was opposed by Bill Jones. When the vote was taken the 56 members present all voted against the motion.

In the short term, however, the battle against the ban was lost. Once again, the London Bus Section witnessed an upsurge of unofficial activity. The officials appear to have had their hands full, and the fact that those hands were so often heavy, leads one to believe that they were uncertain of their own strength.

When Dalston passed a motion ironically congratulating the full-time officers on their 15s. per week wage-rise, whilst pointing out that London busworkers had only been able to achieve increases of 15s. 6d. over the previous four years, the response of the officials appears to have been out of all proportion to the 'offence'. A Divisional Officer called on Dalston's Branch Secretary, Harding, handing him a letter in which the Regional Secretary requested the surrender of the branch minute book (Areas were by this time re-named Regions). Upon being informed that this was in the possession of Crossman, the minute secretary, the officer telephoned the garage, obtained Crossman's address and persuaded Crossman's wife to part with the book. The following day, another official visited the printer used by the Dalston branch, brandishing a letter signed by J.T. Barrett, the Passenger Group Secretary, and requesting information regarding the leaflet upon which the motion was reproduced. The printer referred the matter to his solicitor.[15]

An investigation in 1951 into *The Platform*, an unofficial publication, led to a lengthy exchange of correspondence between Jones and Brandon, the Regional Secretary. Brandon reported that allegations had been made that Jones was a member of the 'Brains Trust' associated with the journal and that, indeed, certain articles appeared to be signed by him. Jones was reminded that he had been issued with a final warning in June 1950 and that he had undertaken to observe the rules and constitution of the union. Jones dropped a broad hint that legal action might follow if the matter was pursued further and, in a characteristically impish postscript, asked if Brandon would object if the correspondence was made public. Brandon replied that he could not agree to this and that rather than being submitted to the GEC as originally intended, the whole matter would be given 'further investigation' at Regional level.[16]

In a later case, a solicitor's letter had the desired effect – at least in the short term. The Dalston branch called a mass meeting for Sunday 31 August 1952 to which members of other branches were invited. The London District Secretary circulated all branches to the effect that the meeting was unconstitutional. The meeting went ahead. As a result the Regional Secretary, Brandon, suspended from office all the branch officers and the entire branch committee. A solicitor's letter on behalf of the garage engineering shop steward to Deakin pointed out that the suspensions were contrary to the TGWU rule book and demanded the lifting of the suspensions by noon, four days later. The suspensions were lifted – within the deadline. That was not the end of the matter, however, for after an investigation by the Regional Committee the branch officers and committee members were all debarred from office until the end of the 1952-53 electoral period.

The unofficial activity of this period produced one long-lasting achievement: *The Platform*, a journal which was to appear regularly, month after month, for no less than seventeen years. It was founded late in 1949 when, following the ban on Communists:

> Busmen were indignant. Not only the Communists, but non-Communists who objected to political discrimination in their Union.
>
> It was in this atmosphere that a group of London busmen met in a room in Gray's Inn Road towards the end of 1949 and decided to start a Busmen's journal. Only one or two were Communists, the others were far from being so ...
>
> ... A man with some knowledge of the laws relating to libel, a man with the know-how for laying-out, editing and producing a paper was needed. Such a man was invited to act as technical editor, working with a team of busmen who would determine the paper's policy. That man is now known to thousands as George Moore.[17]

George Moore was a pen-name for our old friend George Renshaw. The former RILU man, no longer a member of the Communist Party, was to perform the same function for *The Platform* as Emile Burns had for the *Busman's Punch*. This time, however, although *The Platform* enjoyed a mass *readership*, the creation of a mass rank-and-file organisation around the journal was never achieved – or, indeed, even seriously attempted. This was due partly to the climate created by Deakinism and partly, as we shall see, to the changes which had taken place within the London Bus Section itself.

Notes

1. Allen, op.cit., pp.5-6.
2. Ibid., p.6.
3. Hutt, op.cit., p.174.
4. Ibid., p.179.
5. A. Deakin, letter to C.J. Van Ryne, J.J. Kane and E.A. David, 25 August 1947.
6. Hutt, op.cit., p.180.
7. Ibid.
8. Ibid., p.177.
9. Max Egelnick, interviewed by the author, 24 August 1984.

10. Bill Jones, interviewed by the author, 18 August 1984.
11. Max Egelnick interview.
12. Larry Smith interview.
13. Harry Selmes interview.
14. A.J. Townshend to J.W. Jones, 11 November 1949.
15. Circular issued by Dalston Branch, undated.
16. Charles Brandon to J.W. Jones, 9 April 1951; J.W. Jones to C. Brandon, 17 April 1951; J.W. Jones to C. Brandon, 26 April 1951; C. Brandon to J.W. Jones, May 1951.
17. Bill Waters, 'The First Twelve Years', *The Platform*, May 1962.

CHAPTER NINETEEN

The Loss of Status, 1950-70

> In the six years following 1950, the money passing across British shop counters increased by almost fifty per cent.' Harry Hopkins, *The New Look*, 1963.

In the 1950s and 60s Britain became a mass-consumption society as post-war capitalism based its expansion on the satisfaction of the needs, real or created, of the working-class market. In 1956 only 8 per cent of households boasted refrigerators; by 1962 this figure had reached 33 per cent. By 1961 three-quarters of all households had television sets; ten years later 64 per cent of households had washing machines.[1] The 'traditional' labour aristocracy, having seen the wage differential between itself and unskilled workers eroded since 1914, now saw its privileges further eroded as the industrial base of Britain declined and the wages of the working class as a whole were improved, especially in the 'new' industries and the service sector.

The London Bus Section was also a victim of the changes which took place during those twenty years. One of the most important components of the new, 'consumer' style of working-class life was car-ownership. The demand for private cars was, of course, assiduously encouraged by the motor companies and the Tory administrations which held office between 1951 and 1964. Hand in hand with this, the voracious appetite of the road lobby was satisfied by Dr Beeching's massive cuts at British Rail and the path, pursued by Ernest Marples at the Ministry of Transport, of encouraging road-building for private cars at the expense of public transport.

Between 1948 and 1965 the number of private cars licensed in the London Transport area increased by more than 400 per cent.

1948	416,000
1950	480,000
1955	803,000
1960	1,279,000
1965	1,920,000

Such a development had two effects. First and foremost, traffic in the capital was slowed by congestion and the demand for bus-services declined; secondly, driving-skills became commonplace.

The television set, another major component of the consumer lifestyle, contributed to the decline of public transport in that people increasingly stayed at home during the evening; cinema attendances, which had peaked in the immediate post-war period, began to fall sharply.

The population of London, which had risen steadily to a peak of 8,728,000 in 1939, began to fall after the war, as the following figures show:

	Greater London	*GLC Area*
1951	8,350,000	
1961	8,174,000	
1964	8,187,000	7,940,000
1969		7,703,000
1971		7,379,000

Source: Barker and Robbins, op.cit., vol. II, p.2.

This combination of factors led to a dramatic decline in passenger demand, as shown in the table on the following page.

Chronic staff shortages also contributed to the decline, for London Transport's remedy was to axe services. At the end of 1958, 732 buses were withdrawn, amounting to a cut of 62 million miles per year. This in turn led to an 11 per cent decline in passenger demand.[2] London Transport approached this phenomenon in a similarly unimaginative manner – by raising fares. Between 1954 and 1964 they rose by 89 per cent, accompanied by a reduction in vehicle-miles of 24 per cent; passenger-loss during the same period amounted to 36 per cent.[3] This response to the objective problems facing the industry proved over the years to be extremely counter-productive, as the service-cuts and fares-increases merely contributed to the unattractiveness of the product. The service-cuts, of course, seriously reduced the size of the London Bus Section. In the ten-year period 1954-63, the establishment of drivers and conductors was reduced from 39,749 to 31,277. In part, the service-reductions were made in order to try and match frequencies to the availability of staff. Most disturbingly, the following table shows that this aim was most certainly not achieved, as the staff shortage obstinately refused to respond to treatment. This is, perhaps, the most eloquent

Passengers Carried, London Transport, 1948-1962
(millions)

Year	*Central Buses*	*Trams*	*Trolley-buses*	*Country Buses*	*Coaches*	*Total Road Services*	*Railways*	*Total*
1948	2,430	302	909	288	26	3,955	720	4,675
1949	2,432	292	891	289	25	3,928	703	4,631
1950	2,412	266	857	282	23	3,841	695	4,537
1951	2,594	145	814	290	27	3,869	694	4,564
1952	2,591	29	764	297	30	3,711	670	4,381
1953	2,583	—	747	296	33	3,658	672	4,330
1954	2,483	—	718	297	33	3,530	671	4,202
1955	2,405	—	683	297	35	3,420	676	4,095
1956	2,288	—	630	284	34	3,236	678	3,914
1957	2,234	—	607	281	36	3,159	666	3,825
1958*	1,759	—	477	218	30	2,484	692	3,176
1959	1,995	—	475	250	36	2,756	669	3,425
1960	1,995	—	312	250	36	2,593	674	3,267
1961	2,098	—	145	244	34	2,522	675	3,197
1962	2,215	—	†	238	32	2,485	668	3,153

* Road services strike, 5 May-20 June 1958.
† Included in Central Bus figure.
Sources: BTC Reports and Accounts, 1948-62; London Transport reviews, 1955-62. The L.T. railway carryings differ from the figures published in the earlier BTC reports – the figures above show all rail journeys over LT including those on tickets issued by British Railways.

Note: Individual figures are rounded to millions, and totals may not be the sum of the components as shown.

Taken from Barker and Robbins, op. cit., p.350.

statement on the status enjoyed by London's busworkers in the eyes of the capital's working class.

	Establishment	*Shortage*	*Percentage*	*Recruitment*	*Wastage*
Drivers					
1954	19,874	1,074	5.5	1,768	3,127
1955	18,829	1,538	8.2	1,393	2,776
1956	18,463	1,396	7.6	1,724	1.169
1957	18,329	1,113	6.1	1,396	1,861
1958	17,594	1,405	8.0	912	2,274
1959	16,074	1,203	7.5	1,021	2,106
1960	16,063	2,153	13.4	1,470	2,186
1961	15,888	1,955	12.3	2,021	1,525
1962	15,719	1,639	10.4	2,149	2,218
1963	15,604	1,849	11.8	2,001	2,717
				15,855	21,959
Conductors					
1954	19,875	1,166	5.9	5,317	6,795
1955	18,834	1,584	8.4	5,127	6,023
1956	18,467	1,188	6.4	5,835	5,571
1957	18,377	977	5.3	4,846	4,816
1958	17,624	1,165	6.6	3,034	4,970
1959	16,100	1,081	6.7	3,933	4,645
1960	16,057	1,835	11.4	4,633	4,962
1961	15,873	1,413	8.9	4,806	4,590
1962	15,723	1,035	6.6	4,499	4,366
1963	15,673	1,170	7.5	3,595	4,237
				46,625	50,975

Source: The Platform, May 1964.

Whereas before the Second World War wastage was approximately 2 per cent per year, the above table shows that during this period it was often 25 per cent.

The staff shortage was the result of the *relative* unattractiveness of the occupation. As the consumer boom got under way and the British economy began to experience levels of employment unknown (with the exception of the war period) since before 1920, the job-security offered by employment with London Transport ceased to be an attraction. As other groups of workers improved their conditions of employment, the negative aspects of buswork, especially the shift and weekend-work, became barriers to the retention of staff.

Wages, too, played a part in the high staff turnover. As we saw previously, London bus drivers had topped the wages league for semi-skilled men in 1935. In the following table, we see that the growth of average hourly rates for manual workers as a whole exceeded by a considerable margin that for London bus drivers in the years 1951-60.

Year	*Average Hourly Wages (Manual Workers)*	*Hourly Wages, London Bus Driver*
1950	100	100
1951	109.2	106.25
1952	118.8	111.4
1953	125.0	
1954	132.3	
1955	143.4	131.25
1956	155.5	142.9*
1957	163.5	
1958	167.5	149.26
1959	176.7	
1960	190.1	162.58

* The figures for London bus drivers from 1956 onwards are based on a 42-hour week, while those preceding that year relate to a 44-hour week.
Source: F. Burdjalov, *State Monopoly Incomes Policy*, Moscow 1978, p. 32, and various TGWU/London Transport agreements.

The *full* extent of the decline in the status of the London Bus Section may be seen in the table on the following page.

Thus, by 1955 the London bus-drivers had dropped from first to sixth place in Routh's wages league, while by 1960 they were ninth.

London Transport appears to have taken full advantage of the Section's reduced bargaining power in order to worsen conditions or, at the very least, to hold back improvements. Thus, in June 1950 when the TGWU Passenger Group Committee made an application for a sick-pay agreement, John Cliff for the LT Executive reported a month later that he was 'unable to accede' to the demand, as such a scheme would be 'a financial burden which they were unable to shoulder ...'[4] Whereas, on a simple supply-and-demand basis, some employers would have considered raising wage-rates to ensure an adequate supply of staff, London Transport advocated increased overtime, a relaxation of the loan and transfer agreement and the recruitment of women conductors. Each of these measures was resisted by the militant elements within the Section. If the membership came to rely upon overtime for increased earnings the impetus for a higher basic rate would be lost; any relaxation of

Earnings or rates for semi-skilled men (occupational class 6), various years 1906-1960 (pounds)

	1906	*1924*	*1935*	*1955*	*1960*	*Percentage of 1906*
Packers, The Potteries	88	153	159	...	653	742
Other semi-skilled pottery workers	77	171	173	...	585	760
Engineering machinemen:						
time	73	(151)	168	547	672	921
piece	84	...	...	634	808	962
Railway platelayers	55	147	128	549	720	1309
Railway engine firemen	71	199	203	507	712	1000
Railway ticket collectors	64	166	164	510	680	1062
Railway horse carters	65	151	147	458	634	975
One-horse carters average rates	66	139	135	372	492	745
Bus and tram conductors (London) rates	72	147	157	399	485	674
Bus and tram drivers (London) rates	107	190	218	476	546	510
Postmen (London) rates	81	160	149	430.5	527	651
Weighted average	73	158	168	532	662	908
Shop-assistants	83	120	113	390	487	587

Source: Routh, op. cit., p. 107.

agreements would entail a worsening of conditions; and the re-introduction of women conductors was perceived as dilution and a means by which London Transport sought to evade the payment of a more attractive wage-rate.

At its meeting with London Transport in March 1950, the Passenger Group Committee informed the Executive that a conference of all three sections had 'declined to agree' to the recruitment of women conductors. F. Coyle, the National Passenger Secretary,* suggested instead that physical standards be relaxed and that the Executive reduce the period before the maximum wage-rate was paid and give more sympathetic consideration to re-engagement.[5] Despite extensive advertising, the opening of additional recruitment centres and combing areas such as Scotland, Wales and Northumberland, the Executive replied that there was no alternative to the employment of women conductors.[6] At its August meeting with London Transport the Passenger Group Committee agreed to relax the loan and transfer agreement, provided that the staff affected worked within a spreadover of ten hours. On women conductors, J.B. Burnell, the Operating Manager, indicated that he would be writing to the Assistant General Secretary, informing him that London Transport proposed to go ahead with their recruitment. At a joint conference of all three sections in September the employment of women conductors was reluctantly accepted. While such an attitude would be considered backward today, it must be remembered that a once-proud section of workers was seeing its status reduced and its industry transformed beyond recognition.

As the staff shortage proved intractable, London Transport turned to the recruitment of labour from the Caribbean, establishing a recruitment office in Barbados. Initially, this produced the same fears as had earlier been expressed about women, i.e. that immigrant labour would be used as a means of depressing wages and conditions and that they would prove less trade union-oriented than native staff. The 1958 strike seems to have calmed these fears somewhat, for Brookes quotes a woman conductor as saying: 'They stuck by the Union in the big strike, although no one expected them to. It was OK after that.'[7] Even so, the London Bus Conference of May 1961 passed a resolution by a majority of two to one, 'opposing the influx of immigrants into this country and their

* Coyle's predecessor, the Communist Sam Henderson, had taken the honourable path after the imposition of the ban. For some time, he worked in the Industrial Department of the Communist Party and later was a bus conductor at Southall Garage. Over a year after leaving the Communist Party he was re-appointed as national Passenger Secretary of the TGWU.

employment in London Transport'.[8] However, this appears to have been due more to fears about cheap labout than racism (although, of course, it would be foolish to pretend that this did not exist), for a month later the same conference passed a resolution opposing racial discrimination.

In 1963, when London Transport attempted to recruit in Malta, the London Bus Section took a firm stand against this policy, its Conference voting by 70 votes to six against accepting further recruits from outside Britain until acceptable wage-rates and conditions were established. Predictably, this provoked allegations that the Section's stand was racist. In a centre-page article in the September issue of *The Platform*, Bill Jones set out the true position in his familiar, pungent style:

> Having temporarily run out of 'whores', 'procurers' and brothels with which to titillate the breakfast-table appetite,* some Fleet Street organs have seized the opportunity to fasten a colour-bar tag on London busmen. They lie in their teeth. Nowhere in Britain has the integration of white and coloured staff taken place so happily and with so little friction as on London's buses.
>
> ... I believe the central bus delegates to be a thousand times RIGHT in the decision they have taken – for, in fighting London Transport on this issue, we are defending the true interests of ALL workers – white and coloured alike.
>
> Does anyone really believe that, in flying a recruiting squad to Malta the gentlemen at 55 Broadway are showing genuine concern for the well-being of the coloured man? On the contrary. The coloured man is seen simply as a source of CHEAP LABOUR – as an instrument for perpetuating wage levels on London buses that the average British worker won't touch with a forty-foot barge pole.
>
> Far from showing prejudice against the coloured man, we are, by opposing his recruitment under present conditions, protecting him – and ourselves – from the worst possible kind of exploitation.

It should also be borne in mind that the London Bus Section was at this time heavily involved in the public campaign which was to lead to a committee of inquiry into wages and conditions. John Stevens, the leading busworker in that campaign, recalls:

> We felt it was morally wrong that London Transport should scour the world for competing labour for the peanuts they were paying, and that it was not a way to solve the problem; they ought to compete in their own market first. We were against cheap labour. We didn't care who took the job or what colour they were. There were some who were anti-immigrant, but they were by no means the majority.[9]

* Here, Jones was obviously alluding to the Profumo scandal.

The TGWU's General Executive Council, acutely conscious of the fact that the Section was leaving itself open to allegations of racism, refused to support the stand taken. This fear was shared by some rank and file members, as is evidenced by the fact that an English driver from Hanwell wrote in the October issue of *The Platform* that the policy was divisive and could encourage racists in the garages. However, the problem did not turn out to be a major one: while 600 members left the buses between September and October, 1963, London Transport were able to recruit only thirteen men from Malta.[10]

Far from conceding the kind of wage increases which would have contributed to the solution of the staff shortage, London Transport appeared eager to rub salt into the Section's wounds by giving the public a false picture of busworkers' earnings. Reluctant to improve basic rates, London Transport conceded a 'scarcity payment' of 6s. per week to Central Bus drivers and 5s. per week to their Country Services colleagues in July 1963. This was accepted by a divided Conference – 50 delegates voted for, 43 against, while seven abstained.[11] On several occasions during the early 1950s the Passenger Group Committee requested that London Transport's advertising show standard rates rather than fleet average earnings, as these could not be obtained in some garages, thereby misleading new recruits and causing 'domestic strife'.[12] Not only was this request ignored, but in 1956 the Section was further affronted by London Transport's display of publicity material which cited wage-rises as the cause of a fares-increase.

Of course, improvements *were* won during this period. In 1956 the 84-hour, eleven-day fortnight was introduced. In the same year, a sick-pay scheme was brought in – although, significantly, not by London Transport alone, but by the British Transport Commission, covering staff employed at BTC headquarters, in British Rail, the docks, waterways, hotel and catering services, British Road Services and London Transport. In 1964 it was agreed that as soon as practicable, a 160-hour, 21-day, four-week cycle would be introduced in 1965, along with longer holidays. The five-day, 40-hour week was achieved in 1967.

Even so, the staff shortage grew steadily worse throughout the 1960s, as the following table shows.

By 1966, two years after the Phelps Brown Report had brought substantial short-term increases in earnings (see Chapter 20), the London Bus Section was once again losing ground to other groups of workers. To re-establish parity with Underground drivers (a demand voiced during the Phelps Brown Inquiry), a weekly increase of £4 would be necessary. For the Section to re-establish its pre-war position, a weekly increase of

Date	*Total Shortage, Drivers and Conductors*
April 1964	3, 386
September 1964	3,649
April 1965	3,878
June 1965	4,059
March 1966	4,044
May 1966	4,769

Source: The Platform, August 1965, May and June 1966.

no less than £7 would be required.[13] *Platform* summed up the situation (although not without some exaggeration) in its usual acerbic style:

> Let us tell the truth – and shame the devil. The London bus section has become the 'bastard child' of the trade union movement. No section of workers – be they dockers or dustmen – guards or grave-diggers – postmen or pork-butchers have lost so much ground in the post-war years as have the London busmen.[14]

In the wage-round that year London Transport was prepared to settle for an increase of 6.6 per cent – approximately £1 extra. However, the Labour government which was then pursuing a policy of wage-restraint intervened and the claim was referred to the Prices and Incomes Board. The PIB agreed the increase, but on terms which turned the thinking of the Chambers and Phelps Brown Reports on its head:

> We consider ... that pay settlements in the bus industry should not primarily be directed to attract more labour for the practical reason that in an area of general labour shortage, pay adjustments designed to do this are likely to be ineffective. The most effective remedy for an undertaking suffering from a shortage of labour in such an area is to make better use of the existing labour which it already has. A pay increase which is justified by a better use of the existing labour force also has the secondary effect of protecting it against the loss of man-power.[15]

Elsewhere in industry the Labour government's 'productivity bargaining' policy was being used not as a means of remedying staff shortage but, on the contrary, of shedding labour. By agreeing to increase productivity in exchange for wage-rises, workers were paying for their own increases, concurring in the reduction of the labour force and thus increasing the rate of exploitation of their own labour-power. This, indeed, was the prime purpose of the policy. *Platform* noted, with considerable insight:

> Indeed, as all the evidence shows, 'productivity' from the peculiar angle of London Transport means not MORE activity but LESS – not INCREASING service but REDUCING it – not running the job BETTER but only CHEAPER. To the LTB, 'efficiency' is but another word for 'economy'.
>
> Their sole yardstick of measurement takes no account of public needs nor of staff requirements – but only of the state of their balance sheet.[16]

Throughout that spring and summer London Transport put forward a number of proposals for coping with the staff shortage: the employment of students as conductors and of women drivers, the compulsory working of five rest-days out of every eight and the allocation of garage maintenance staff to drivers' duties on an overtime basis. Only that concerning the employment of students was adopted at the time. However, the main thrust of London Transport's 'productivity' proposals concerned the introduction of more one-man buses.*

One-man buses were first introduced at Uxbridge, Sidcup and Slough garages as early as 1930. At the time the Central Bus Committee's demand for an increase of 10 per cent in the wages of the drivers concerned was refused by the LGOC, but it was anticipated that a maximum of only 25 vehicles would be introduced and that they would be confined to the outlying areas. By November 1930 J.J. Mills, the London District Secretary, was suggesting that the Company re-open discussion of the principle of one-man operation (OMO), as in the union's opinion experience had demonstrated the inadequacy of this form of operation. Frank Snelling warned that the members of Merton would resist the introduction of OMO vehicles on route 103, a stance which the LGOC warned would be 'seriously regarded by the Company'.[17] Things went from bad to worse. Soon the Company was using drivers trained in OMO as conductors on crew routes. When Cassomini, acting as London District Secretary in Mills' absence, demanded that the practice cease, he was met with a blank refusal. During the Second World War, however, monetary compensation for OMO drivers was conceded – in principle at

* The term one-*man* operation' was appropriate until the fairly recent employment of women drivers; nowadays, the term 'one-person operation' is not only accurate but, indeed, widely used.

least – with an allowance of 5s. for all such drivers on routes authorised to take six standing passengers.

The extension of OMO in the outer area was proposed in the late 1950s. In 1959 the CBC suggested that this would be acceptable as long as each route was considered on its merits, that there were no standing passengers, a maximum seating capacity of 39, that allocation of staff to OMO duties be determined on a rota basis at local level (thus preventing the development of a separate, higher-paid OMO grade) and that the whole proposal be subject to agreement on the proportion of the 'savings' made which would go to the staff. London Transport refused to agree to no standing passengers, argued the need for 'further reflection on both sides' regarding the method of allocation and indicated general agreement on the other demands, offering an allowance of 15 per cent to OMO drivers.

Following the Phelps Brown Inquiry in 1964, a supplementary agreement was concluded which gave the go-ahead to 'technical improvements designed to improve the service to the public and to provide economies in vehicles and manpower in the interests of the public, the staff and the Board'. This entailed an extension of OMO in the Country Area 'and the introduction of this type of vehicle in the suburban districts of the Central Bus Area' in return for an allowance of 15 per cent; in addition, a 'productivity allowance' of one (pre-decimal) penny per seat per duty was conceded to OMO drivers.

Even allowing for the limited nature of these proposals (there being, as yet, no intention that OMO vehicles be introduced into the inner districts of the Central Bus Area), there was considerable opposition to them from within the Section. Harry Selmes recalls Bill Jones' attitude during the early stages of the OMO discussions:

> I can picture the meeting now, on a Sunday morning at the Stratford Town Hall. Old Bill was up on the platform and he said, 'OMO? Over my bleedin' dead body!' Sam Henderson said, 'You know, Bill, it's the simplest thing in the world to run over a dead body.' Just as calm as that.[18]

Following the 1964 agreement on OMO, there was evidence that the exercise was far from being economic. It was found that revenue fell dramatically, as the table on page 213 shows.

By the second half of the decade, however, pressure for an extension of OMO was growing: not only was the staff shortage proving intractable but, as we have already seen, the Labour government was tying wage increases to the acceptance of such 'productivity measures'. (Frank Cousins, who by this time had entered the government as Minister of

Route	*Reduction in Revenue*	
201	31 per cent	
206	27 per cent	Five 4-weekly
216	26 per cent	periods
250	25 per cent	
237	36 per cent	Three 4-weekly
251	39 per cent	periods

Source: The Platform, April 1966.

Technology, stood by his principles and resigned when workers were made liable for fines of £500 if they went on strike for wage-increases outside of the guidelines laid down by the Prices and Incomes Board.)

Larry Smith recalls that

> The Prices and Incomes Act meant that we were never going to get movements of pay justified by movements in the cost of living or anything like that. If we really wanted improved pay and conditions we were going to have to do it via productivity.[19]

London Transport unveiled its 'reshaping plan' in 1966. According to this, 'fewer but higher paid staff need to be employed on the buses'.[20] Not only did this approach contradict the recommendation of the Phelps Brown Report, but it went against the spirit of an agreement reached in October of the same year. Following the overtime ban of 1966 (see Chapter 20), a Joint Working Party had been set up by London Transport and the TGWU to review conditions which might, in the view of the working party, be causing staff wastage and practices which militated 'against the provision of a regular and satisfactory service to the public ...'[21] The agreement resulting from this investigation gave London Transport several productivity measures and the London Bus Section the 40-hour, five-day week. On OMO in the Central Area, the agreement was characterised by extreme caution:

> The parties recognise that work on one man operation presents certain problems. There might be an extension of OMO work on Sundays; possibly withdrawn routes could be re-introduced on this basis or consideration be given to the conversion of the whole or part of a double deck route.[22]

Now, with its document entitled *Reshaping London's Bus Services*, London Transport was throwing such caution – and the part of the agreement which embodied it – to the winds. However, as the document referred to the Prices and Incomes Report quoted above (see page 210) it might be said that London Transport, if not actually being pushed along by the government, was certainly leaning upon it for support. In common with other sections of workers, London busworkers were, in fact, to find themselves negotiating with an employer whose hands were tied by government policy (and who seemed to be enjoying the experience) for the next three years. In the 1970 general election this very policy, plus an additional attack on trade unions in the form of the White Paper entitled 'In Place of Strife', was an important element in the Tories' victory.

The negotiations triggered off by publication of the reshaping plan dragged on for eighteen months – in large part due to a further intervention by the Prices and Incomes Board.

In March 1967 another Joint Working Party was set up. Much of the discussion here centred around how the 'savings' from the extension of OMO should be divided; the trade union side was anxious that crew drivers and conductors should not be excluded. There was further disagreement over what proportion of the global amount should go to the staff. London Transport initially argued that the sum should be split three ways: a third to the employer, a third to the public and a third to the staff. Against this the union argued that the split should be evenly divided between staff and employer, as the public and the employer were really one and the same.[23] With agreement still not forthcoming, the management proposals were put to a Joint Delegate Conference in August 1967 and rejected. Some months later Bill Jones explained:

> From the very moment of the rejection by the bus branches of the proposals before the August Conference, the view of the majority of the Negotiating Committee was that we should oppose any wage increase based on increased productivity.[24]

It was at this stage that the government intervened again with the publication of its Prices and Incomes Report No.50. This recommended a payment of 10s. to all staff (this had already been put forward by the employer) and a premium payment of 20 and 22½ per cent respectively for single and double-deck OMO drivers in the Central Area. At the same time it argued that the 'double share' of the receipts bonus and the capacity allowance (the penny per seat) received by OMO drivers should be discontinued.

As the talks with London Transport got underway once more *Bus Stop* (the unofficial journal published by Bill Jones and others which succeeded *Platform*) commented sympathetically on the difficulties of the union's Negotiating Committee:

> They are not negotiating with the LTB. They are negotiating with the government. The meetings they have had and are having with the LTB are purely discussions about what both sides can or cannot do about the government's Prices and Incomes policy. It might almost be said that the LTB are the government's unwilling or willing agents.[25]

In March 1968 the Negotiating Committee, believing that the negotiations had been exhausted, agreed by six votes to two that a Joint Delegate Conference be called to recommend the Board's proposals, i.e. the 10s. recommended by the Prices and Incomes Board and a further 10s. for productivity items negotiated during the discussions. It further recommended that the question of the capacity bonus be referred back to the Prices and Incomes Board. Three weeks later the full-time officers met Barbara Castle, the Minister of Transport, who said she could not recommend 10s. for productivity as she believed that only productivity worth 5s. was being given by the Section. This meeting was reported to the Negotiating Committee in early April as a result of which a further Joint Delegate Conference was called. That Conference, by 68 votes to 29, called for continued negotiations on the basis of the two payments of 10s., both of which to be consolidated at a later stage, an OMO allowance of 20 per cent and double receipts bonus.

When the London Bus Conference met separately, however, it decided to add a little muscle to the demand. The Conference voted unanimously for a joint approach, along with the Country Services Section, to the General Executive Council with the aim of securing plenary powers 'to take strike action of a limited character' in order to break the deadlock.[26] This did the trick. The Chairman of the LTB agreed to meet Jack Jones, Assistant General Secretary of the TGWU, and Alan Thompson, the National Passenger Secretary, and a formula was agreed. Instead of the proposed 20 per cent OMO allowance each single-deck OMO driver would receive an allowance of £4 10s. per week; all drivers and conductors would receive 10s. per week, to be consolidated in January 1969, with a further 10s. for productivity items. With the introduction of double-deck OMO vehicles, a more complicated formula was needed. In 1970, single-deck drivers received an allowance of £4 14s. while double-deck drivers received £5 7s. and £5 12s. (26 per cent of the basic driver's basic rate), depending on which model they drove. Later, the allowances were consolidated to give OMO drivers a separate basic wage. On the thorny question of receipts bonus and capacity allowance it was proposed that this amount would be shared among the staff by agreement with the union.

The 1968 agreement found universal favour with neither the Negotiating Committee (which agreed to recommend it by only five votes to four) nor with the Joint Delegate Conference (which voted by 56 to 43 for its acceptance).[27] *Bus Stop*'s view seems, in retrospect, a sensible one:

> Was it a good or bad agreement? Well, we are sure that that argument will go on for a long time. We understand that some of the branches whose representatives voted in favour of accepting it turned it down, while other representatives had a tough time getting their lads to accept it.
>
> We don't find that difficult to understand; even the mover of the resolution of acceptance described it as a *bad agreement*, while the seconder called it a *good agreement*. We disagree with both of them. We hold the view that whether it is a good or bad agreement is not the real issue: the basic issue is – could we have got a better agreement in the present political climate and circumstances in which we find ourselves?[28]

That indeed *was* the basic issue. The fact was that an agreement for the introduction of OMO buses into Central London was practically inevitable under the circumstances: the staff shortage and the government's hard line on productivity bargaining, coupled with the changed character and outlook of the Section's membership together made it so. Also, it must be remembered that the extension of one-man buses threatened no one's job in 1968. Whether the *actual* agreement was the best possible one may be judged by the fact that early on in the negotiations London Transport put forward a shopping list of twelve productivity items (including the lengthening of duties and spreadovers, an increase in the percentage of spreadover duties and a 10 per cent cut in running time at certain times of the day and all day Sundays). Only two of the more innocuous of these items were eventually incorporated in the agreement and a third, that concerning running times, resulted in a 5 per cent cut instead of the 10 per cent originally proposed.[29]

The London Bus Section had not had its last brush with the Prices and Incomes Board, however. The following year, in reply to the Section's demand for an increase of £1 on the basic rate and 12s. for London weighting, London Transport replied with an offer of 12s. on the basic rate, no London weighting and a string of further productivity proposals. With the staff shortage running at over 5,000, the Section decided that the time was ripe for an overtime ban. As this began to bite seven East London garages struck every Saturday and Seven Kings remained out for a complete week. Jack Jones, by then General Secretary-elect, intervened and London Transport withdrew the productivity proposals, improving their offer to 17s. on the basic rate, with a further 3s. from October, subject to agreement on the rate for a new model OMO bus.

The extension of OMO did nothing to solve the staff shortage, as we will see later. If anything, it contributed to the decline of London's bus service, for boarding times increased, leading to an increased tendency to 'bunch' and thus to irregular headways. Moreover, they proved unpopular with the public. By February 1969 George Leeks was writing in *Bus Stop*:

> After the songs of praise about OMO, what do we find is the policy? None other than the old procedure of cuts, increased running times, at the expense of frequency. If Beeching used the 'axe' on the railways, we've come up against the 'Black and Decker'. What a shock!

There were more shocks to come.

Notes

1. Marwick, op.cit.
2. John Stevens in *Tribune*, 11 December 1959.
3. *Taking London for A Ride*, A Group Of Rank And File Busmen, undated.
4. Minutes of Passenger Group Committee/London Transport meeting, 7 July 1950.
5. Ibid., 23 March 1950.
6. Ibid., 2 August 1950.
7. D. Brookes, *Race and Labour in London Transport*, London 1975, p.62.
8. Ibid., p.61.
9. John Stevens, interviewed by the author, 12 September 1984.
10. *The Platform*, October 1963.
11. Ibid., September 1963.
12. Minutes, Passenger Group Committee/London Transport, 6 May 1952.
13. *The Platform*, March 1966.
14. Ibid.
15. Quoted in *Reshaping London's Bus Services*, London Transport, 1966.
16. *The Platform*, April 1966.
17. This paragraph is based on minutes of various meetings between the CBC and the LGOC, 1930.
18. Harry Selmes interview.
19. Larry Smith interview.
20. *Reshaping London's Bus Services.*
21. Agreement Between the London Transport Board and the TGWU, 24 October 1966.
22. Ibid.

23. Larry Smith interview.
24. *Bus Stop*, April 1968.
25. Ibid., February 1968.
26. Ibid., June 1968.
27. Ibid., July 1968.
28. Ibid., August 1968.
29. Ibid.

CHAPTER TWENTY

Forms of Struggle, 1950-70

Why, as members became increasingly disgruntled with their conditions of employment, was there no really effective fightback? If the situation may be gauged accurately from the pages of *Platform*, there seems to have been widespread agreement that the level of trade union consciousness, organisation and militancy had declined. In late 1963 this had reached a stage where the *Daily Express* was able to report:

> Two 'left-wing' members of the nine-man Central Bus Committee, the traditionally militant leadership of London's 33,000 busmen, have been defeated in their efforts to gain re-election. The beaten pair are Mr Alf Mezen (Enfield) and Mr Charles Young (New Cross). In Putney, Mr John Stevens, one of the best known 'left-wingers', only retained the backing of his colleagues by 130 votes to 117.[1]

Among the rank and file there appears to have been two schools of thought both of which neglected to consider the objective factors influencing the decline. The April 1965 edition of *Platform* asked why the London Bus Section was so far behind tubeworkers, and answered:

> Bus drivers are covered by the TGWU. The TGWU is SIX TIMES as big as the other two unions [i.e. the NUR and ASLEF] put together. Clearly it is not SIZE – then is it LEADERSHIP?

The following month, Harry Shaw of Elmers End pointed out that

> there may be room for improvement at the top, but our worst enemy is the widespread apathy in most branches ... To those who keep attacking our present leaders I say: Look around and ask yourselves where your leaders will come from a decade from now. So, stop rocking the boat and get in and pull your own oar.[2]

A similar debate had appeared in the pages of the journal three years earlier, when Fred Walsh of Chalk Farm had agreed that 'BRANCH life is the HEART of trades unionism'.

> If the passenger section of our union is to be the fighting force that it should be (and once was) then we have to begin at branch level. The regular five or six attenders do not represent the true feeling and desired policy of the branch. Particularly in respect of new members (and staff wastage produces thousands every year) ways and means must be found to initiate them into regular participation in branch life.[3]

It is worth remembering that by the time the above debate was taking place, Frank Cousins was General Secretary and the winds of democratic change were blowing throughout the TGWU. Chalk Farm's Fred Walsh had identified one of the major underlying reasons for the lower level of consciousness and activity in the Section when he spoke of new members. He pointed out wastage produced thousands of these every year. Such members would have, of course, no experience – or even knowledge – of the militant traditions of the London Bus Section. Whereas in an earlier era many recruits had been discharged soldiers, sailors or fire brigadesmen used to discipline, and the recruitment process so selective that in 1927 and 1928 less than 2,000 men out of 61,000 applicants were actually employed, in the 1950s and 60s the picture was very different.[4] Now, in the consumer-led 'boom', many recruits to London Transport would have been among those manual workers described by Hobsbawm who, paradoxically in this period of increased social mobility and technological development, found:

> they were oppressed more than others by the vicious circle of modern industrial society in which the underprivileged found their lack of privilege reinforced, the uneducated their lack of education a permanent barrier, the stupid their stupidity fatal, the weak their weakness doubled.[5]

Such a phenomenon goes a long way towards explaining the apathy Harry Shaw describes. Hobsbawm finds, however, that 'consumerism' had yet another demobilising effect. The isolation of working-class culture was gradually broken down and sections of the working class began to move towards 'middle-class' life-styles, thus shifting 'the centre of working-class life from the public and collective (the pub or football match) towards the private and individual ...'[6] This would have had the long-term effect of undermining the collective consciousness necessary for any effective form of class action and replacing it with a self-centred consciousness concerned with the acquisition of consumer goods. More recently in London Transport, this has allegedly led to a reluctance to strike arising from the need to maintain mortgage payments (leading some to believe that London Transport had ulterior motives when it introduced its Staff Mortgage Scheme).

It has already been noted that no mass rank and file movement was created around *Platform*. In the early stages of the journal's life full conferences of sellers and supporters were held, 'but as they tended to deal with matters of union policy as well as the policy of the paper, they were discontinued'.[7] It would appear from this that it was decided, in the climate created by Deakinism, that the open existence of an unofficial organisation would have proved counter-productive. This is not to say that unofficial meetings were not held. They were, but they were convened by personal notification (often by telephone) and were largely confined to branch oficers and activists.[8] This meant that there was no *systematic* attempt to mobilise the membership as a whole. Also, *Platform* appears to have made no serious attempt to raise the level of *political* understanding of its readership, for its pages were concerned almost exclusively with wages and conditions. According to Harry Selmes this was quite deliberate, the aim being to minimise political differences and to build the maximum degree of unity around the wages and other questions.[9] It must be borne in mind, of course, that wages were a highly political issue as successive governments, never more so than during the 1958 strike, attempted to impose wage restraint on the trade union movement, using the public sector as a testing ground. But, as was the case elsewhere in the labour movement, the propagation of *socialist* politics seems to have been given little priority during this period.

As we saw in the previous Chapter, Communists were still very much in evidence in the Section during the early part of the period, although the ban imposed in 1949 kept them from office and had a significant impact on militant representation within the Section. Even so, militant *organisation* within the garages continued, with large Communist party branches in several of these. We may take it for granted that there would have been liaison between them, but this was hardly the same as a broadly-based *mass* movement. Also, there are indications that throughout the early 1950s the party was losing a steady trickle of members in the Section – although often for the best of reasons. Harry Selmes was one such member:

> We would get nothing by me stopping outside and I could see that the leadership was going the wrong way. I could have stopped out in the wilderness for ever. But to me it was not a bit of good coming to the branch and voicing opinions when I knew perfectly well that the officers of the branch were in no way prepared to further it. So I thought: alright, get inside and take over. And that's what happened.[10]

After the Soviet intervention in Hungary in 1956 the decline of Communist Party membership and influence in the Section became more serious, especially as leaders like Bill Jones now opted out and regained leading positions. But the party was in decline anyway. Hobsbawm remarks that during this period the 'embattled aristocrat' turned to the left and that 'the characteristic working-class Communist cadre was a metal-worker'.[11] Like the London Bus Section, however, the industrial bases of such cadres were shrinking rapidly and from the mid-1960s the Communist Party attempted to make the transition to a more 'community-based' form of organisation, as exemplified by the renaming of the *Daily Worker*, with its industrial connotations, into the more anodyne *Morning Star*. By 1970 there were a mere handful of Communists in the London Bus Section. Paradoxically, the decline of the Communist Party was accompanied by the re-emergence of a militant official leadership within the Section, for Communists like Bill Jones who left the Party after Hungary took up their old positions almost immediately – and Jones was later elected to the General Council of the TUC.

In the Deakin era unofficial activity was organised largely through the mass meeting or, by taking a page out of Chelverton Road's book in 1932, by the militant branches – principally Dalston – circulating their resolutions throughout the fleet.

In September 1950, nine days after a conference of all three sections had accepted the principle of women conductors, Dalston organised a mass meeting at Stratford Town Hall at which it was decided to call upon all branches to 'let both the General Executive Council, and our Trade Group Representatives know by resolution that they have lost our confidence', to refuse to relax the loaning agreement and to press for a fleet ban on overtime and rest-day working until the Section's wages demands were met. Most significantly, the meeting demanded the 'rescinding of the GEC agreement with the LTE along the lines of "one woman in, all out".'[12] Three days later more than 13,000 drivers and conductors from 14 bus garages and several tram and trolleybus depots were on strike over the issue of women conductors. Despite the Passenger Group Committee's call for a resumption of work the action lasted for five days.

Throughout the 1950s unofficial industrial action showed a marked tendency to increase. In January 1952 Dalston struck for two days when staff were suspended for refusing to work new schedules. In October 1953 Middle Row and Clay Hall garages struck for a day over new winter schedules. Later the same month, Dalston and Peckham were out for two days due to the delivery of 'black' petrol during a strike by tanker drivers. In its resolution recommending a return to work Dalston bitterly criticised the leadership:

> We feel compelled to take into account the fact that the leadership of our Union, both at national and local level, have succeeded by the use of the Union machinery, in holding down any effective expression of trade union solidarity with our fellow-members engaged in the oil industry.
>
> ... We express our shame, having regard for the fighting history of the London bus section, that we are now being used for the first time in our history as scab labour. We feel confident that the oil workers will understand that the power of our reactionary leadership has created this apparent indifference by the London busmen to their struggle.

By 1954 dissatisfaction on the wages question had reached boiling point. At the end of July Dalston passed a motion calling for the limitation of overtime. By 12 September 35 branches had imposed an unofficial overtime ban. When some members at Willesden were enticed to break the ban the garage struck for three days. On 15 September New Cross struck for three days over new schedules. As the overtime ban spread there is evidence that an attempt was made to devise a centralised leadership, for a circular issued by thirteen branch representatives and one branch secretary on 4 October stated:

> This movement has grown spontaneously without fleet organisation and against opposition from all quarters. Without guidance the movement can be diverted into harmless channels. It is our desire to place this movement, which is now practically fleet wide, on an organised basis. We realise that this cannot be done through the present machinery of the Transport and General Workers' Union and so we intend to call a meeting of all the representatives of garages and depots ... in order to maintain the determination of our members and to keep them organised.

London Transport responded to the ban by introducing emergency schedules. This resulted in an eight-day unofficial strike involving 16,550 drivers and conductors (roughly half the fleet) and 87 garage engineering staff.[13] 1955 saw two unofficial strikes – a three-day stoppage by Bexley, Highgate, Ilford and Loughton over schedules in February, and a one-day stoppage by 29 garages over revised Sunday schedules in May. The following two years appear to have been fairly peaceful. Below the surface, however, resentment over low wages and the consequent staff shortage was building up, and 1958 was to witness the longest strike in the history of the London Bus Section.

Two events in the mid-1950s contributed to the development of militancy within the Section, making the full-scale *official* stoppage of 1958 possible. In 1955 Arthur Deakin died after collapsing at a May Day rally, and in 1956 the Soviet Union intervened in Hungary.

We have already noted the effects which Hungary had on the leadership of the London Bus Section. Deakin, who had been due to retire anyway, was succeeded by 'Jock' Tiffin. The latter was so ill by now, however, that Frank Cousins, the new Assistant General Secretary, took over his appointments. Tiffin died in December, and in May 1956 Cousins was elected General Secretary.

Larry Smith recalls that Cousins' election:

> ... made a tremendous difference. The Section saw in Frank Cousins an absolute turning of the tide away from Deakinism and I was surprised that he didn't get an even greater vote than he did; but the London Bus Section was certainly 100 per cent behind him.[14]

From the outset Cousins was against wage restraint, much to the horror of his right-wing colleagues on the TUC General Council. At the meeting of the TGWU General Executive Council in December 1955 Cousins made his position on this question perfectly clear:

> While prices rise, wages must rise with them. In other words, wage increases that result from rising output are the workers' share of the extra wealth they are helping to create. To re-state our position as a union in a single sentence: we are not prepared that our members should stand still whilst the Government continually hand out largesse to those who are more favourably placed.

With this statement, according to Cousins' biographer Geoffrey Goodman, 'the tide of TGWU affairs turned'.[15] However, Goodman recognises that this was not merely the achievement of one man, for if 'it hadn't been Cousins, then it is almost certain that these changes would have thrown up someone else who would have understood the impulses of the moment, and would have been able to respond to them.'[16] In fact, democratic changes, perhaps the most significant of which was the expansion of the shop steward system, were taking place throughout the trade union movement. In the Amalgamated Engineering Union the number of shop stewards is estimated to have increased by as much as 60 per cent between 1947 and 1961, half of this increase occurring between 1957 and 1961.[17] In the TGWU the most likely explanation of Cousins' victory (or, more to the point, of the democratic tendencies which he represented) would appear to be that there was a similar development of the shop stewards movement in the increasingly important motor industry and that this combined with a revolt in the traditional sections, such as passenger transport and docks, against the centralist approach of Bevin and Deakin. In short, the organisational needs of the expanding industries and the resentment of Deakinism which was smouldering in the London Bus Section and other trade groups would not have permitted another term of right-wing leadership. From this point on the leadership of the TGWU moved steadily to the left, embracing both industrial militancy and the major political issues of the day such as nuclear disarmament. As it turned out, however, this on its own proved inadequate to arrest the relative decline of the London Bus Section, for even with the granting of plenary powers in 1958 it was to find two formidable adversaries ranged against it: a Tory government bent on implementing wage-restraint and a right-wing TUC General Council which objected to Cousins' radicalism.

The 3 per cent wage increase granted to the railwaymen in 1957 was considered to be the norm by the government, although the London Bus Section achieved a rise of 5 per cent. In October of that year Chancellor Thorneycroft announced that public spending would be cut and that wage rises would be subject to a *ceiling* of 3 per cent. The same month a claim for the London Bus Section of 25s. – almost 12 per cent – was submitted to London Transport. London Transport rejected the demand by the end of November. The Joint Delegate Conference the following month voted, by 105 votes to 25, for continued discussions, the failure of which would signal their request for plenary powers.

In January 1958, Sir Wilfred Neden, the Chief Industrial Commissioner at the Ministry of Labour, met Harry Nicholas, the Assistant General Secretary of the TGWU and Anthony Bull of London Transport. Before the meeting Neden received a telephone call from Harold Watkinson, the Minister of Transport, instructing him not to give the union the impression that concessions would be forthcoming. When Neden checked with Iain Macleod the Minister of Labour, the latter, Watkinson's senior in the Cabinet, claimed that he knew nothing. Neden felt free, therefore, to offer an inquiry. At a conference called the following week, Nicholas, after six hours of debate, persuaded the delegates to accept the inquiry.

Then came the bombshell.

Macleod announced a week later that there would, after all, be no inquiry, leading Neden to suspect that he had been overruled in Cabinet. Sir John Elliot, Chairman of London Transport, later admitted that without government interference the Executive would have negotiated. 'The whole thing,' he said, 'was laced with politics.'[18] On 3 February the Conference voted 83 to 48 in favour of a strike. As this was less than the two-thirds then needed, a further debate led to a decision to go to arbitration.

On 13 March the Industrial Court delivered its verdict: 8s. 6d. for Central busworkers and nothing for those in the Country Services. Moreover, the Ministry of Transport stated that the costs of the increase would have to be found internally – presumably by service-cuts. Cousins' request that the global amount be spread over all busworkers employed by London Transport, giving them 6s. 6d. each, was refused by Elliot. Conference endorsed a final claim put forward by the Central Bus Committee of 10s. 6d. voting by 128 votes to four for strike action. On 2 April the Finance and General Purposes Committee granted plenary powers to the London Bus Section for the first time in 21 years. London Transport was given notice that there would be a withdrawal of labour commencing on 5 May.

The strike was faced with the same problems as those which had contributed to the defeat of the 1937 strike – the availability of other methods of transport, exacerbated this time by widespread car ownership. Although *The Times* was sufficiently alarmed to headline an article 'Strike Would Halt Buses Over 2,000 Square Miles. Stoppage on 600 Routes', the government had ample room for manoeuvre and arranged for the central London parks to be turned into massive car parks for the duration of the dispute. It was estimated that the number of passengers using the underground rose by 10 per cent and that British Rail's takings in the London area rose by almost one quarter. *The Times* was able to report 'London Takes Bus Strike in its Stride'; unfortunately, this was an accurate summary of the situation.

On 2 May 6,000 busworkers flocked to the Empress Hall, Earl's Court, to hear Frank Cousins speak. Despite the fact that the General Secretary made no secret of the fact that the situation was bleak, enthusiasm for the strike action was undaunted. Indeed, some members were already taking a long-term view of the dispute. A notice was posted by the Kingston branch stating that 'Members will not be required to picket on August Bank Holiday, Christmas Day and Boxing Day.'[19] As in the 1937 strike, London Transport collated reports from local level and assessed the situation on a day-by-day basis. These reports indicated that no more than a handful of members reported for work on any one day. Indeed, feeling for the strike was so high that despite the great financial hardship which must have been caused, a report on 23 May recorded that at 'a number of garages a considerable number of men failed to collect the income tax refunds due to them.'[20]

It is all the more tragic, in view of such determination and sacrifice, that the strike was betrayed by the TUC.

From the very outset Frank Cousins' left-wing stance on the General Council (and, moreover, the fact that the TGWU was reversing many of the TUC's previously-held policies) had been resented by many of the rightwing members of that body. Now, as he could see little chance of the London busworkers achieving victory on their own, it was these very men to whom Cousins was forced to turn for assistance. During the second week of May Cousins' request for a special meeting to issue a financial appeal was refused, although it was agreed that this would be recommended to the General Council meeting 21 May. In Goodman's opinion the cross-examination to which Cousins was subjected when the special meeting was finally convened was

> part of a carefully worked-out strategy to cover the TUC's retreat ... Several senior members discussed this privately with Sir Vincent Tewson [the TUC General Secretary] and agreed to halt what they feared might develop into a headlong confrontation between the TUC and the government.[21]

Tewson, after a visit by Cousins and Nicholas, agreed to lead a TUC deputation to the government. When Macleod refused to re-open talks, Prime Minister Harold Macmillan was approached. When he met the TUC leaders on 30 May Macmillan must have been supremely confident, for without Cousins' knowledge members of the General Council had been communicating regularly with him. 'Not until some months after the strike ended,' writes Goodman, 'did Cousins realise the full extent of what had been going on behind his back.'[22] Macmillan suggested acceptance of the offer of 8s. 6d. with the inclusion of the Green Line coach men in this deal and negotiations between the parties to fix a date for those not included in the settlement. The same day troops' leave was cancelled in case they were called upon to move oil in the event of solidarity action by the TGWU-organised tanker-drivers.

Talks were re-opened but lasted only two days, producing no concrete offer for the Country Services men. By early June the TUC General Council was intimating that Cousins should retreat and that they were not prepared to see the action extended to other sections. On 4 June Sir John Elliot offered to come to terms on the basis of a mutually-agreed figure for the Green Line men and an immediate review of the excluded grades. Intimating that he knew something of the skulduggery which had been going on in certain quarters, he added that the statement was made on his own initiative and that he had had no contact with any Minister.[23]

Two days later a Delegate Conference heard Frank Cousins argue against spreading the strike, even though the Central Bus Committee had voted, by a majority of one, for this to happen. In fact, the chances of solidarity action were looking increasingly remote, given the attitude of the TUC. Local NUR leaders had voted to strike every Monday in support of the busworkers, but their General Secretary Sidney (later Sir Sidney) Greene had instructed them to work; some railwaymen who stood by their original decision were sacked. Nevertheless, the Conference voted to continue the strike.

A week later Conference acknowledged defeat and voted to return to work. When this recommendation arrived back in the branches the determination of the members resulted in a vote of 64 to 54 for sticking it out, as London Transport had in the meantime posted schedules embodying a 10 per cent cut in services.

On 19 June London Transport put forward a formula whereby the Country Services would receive an 'agreed increase' upon resumption and the other excluded grades would have their wages reviewed. The new schedules were withdrawn. This was accepted by Conference and confirmed by the branches on the understanding that the rise for the Country Services would be no less favourable than for Central busworkers. Certainly, the agreement signed by Cousins and Elliot on 19 June gave the impression that this would be the case:

> In so far as the Country Services staff are concerned, it is not the intention that any decision arising from the review shall leave the wages of such staff in an unfavourable position with other staffs inside the London Transport Executive Road Services or comparable grades elsewhere.[24]

After the return to work on 21 June Elliot refused to include the Country Services in the full award, and in July the union was forced to settle for 5s., with Green Line single-deck coach drivers receiving 7s. 6d., while Central busworkers received the full 8s. 6d. According to Goodman the evidence suggests that Elliot intended to pay the larger amount but was restrained by 'the severest pressure from the government'.[25]

It has been said that the strike resulted in other groups of workers breaking through the government's wages-ceiling and, perhaps more significantly, in a transformation of the basis upon which the TUC conducted its relationship with the government. For the London Bus Section, however, there is no escaping the fact that it was a defeat of major proportions. Hereafter, the London Bus Section would become cautious in its approach to major industrial action and the negative lessons of 1958 would be retailed in garage canteens for years to come.

The major lesson of the seven-week strike is still being learned. No matter how it may affront lingering aristocratic sensibilities, the London Bus Section needs allies in any major confrontation, be it with the employer or with the government. The dispute also pointed towards the fact that the Section's future could not be determined by industrial strength alone, but that it would depend upon a combination of industrial muscle and the political advances of the labour movement as a whole.

The need for action of a political nature was appreciated readily enough by the activists in the Section. With the wages question still uppermost in the minds of busworkers, and with the staff shortage still failing to respond to London Transport's treatment, an unofficial campaign was organised with the aim of forcing the government to establish a committee of inquiry into London Transport.

The campaign was launched in August 1960 by eleven garage branches. When the number of sponsoring branches had reached 41 an article outlining the campaign's demands was published in *Platform*. Here, the campaign organisers were dubbed the 'Group of 41', a name which was to stick even though 52 branches were eventually affiliated.

The Group of 41 was to function not only as a public campaigning body but as a ginger-group within the London Bus Section. Meetings were normally convened before each London Bus Conference in order to arrive at a common approach to the most important items on the agenda. Those involved were 'not all left-wing, but they all supported a firm line on wages.'[26] There were, however, few points of similarity between the Group and the old Rank and File Movement, for the Group had no political objectives other than those concerning the future of London Transport and participation in its activities was largely confined to branch officers and members of the Central Bus Committee.

With the launching of the campaign every London MP and borough council was circulated, several of the latter passed resolutions demanding an inquiry. At a mass meeting in St Pancras Town Hall in September 1960 a petition was launched. Within three months 100,000 signatures had been collected. A lobby of Parliament was arranged for November. John Stevens, a driver at Putney and a new member of the Central Bus Committee, conducted what amounted to a one-man media campaign, contributing articles to the *Star* (the now defunct evening paper), *Tribune* and other papers. Frank Cousins added his voice to the clamour for a public inquiry and it was in this climate that London Transport, faced with a staff shortage of 5,200 on the buses, offered an increase of

18s. per week on the basic rates.[27]

The campaign failed to achieve its main objective, however. The government refused an inquiry and London Transport continued to cut services. It took a threatened strike in early 1961 to force the employer to withdraw planned cuts at 13 garages. Even so the agreed peace formula was far from satisfactory – the cuts would merely be spread over a wider area.[28]

In the same year leading members of the campaign met in a room in Gray's Inn Road and concluded that the time had come to draw the public into the campaign. On 23 September 200 delegates representing 100 organisations attended a meeting at St Pancras Town hall, where the London Passenger Transport Campaign Committee was launched. Again, the main aim was to secure a public inquiry on the grounds that London Transport was failing in its duty under Section 7(I) of the Transport Act, 1960, i.e.

> to provide or secure the provision of an adequate and properly co-ordinated system of passenger transport for the London Passenger Transport Area, and to have due regard to efficiency of operations as respects the service and facilities provided by them.

By the time the campaign got into its stride it was claiming affiliates representing 500,000 members: 23 trade councils, 18 constituency Labour Parties, eight trade union District Committees, 87 trade union branches from 14 trade unions, six local branches of the Liberal Party, nine tenants' and ratepayers' organisations and seven miscellaneous organisations. A conference in July 1962 agreed the following demands: that the Exchequer should take responsibility for London Transport's central charges and capital developments; that diesel fuel tax be abolished for all public passenger transport; that London Transport be required to concede wages and conditions adequate to attract and retain staff; that a system of lower fares, with special attractions such as cheap off-peak travel, be introduced. The conference also suggested a number of measures to reduce traffic congestion and demanded a single London Authority (as opposed, that is, to one controlled by the government) responsible to the public for the capital's transport. One suggestion for the easing of traffic congestion, that industry be encouraged to move out of London is now recognised as having been misguided and in 1983 London Transport was citing such moves as an important cause of reduced passenger-demand.

Despite the breadth of the organisation, the campaign was unable to maintain the momentum which had been set by the Group of 41. Thus, a lobby of Parliament called for 12 April 1962 attracted only 25 people. A new petition calling for a public inquiry was launched with the aim of collecting a million signatures by the end of 1962 but, after several extensions of the deadline, only 22,000 had been collected by September 1963. John Stevens suggests that the petition fell flat because 'the busmen had done it once and they never saw it as quite the same' when the campaign went public. In addition many of the affiliated organisations did not enter into the petition campaign with the enthusiasm which would have been necessary to achieve the target set.[30]

The campaign was kept in the public eye by a number of publicity exercises. In September 1963 John Stevens wrote an open letter to the London Transport Board* inviting any member of the Board

> to come on to the back of my bus as a conductor for a period of three weeks ... listen with me to the frustrated passengers cursing the name of London Transport. Then at the end of three weeks call a press conference and honestly repeat the claim that London bus work is 'a well-paid and worthwhile job'.[31]

When there were no takers the Group of 41 announced a debate between Bill Jones and the London Transport Chairman, Anthony Valentine. The motion to be debated was:

> This meeting of LTB staff and passengers hold that the LTB, with the complete support of the Minister of Transport, have failed to carry out the responsibilities laid upon them to:
> (a) provide an adequate and efficient service to the public
> (b) provide decent wages and conditions to the staff.

Needless to say the debate, due to the absence of one of the speakers, did not take place.

It was obvious to the London Bus Section that the public campaign had its shortcomings and that some form of industrial action would be needed to put pressure on the government. Thus an overtime ban which started at Southall in September 1963 in protest against service cuts quickly spread to all garages.

> The tactic of the overtime ban was deliberately chosen. We knew what the Chamber of Commerce would do in Oxford Street. They would go berserk. So it was quite deliberately chosen to put pressure on the Government

* The British Transport Commission was abolished in 1962 and independent management boards were set up for London Transport and the other concerns which had been under the BTC's umbrella.

> through the Chamber of Commerce. We wanted someone else to start screaming at the government that we were screwing them for trade. And we were, because in the pre-Christmas period they weren't getting the people up there. We literally starved the West End. People just didn't take the chance on a bus – you could wait two hours for a bus. Everybody kept screaming at us and we'd say: 'But we're doing our normal work. What do you want us to do – work overtime? You don't *force* people to work overtime!' And people would say: 'Well, if you're doing your normal work, we can't criticise that.' So London Transport took the stick.[32]

In November, with Christmas drawing nearer and no end to the ban in sight, the government surrendered. A Committee under the chairmanship of Henry Phelps Brown was established to review the pay and conditions of London Transport drivers and conductors. Three years of effort had finally paid off. Despite considerable pressure to call off the ban, however, it was maintained until the Inquiry had made an Interim Award. The Phelps Brown Committee published an Interim Report on 16 December with a recommendation that London Transport should negotiate wage increases and the ban was lifted two days later, one week before Christmas.

The Final Report was published in February 1964. Not surprisingly, the Committee found that London Transport's inability to recruit and retain staff was 'evidence of the relative inadequacy of pay'.[33] More seriously, it found that the current situation had in fact been anticipated by the Chambers Committee which, in January 1955 had concluded:

> Unless, in fixing remuneration, London Transport take into account the remuneration of staff at all levels in comparable employment in industry it will be impossible to attract and retain the right men and women ... If the present policy, which in our judgement produces a false economy, is maintained, there will be a chronic inability to get staff of the right quality and a fall both qualitatively and quantitatively in the standard of service given by London Transport, which in turn will encourage the use of other forms of transport with its attendant consequences for London Transport in the shape of diminished revenue, increased traffic and congestion and difficulty of operation.[34]

The Phelps Brown Committee now recommended the phased introduction of the 40-hour week, improvements in holidays and sick pay and the separation of the Board's pension scheme from that of the British Transport Commission. The Interim Report had gained drivers and conductors an increase of 15s. and 10s. per week, respectively. This was followed by a further increase of 16s. for both grades in July 1964.

The three-year struggle provided an example of the gains which could be made by a skilful combination of political campaigning and industrial action. The results more than compensated for the defeat of the 1958 strike and represented a turning point for the wages and conditions of London busworkers. The episode also provides a text-book illustration of how such results may be achieved by a period of rank and file activity and action, followed by a trenchant advocacy of the members' case by union full-time officers. Larry Smith bridged both phases. As a lay member he had played a leading role in the Group of 41 and, by the time the Inquiry was announced, was the London Bus Section's Schedules Officer. The TGWU presented some 60 papers to the Inquiry, one of the most crucial being that concerning schedules. There is widespread agreement that Larry Smith's presentation of that case was outstanding. Apart from immediate concessions the arguments marshalled for the Inquiry would also bear fruit in later years – financial compensation for shift work, for example. 'I always contended,' recalls Smith, 'that the worst possible unsocial hours were worked by busmen, who didn't receive a penny shift pay. It was always argued by the employer that it was in the basic rate.'[35] Later the London Bus Section would achieve its own unsocial hours agreement which tied payment to the duty actually worked. Elsewhere in the country other busworkers were to opt for a weekly shift premium. These agreements would cause many employers a few disturbed nights.

While the Phelps Brown Report was an important turning point in many respects, it is questionable whether London Transport really absorbed some of its more general findings. Notwithstanding the fact that the Report had stated that 'the labour force required in the London bus service is at least as great as the present establishment,'[36] London Transport announced a summer programme for 1964 which entailed the loss of 101 rota crews, while the winter programme which followed it saw the need for a further 181 rota crews to disappear. Despite successive cuts, however, the staff shortage remained an obstinate as ever.

In the next few years the industrial tactic favoured by the Section was the overtime ban, which had proved so effective in the autumn of 1963. While this may have been due in part to a reticence concerning strike action after the 1958 strike, the overtime ban was seen as doubly effective because the suspicion was widely-held that London Transport was holding down recruitment in order to *create* overtime, for in this way effective pressure for increased basic rates would be deflated. With so much overtime being worked, a ban would throw the services into chaos, thus making London Transport a victim of its own tactic. Also, it was possible to whip up considerable feeling. In November 1963 *Platform* reported the case of a driver who, having signed on at 4.15 a.m., had killed a woman pedestrian while working overtime at 6.30 p.m. Fining him £30 and banning him from driving for three years, the judge stated that he was 'satisfied that at the time you killed this woman you were incapable of driving because of your fatigue'. Some indication of the way overtime working was viewed by London Transport is shown by the fact that because Shepherds Bush, Crawley and Hemel Hempstead took a little longer than other garages to lift the ban in December 1963, deductions were made from the *basic pay* of staff at those garages.

During the course of 1964 Norbiton, Bromley, Poplar, Southall, Chalk Farm, Hackney, Hanwell, Barking and Seven Kings all operated overtime bans – either over service cuts or schedules. With the announcement of further cuts for 1965, a Joint Delegate Conference in December 1964 voted to impose a ban from 6 January 1965. However the Conference was recalled the day before the ban was due to start and it was agreed to call it off. The terms, described by *Platform* as 'truly monstrous',[37] included the withdrawal of one programme of cuts in return for the postponement of the shorter working week until October, the compulsory working of one rest-day per month and the right of London Transport to take 'any action' against any garage imposing an overtime ban. Notwithstanding the Conference decision, at least 70 garages were affected by an overtime ban on 6, 7 and 8 January. In the months which followed it was a matter of fierce controversy as to whether there was in fact an 'agreement' along the lines outlined at the December Conference. When London Transport finally admitted that the 'agreement' was unsigned, the London Bus Conference debated whether to ban overtime from 10 March 1965, but this was defeated by 36 votes to 34. Eventually the agreement, minus one of the offending clauses, was signed, and from 17 March crews received an extra 21s. 3d. per week in lieu of the shorter working week.

On 16 December 1965 the Conference debated a motion from the floor calling for a strike on Boxing Day in support of a demand for improved pay and conditions at Christmas. The motion proved a source of disagreement between Bill Jones, who was chairing the Conference, and Larry Smith, then the London District Secretary. The latter recalls:

> I said, 'You're not permitted to take a strike motion because it's unconstitutional, and if you as chairman take the motion then I must withdraw the Officers from the Conference and the Conference will then be unofficial.'
>
> I'll always remember Bill saying 'The London District Secretary is absolutely correct; there's nothing he's said that one could disagree with.'

Now the *pièce de résistance*: 'I'm taking the motion!'

He came to me afterwards and said, 'Well, now we've gotta get out of the mess, ain't we?'[38]

A few days later talks were held with the LTB, after which an emergency Conference was called at which the strike call was reversed on the understanding that talks on Christmas operations would continue. In the event, Chalk Farm, Hackney, Putney, Palmers Green, Peckham and Turnham Green went ahead with unofficial strikes on Boxing Day. Eventually, London Transport agreed that all duties on Boxing Day would have a maximum length of five hours.

The last overtime ban of any significance occurred early in 1966. This was unusual in that it was official, having the aim of compelling London Transport to introduce the five-day, 40-hour week. Larry Smith, by this time National Officer for the Passenger Group, put the case to Jack Jones for official support on the basis that it would demonstrate that the Union supported the Section in its fight and

> because of the success we had achieved with the overtime ban that culminated in the Phelps Brown Inquiry I was pressing the lads to have an overtime ban in order to do much the same thing again ... I was also involved with the company and municipal busmen, who were fighting it out against the Prices and Incomes Board, and I needed a united front. Accepting the proposal [for an overtime ban] from the London Bus Section would, I thought, assist us in both the company and municipal negotiations.[39]

The action lasted for five weeks. In February Catford, Camberwell and Stockwell struck against the employer's attempts to break the ban. In March Southall and Hanwell struck over cuts in services (it was London Transport's policy to attempt to introduce cuts during overtime bans). On 14 March a crew was put out on overtime at Hounslow after the members at the garage had re-imposed the ban in protest against cuts. When management ignored an ultimatum that the garage would stop unless the bus came in, a strike ensued. The performance was repeated the following day, after which it was agreed that eight additional buses would be placed in Hounslow on a 'supplementary basis'. The original fleet-wide ban was successful in that London Transport agreed to participate in a Joint Working Party to inquire into conditions of service and the part these played in wastage. As a result the five-day, 40-hour week was introduced in 1967.

Since then there have of course been isolated schedules disputes and other local forms of action. But with the exception of the occasional day's protest stoppage and a brief overtime ban in 1969, there has been no major industrial action by London busworkers since the overtime ban in 1966. The changes which had been taking place in the industry and in the Section had led not only to a loss of status, but to a loss of self-confidence as well.

Notes

1. Quoted in *The Platform*, October 1963.
2. *The Platform*, May 1965.
3. Ibid., May 1962.
4. For the earlier period, see Barker and Robbins, op.cit., Vol.II, pp.317 and 412, n.11.
5. E. Hobsbawm, *Industry and Empire*, London 1968, p.248. Chapter 14 of this work has special relevance for this period of the present study.
6. Ibid., p.242.
7. Bill Waters, 'The First Twelve Years', *The Platform*, May 1962.
8. George Leeks, in conversation with the author, 23 May 1984.
9. Harry Selmes interview.
10. Ibid.
11. Hobsbawm, op.cit., p.248.
12. Dalston Branch Circular, undated.
13. LTB, *Record of Industrial Disputes …*
14. Larry Smith interview.
15. G. Goodman, *The Awkward Warrior, Frank Cousins and His Times*, London 1979, p.110.
16. Ibid., p.112.
17. Hobsbawm, op.cit., p.228.
18. Goodman, op.cit., p.168.
19. *The Platform*, July 1958.
20. Report to the Operating Manager now in the possession of London Regional Transport. Some of these reports are so detailed that the intelligence must have been passed to local managers and officials by busworkers. One of these, named in a report, was a Branch Representative in a west London garage.
21. Goodman, op.cit., p.182.
22. Ibid., p.185.
23. Press Association statement, 4 June 1958.
24. *Proposals For Settlement of Bus Strike*, 19/20 June 1958.
25. Goodman, op.cit., p.190.
26. John Stevens, interviewed by the author, 12 September 1984.
27. John Stevens, *Tribune*, 28 October 1960.
28. Ibid., 3 March 1961.
29. Various minutes, London Passenger Transport Campaign Committee.
30. John Stevens interview.
31. *Evening News*, 13 September 1963.
32. John Stevens interview.
33. 'Report of the Committee of Inquiry to Review the Pay and Conditions of

Employment of the Drivers and Conductors of the London Transport Board's Road Services', HMSO, 1964, p.31.

34. Ibid., p.56.
35. Larry Smith interview.
36. 'Report of the Committee ...', p.55.
37. *The Platform*, January 1965.
38. Larry Smith interview.
39. Ibid.

CHAPTER TWENTY-ONE

London Busworkers and the GLC

In January 1968, *Bus Stop* reported that the Labour government had announced that control of London Transport would be handed over to the Greater London Council. The unofficial journal went on to speculate whether 'our new guvnors' would allow a 'greater opportunity and freedom to improve our wages and conditions' or whether fares would be kept at an artificially low level at the expense of wages.

The GLC took over the Underground and the Central buses on 1 January 1970. The Country Services and Green Line coaches were transferred to a new company, London Country Bus Services, a subsidiary of the state-owned National Bus Company. Three weeks prior to the GLC takeover, uncertain of the future and concerned about future service-cuts and conversions to one-man operation, the London Bus Conference called for a one-day stoppage on 1 January. The London Transport Joint Committee, an unofficial body linking bus and tubeworkers, associated itself with the call.

On 19 December Jack Jones, the new General Secretary, took the officers and committee of the London Bus Section along to a meeting with the Transport Minister to discuss the deterioration in the bus service and the crews' deteriorating working conditions. Arising from this and subsequent correspondence, it was agreed that the Chairman of the GLC would meet Jones and and the Central Bus Committee at an early date. A meeting with Sir Richard Way, the London Transport Chairman, was arranged for 7 January. However, as late as 30 December Larry Smith, the National Passenger Officer, was still unable to get the Central Bus Committee to recommend that the action be called off.

Later that evening, however, it became known that the London Transport Joint Committee had decided that the tubes would work normally on 1 January, compelling the CBC to call a special London Bus Conference the following night. Larry Smith pointed out that the proposed action was unconstitutional, as the GEC was the only body empowered to call strikes, and outlined the events since Conference had

London Buses, 1970-1983

Year	*Passenger miles, millions*	*Bus miles (crew) millions*	*Bus miles (OPO), millions*	*Average fare per passenger mile*	*Operating staff*
1970	2,990	175	24	2.2p	25,972
1971	2,907	156	42	2.3p	25,015
1972	2,856	135	55	2.5p	23,415
1973	2,958	119	63	2.5p	21,937
1974	3,061	109	66	2.5p	22,348
1975	3,039	109	69	3.1p	23,888
1976	2,980	111	71	4.3p	20,847
1977	2,919	106	73	5.0p	20,045
1978	2,819	98	74	5.6p	19,961
1979	2,690	92	73	6.1p	19,739
1980	2,593	95	78	8.0p	19,851
1981	2,511	90	84	8.3p	19,775
1982	2,332	85	79	10.8p	18,992
1983	2,400	78	95	10.8p	18,800

Sources: London Transport Reports, 1975, 1980, 1982, 1983.

taken its decision. The decision to strike was withdrawn, pending the meeting with the Chairman of the GLC and London Transport.

The Section's concern was to prove justified, as over the ensuing periods of Tory control at County Hall the policy of service cuts and fares-increases was pursued mindlessly. The results of this policy are summarised in the above table.

In the mid-1970s, during Labour control of the GLC, fares were held constant, and the effect of this may be seen in the increase in passenger mileage. The 1974 wage agreement secured a sizeable increase in basic rates, a system of unsocial hours' payment, London Weighting Allowance and a threshold agreement to counter the effects of the rampant inflation of the period. This dramatically improved the staff position and resulted in the increase in numbers of operating staff observed in the years 1975 and 1976.

Of course, growing unemployment and the economic recession which steadily deepened throughout the 1970s, tended to act as a deterrent to bus travel. From the middle of the decade this factor assumed increasing significance and with the Tories installed at County Hall once more, London Transport resumed its practice of regular fares-increases. By the latter part of the 1970s, the downward spiral witnessed in the 1950s and 60s was being repeated. Other factors in the decline were the continued decrease in the population of London and the seemingly inexorable rise of the private car:

Vehicle and Passengers Entering Central London in the Morning Peak

	1970	1975	1980
Cars	111,800	118,000	137,000
Car Passengers	159,900	166,000	184,000
LT Buses	4,000	3,200	2,600
Bus Passengers	152,400	148,000	103,000

Source: LT Annual Reports, 1975 and 1980.

Because of a fall in the number of passengers in each vehicle, 19,000 extra cars were bringing a mere 18,000 more people into central London between 1975 and 1980, while 600 fewer buses were conveying 45,000 fewer passengers. There was a misguided tendency to look upon such problems as God-given. In his foreword to London Transport's 1980 Report, the Chairman, Sir Peter Masefield, merely noted the 4.2 per cent decline in passenger traffic as 'a trend which has been a feature of the past 30 years'.

Apart from the worsening of the industry's crisis by the actions of a Tory GLC, the Section also had to contend with three other major threats during these years. A shortage of spare parts which kept buses off the road, cuts in public spending and wage-restraint imposed by a *Labour* government and, sadly, an escalation of assaults as the deepening economic crisis gave rise to anti-social acts among demoralised sections of the working class, especially youth.

The shortage of spare parts meant that in the summer of 1975 a daily average of 200 SMS and 200 DMS type buses were off the road. Out of a total of 1,600 DMSs (an OMO type), 1,200 had experienced gearbox problems.[1] Significantly, this led Ralph Bennett, Vice-Chairman of the London Transport Executive, to suggest that the situation was actually a blessing in disguise, as it had allowed London Transport to avoid imposing the 20 per cent cut in *scheduled* mileage suffered by the national and municipal bus undertakings.[2]

The Labour government announced that it would be cutting the transport supplementary grant for 1976, prompting London Transport to state that as it was dependent upon this and rates-subsidy for a third of its financial requirement, internal economies and fares-increases would be the order of the day. The fares-increases obviously contributed to the loss of passengers already noted. The government's wage-restraint policies, on the other hand, (a £6 maximum in 1976 followed by a £4 maximum in 1977), reversed the improvement in staff-retention achieved by the wage settlement of 1974:

	Week Commencing				
	27 December 1975	*12 June 1976*	*8 January 1977*	*18 June 1977*	*11 February 1978*
Establishment (Drivers/ Driver ops.)	14,417	15,932	14,915	15,370	14,895
Shortage, per cent	190.6	17.2	13.6	17.9	15.6
Establishement, (Conductors)	8, 937	9,446	9,152	9,197	8,655
Shortage, per cent	10.9	16.5	13.2	17.9	14.2

Source: Central Bus Committee Minutes, 1976-1978.

The problem of assaults was painfully and sharply brought into focus when, one Sunday in January 1975, Conductor Ronald Jones, a 44-year-old Jamaican, was the victim of an assault following a fares dispute. He fell from the platform and cracked his head on the pavement. Several days later he died in hospital. The day following Ronny Jones's death Merton garage staged a one-day protest strike. On 29 January the whole fleet stopped and several hundred members of the Section marched behind Jack Jones to a memorial service in Clapham. In the months that followed the Section raised over £10,000 for Ronny Jones's widow and family.

The changes which had taken place in both the character of the Section and in the industry during the post-war years combined with these factors to produce low morale and a lack of confidence in the ability of the Section to fight its way out of the problems besetting it. Thus, although a major campaign called 'Save Our Services' was launched by the official leaders of the London Transport unions, principally the TGWU and the NUR, in 1976, and various lobbies of both the GLC and Parliament were held over the next year or so, by October 1977 Charley Young, the Section's London District Secretary, was complaining that the attendance at these events had been very poor.[3] In June of the same year a motion to ban overtime for a week in order to demonstrate to the public the true level of staff shortage was overwhelmingly defeated.[4]

In the absence of the bold initiatives necessary to tackle the roots of London Transport's problems, both management and the GLC could see no escape. The Horace Cutler régime at County Hall appeared to favour bleeding the patient, and Bus Plan '78 was but the first in a series of planned cuts which sought to axe scheduled mileage from 211 million miles to 199 million miles. This would reduce the total staff establishment figure from 23,500 to 20,800. Paradoxically, this would mean not redundancies but the recruitment of *extra* staff, as there existed at the time a staff shortage of 15 per cent – 3,600 drivers, driver/operators and conductors.

At first the London Bus Conference opposed the plan, resolving to stage a series of lightning one-hour strikes, District by District. The response was less than 100 per cent, with some branches not responding at all. When this was discussed by the Central Bus Committee in May 1978, two members of that Committee resigned. Four days later the CBC met the Managing Director (Buses), Dr D. Quarmby, and heard the latter announce that a part of the programme would be deferred until March 1979, subject to further discussions. On 31 June, by a vote of 33 to 32, the London Bus Conference accepted the programme. Despite attempts at reversing it, the June decision stood, although the cuts were not quite as deep as had been originally intended: by November 1979 the establishment figure was still just over 22,000.

However, after a deficit of £15 million in 1979, London Transport announced further cuts for 1980. In response the Section called a one-hour strike with the intention of creating maximum disruption on 3 March. Again, the response was less than 100 per cent and the

Conference two weeks later resolved that the full-time officers should visit the 'Branches in their District to make sure Conference policy is carried out'.

In 1981 London Transport's attempts to wrestle with its crisis approached the farcical. First, it was announced that scheduled mileage would be reduced to 193 million miles, whilst that actually operated would not be allowed to climb above 168 million miles. Then when it was found that actual performance was exceeding that budgeted for, recruitment, overtime and rest-day working were limited. Despite the fact that the Section was still 14.4 per cent short of establishment, London Transport's General Manager was reported to Conference as saying: 'The main problem was that there were too many staff on books at the present time, in relation to the budget.'[5] The Section rejected this approach, calling for recruitment at the thirty or so garages where the staff shortage exceeded 20 per cent.

But help was on its way.

Despite an unprecedented press campaign against the Labour Party's fare-cutting proposals, the Tories were defeated in the GLC elections in May 1981. Recruitment was increased, the restrictions on overtime working lifted and the budget revised upwards to allow for an extra five million operated miles. Cuts planned for October were scrapped. The new administration immediately went into a process of public consultation during which it discussed the various options for cutting fares and improving the services offered by London Transport. As a result, fares were reduced by an average of 32 per cent on 4 October that year and a zonal system was introduced. The fares-cut was, despite the fanfare, quite modest. In real terms fares had merely returned to their 1969 level.

The results were, in more ways than one, dramatic. Passenger journeys increased by 10 per cent, and passenger mileage by 12 per cent. These figures understate the real effect, however, for as Sir Peter Masefield remarked in his foreword to London Transport's 1981 Report, 'there were indications that the decline in tourism and the general economic recession were going to lead to a further reduction during the remainder of the year' – before, that is, Fares Fair, as the new system was called, was introduced.

In fact, passenger-demand had declined by 4.8 per cent in the first 20 weeks of 1981. Thus, Fares Fair first made good that loss and then went on to win more passengers. Masefield was able to claim that

> for the first time in about twenty years, the steady decline in the use by passengers of public transport services in London was halted and reversed, in

spite of the continuing growth in the ownership of private cars and the declining population of the capital city.

Fares Fair also halted the growth of cars coming into London:

Vehicle and Passengers Entering Central London in the Morning Peak

	1980	1981
Cars	137,000	131,000
Car Passengers	184,000	173,000
LT Buses	2,600	2,600
Bus Passengers	103,000	105,000

Source: LT Annual Report, 1981.

All this was possible by taking the level of subsidy to 54 per cent, something quite acceptable by international standards, being about the same as Paris, Chicago and Copenhagen and considerably lower than Brussels, Stockholm, New York and Milan. However, this subsidy had to be partly-funded by the rate-payers, due to the fact that the Thatcher government had systematically cut its own aid to local government in general and to the GLC in particular. Even though rate-payers who used London Transport services at all regularly would have been better off on balance, it was this aspect of the exercise which was used to torpedo Fares Fair.

Resulting from an action brought by Bromley Council, the Law Lords ruled on 17 December 1981 that Fares Fair was unlawful. Moreover, they proclaimed that London Transport had a 'fiduciary duty' to attempt to break even. There was an outcry at this decision. Lobbies of Parliament and of the GLC led to the first-ever meeting of all trade union representatives and shop stewards on London Transport at Congress House on 17 February 1982. This meeting, convened by the London Transport Trade Union Defence Committee (representing all the unions with members on London Transport), pledged its support for a one-day protest strike. Thus, London ground to halt on 10 March as, for the first time ever, buses and tubes struck together.

The period was also characterised by intense public activity, with large public meetings being held all over London. This identity of interest between London Transport workers and community groups arose from the fact that, in order to meet the new legal position, London Transport had announced that fares would be doubled in March and services cut in July (later postponed until August), with the projected loss of 5,000 jobs over the following three years. Unfortunately, the industrial and political sides of the campaign never achieved the degree of unity demanded by the situation. As we have seen, the political consciousness of the Section had been in decline since the 1950s, and in that time the status of the job had so deteriorated that the character of the London Bus Section's membership had been transformed to the point where political action was regarded with cynicism. On the other side of the coin the character of some of the political campaigns waged around Fares Fair – especially the 'Can't Pay, Won't Pay' exercise, whereby after the fares-increase individuals were encouraged to pay the old fare – tended to alienate potential support from busworkers. In the event only a small minority of London Transport trade unionists involved themselves in the political campaigning at borough level and, once the fares-increase had been implemented in late March, public activity died away, leaving London Transport workers isolated in their fight against the service-cuts later in the year.

On the trade union side the unity of action demonstrated on 10 March was not repeated. In the London Bus Section an open-ended programme of action saw only one token hour-long stoppage, following which the demand for negotiations grew. On 19 June however, 32 signalmen were suspended on the Underground for refusing to feed new rolls into the machine which would operate the new, reduced schedules. On the following Monday morning, when the 32 men were due to appear on Disciplinary Boards, most motormen and guards came out on strike. The same evening ASLEF declared the strike official. On 24 June, although ASLEF had by then instructed its members to return to work after London Transport had offered to postpone the cuts for a month, the Executive Committee of the numerically-stronger NUR decided to make the strike official. Although there were no plans to call upon the London Bus Section for support, NUR Assistant General Secretary Andy Dodds reported that he had received many messages of support from busworkers. That Friday Wandsworth branch pulled its buses off the road for a mass meeting to discuss possible action on the following Monday. That Monday saw nine garages on unofficial strike. The following day, after London Transport had agreed to reinstate the 32 signalmen and postpone the service cuts while a joint working party looked at alternative methods of making savings, the Underground strike was called off. A Special London Bus Conference, which was to have discussed the call for an indefinite strike with the Underground the next day, was cancelled.

On 23 July an entirely different proposition was put to a Special London Bus Conference. London Transport had agreed to restore 115 of the 785 buses they had planned to cut. By a vote of 36 to 27, the cuts were accepted.

During the campaign against the 1982 cuts some lay representatives had warned that if the London Bus Section did not fight as vigorously as possible the government would take this as a sign of weakness and mount an even greater attack upon the industry. Sadly, this proved to be the case.

The 1983 Transport Act gave the Transport Secretary an influential say in setting the level of subsidy for the transport undertakings of the GLC and the other Metropolitan Authorities. Each such undertaking would be required to submit a three-year plan on a rolling, annual basis, and services were to be put out to tender wherever it seemed likely that the private sector could operate those services more cheaply. London Transport produced its first three-year plan in the summer of 1983 which, predictably, provided for 6,000 job-losses (4,000 of them bus operating, maintenance and overhaul staff) out of a total workforce of 57,000.

This plan was produced with no consultation – not even with the GLC, which provided the subsidy. This led to a major loss of confidence by the GLC in the new London Transport chairman, Dr Keith Bright, whom the authority had appointed in September 1983. The GLC now exercised its power to fill vacancies on the London Transport Executive by appointing part-time directors who would suggest policies to improve services and benefit passengers. Earlier in the year the GLC had undertaken a public consultation exercise around its own 'Balanced Plan'; it used the positive responses to that exercise to radically amend the three-year plan put forward by London Transport. As we will see, however, this attempt was scuppered by further legislation.

Many of the job-losses proposed by the three-year plan were to be achieved by an increase in one-person operation (OPO). Already, as a result of a conversion programme launched in April 1983, OPO accounted for 53 per cent of total bus operations; the plan now was to take this to 65 pr cent by 1987. The London Bus Committee (as the CBC had been renamed in 1982) asked the GLC to instruct London Transport to postpone its conversion programme while an independent study of the social benefits of OPO was undertaken. To an increasing number of people, London Transport's plans to achieve 'savings' by ridding itself of conductors made no social sense if this was going to result in a less satisfactory service for the public and a loss to the Exchequer through increased unemployment. Much to London Transport's annoyance, the GLC agreed to commission the study and instruct 55 Broadway to postpone the conversions. By late 1984 a draft report by Professor Goodwin of the Transport Studies Unit, Oxford University, had arrived at the GLC, although its contents have at the time of writing not been published.

But the government was not finished with London Transport. Later in 1983, as part of its attack on local democracy and its commitment to the privatisation of public assets, it published a White Paper in which it announced its intention to remove London Transport from GLC control (prior to the abolition of the GLC itself) and hand it to an appointed body to be called London Regional Transport.

This proposal, coupled with plans for the abolition of the Council itself, generated widespread opposition. Once again, local borough campaign groups sprouted all over London. CAPITAL, an organisation uniting the transport trade unions with the campaign groups and largely founded by the GLC, within short space of time gained the support of some 2,000 such organisations and individuals. As part of a week of events organised against the abolition proposals, Monday 26 March 1984 was dubbed 'Transport Day', a day on which CAPITAL supporters distributed almost half a million leaflets at bus stops and Underground stations. Two days later London Transport workers participated in a one-day strike called by the London Transport Trade Union Council (the Defence Committee of 1982-83 established on a permanent basis).

Given the Tory majority in the House of Commons, it was clear to most observers that the legislative proposals for London Transport were going to be passed. Thus, in the summer of 1984 the London Regional Transport Act passed into law. Predictably, one of the first acts of Nicholas Ridley, the Transport Minister, was to dismiss the GLC-appointed part-time members of the London Transport Executive. Equally predictably, the majority of Ridley's new appointees to the Board of London Regional Transport (LRT) came from business backgrounds with, on the face of it, few qualifications for running one of the largest public transport systems in the world.

There are now a number of major threats facing transport workers (and in particular the London Bus Section) and the travelling public. On April Fool's Day 1985, LRT was split into three subsidiaries – London Buses Ltd., London Underground Ltd. and Bus Engineering Ltd. At the time of writing LRT is discussing the possibility of making each of the six Bus Districts within London Buses Ltd. a separate subsidiary. Indeed, under the terms of the LRT Act each of the three major subsidiaries may be broken down into further subsidiaries, and there are fears that the smaller subsidiaries may be privatised.

As far as bus services are concerned, LRT is busily putting routes out to tender every few months. Twelve routes have completed the tendering procedure so far, of which six were awarded to operators (two of them private) other than London Buses Ltd. In June 1985 a further ten routes were put out to tender with the rider that a further 30, including all those crossing the GLC boundaries into Surrey and Hertfordshire, would follow shortly. A much greater danger looms on the horizon, for the 1985 Transport Bill contains a provision whereby the Secretary of state may deregulate bus services in London at a time of his choosing, without further legislation; this would allow anyone with a bus to compete on any route. Obviously, this latter form of 'competition' would herald the return of the 'pirate' era.

Both of these forms of private operation contain dangers for the public and the London Bus Section. The fact that private operators carry passengers is secondary to the main reason for their existence, which is to make profits. This being the case, their main targets must be the profitable inner-London routes. If this part of the market is captured by the private operator it will obviously impair LRT's ability to cross-subsidise those uneconomic but socially necessary routes in the suburbs. These routes will only be maintained in those circumstances by either reducing frequency or by raising fares. The danger to busworkers is threefold. If such schemes were carried through on a large enough scale members of the London Bus Section would find themselves divided between several different companies as a result of which their negotiating strength would be weakened; in a competitive race to become 'economic', there is a clear danger of service-cuts and, thus, job-losses. Finally, LRT is already indicating that it will be using the *threat* of competition in an attempt to introduce wage-differentials between inner and outer-London garages.

LRT has picked up the three-year plan formulated by London Transport with the intention of forcing through the 6,000 job-losses. Further extensions of One-Person Operation are planned for 1985, with the perspective of 100 per cent OPO by the 1990s. LRT has also been told by the Minister that the level of subsidy, which in 1984-5 was £192 million, will be cut to £95 million in 1987-88. There can be little doubt that, quite aside from all the dangers outlined above, this will entail quite savage service-cuts.

It is therefore quite clear that LRT will be guided not by the transport needs of Londoners but by the requirements of the balance-sheet. This is evident from the attitude being taken to the free passes enjoyed by old-age pensioners. Although the government claims that the passes are safe, no one is prepared to guarantee that they will be valid for the same hours of the day (all day after 9 a.m.), or whether they will still be entirely free. It is proposed that from 1985 these passes (currently funded by the GLC) will become the responsibility of each individual borough. Some indication of their fate was given when, in August 1984, the Tory-dominated London Boroughs Association gave notice that the boroughs were not prepared to continue to fund Disabled Passes for an extra 30 minutes per day – from 9 a.m. to 9.30 a.m. The cost of so doing would have been an average of £3,000 per borough per year.

Significantly, when the London Bus Conference was told of the decision of the London Boroughs Association it decided to advise its members to continue to accept the Disabled Passes from 9 a.m. This simple decision, and the reasoning behind it, symbolises not only the threats facing both busworkers and the travelling public but also the scope which exists for a joint campaign, backed up when necessary by the industrial strength of the London Bus Section and other LRT workers.

Notes

1. Minutes, Central Bus Conference, 12 August 1975.
2. Ibid., 14 October 1975.
3. Ibid., October 1977.
4. Ibid., 14 June 1977.
5. Ibid., 17 February 1981.

Conclusions

We have seen that from 1913 onwards London's busworkers achieved a combination of industrial militancy and political radicalism which was based upon the quasi-aristocratic status achieved by the 'trade' in those early years. The industrial militancy was dampened during the Second World War when precedence was given to political considerations. Despite the experience of 'Deakinism', the militancy of the London Bus Section's membership was rekindled after the war, and it was not until changes of the 1950s and 60s had reduced both the status of buswork in London and transformed the character of the membership that the levels of both industrial and political consciousness declined.

In the earlier periods, when the TGWU was under right-wing leadership, the membership was mobilised by unofficial methods. The situation is now entirely reversed. In the late 1970s the Platform Group, organised around a journal opportunistically named after that edited for 17 years by George Renshaw, represented little more than an attempt by the Socialist Workers Party to apply its fetish for rank-and-file activism to the section where it had all begun almost fifty years earlier. Neither the group nor its journal survived long after its leading personality was voted out of office. Currently within the London Bus Section and other sections of London Transport, a number of ultra-leftist organisations are attempting to gain influence. But they will fail for the simple reason that they have not learned (or, for reasons of ideological 'purity', refuse to learn) the lesson applied so effectively by the Rank and File Movement in the early 1930s: to stop talking *to* busworkers and instead to talk *with* them, mobilising them around the issues with which they are concerned.

The leadership of the TGWU is no longer right-wing. The need of the moment is not to bring pressure to bear upon that leadership to adopt progressive policies, *but to seek ways in which to raise the awareness of the membership to the point where they are prepared to fight for the implementation of those policies which the TGWU has already adopted.* This does not mean, of course, that the leadership of the Section will never need gingering up to achieve this. Thus, contrary to the experience of the earlier periods of the Section's history, the leadership is faced with the task of mobilising the membership.

The problems are not insurmountable. The Section is (pending a thorough implementation of some of the more radical proposals contained in the London Regional Transport Act, anyway) more compact than at any time since 1933. Since the phasing out of the trams and trolley buses (completed in 1952 and 1962, respectively), and the hiving off of the Country Services to London Country in 1970, there has existed an unprecedented unity of organisation. At less than 20,000, the Section is approximately the same size as the LGOC fleet when the 'red button' union first organised the capital's busworkers. Further, in its attempt to mobilise the membership, the leadership of the Section enjoys an advantage not available to the 'red button' men: the resources of the country's largest union, with all which that entails for the production of publicity material, education, etc.

In many ways, the Section has come full circle. Now, as earlier, the need is to link industrial militancy with a socialist political consciousness. While London busworkers will never regain their privileged status, it is by no means inevitable that their decline should continue. Indeed, environmentally and socially it is necessary that *more* jobs be created in London's transport system by an expansion of demand, and that those jobs be both secure and adequately paid. London busworkers also need a *say* in the way their industry is planned and run, something which could feature as a component of an alternative economic strategy pursued by a socialist-oriented Labour government. To safeguard their futures London busworkers must engage in a *political* campaign. In this context the loss of aristocratic status could in the long run prove no bad thing, for it is clear that the London Bus Section will only secure and improve its own position as a part of the advances made by the whole working class movement.

The great question remains – how will the membership be mobilised for this political struggle? Ironically, the indications are that this may best be achieved in the manner demonstrated by the Rank and File Movement: by a vigorous defence of working conditions and wages. The implementation of the measures contained in the London Regional Transport Act will provide ample scope for this. As discussed earlier, the opportunity also exists to link up with significant sections of the community in the course of such a campaign. (There is also scope for campaigning on a *national* scale, for in its Transport Bill 1985, the government has put forward proposals for dismembering the National Bus Company and the Passenger Transport Executives and deregulating the bus industry outside of London to the extent that virtually anyone who takes it into their head to operate a bus will be allowed to do so. At the time of writing the TGWU is planning just such a national campaign.) Such links are not merely tactically sound but *imperative* because the threats facing the industry are political in their origin, and consequently mass *political* pressure is needed to defeat them.

Dark though the immediate horizon may be, if the measures contained in the London Regional Transport Act are fought step by step, and if the campaign is accompanied by a painstaking explanation of the alternative for which the Section must strive, the militant heritage will be regained and the vision of the Section's socialist pioneers will be brought closer to realisation.

Index

CHAMPION!

THE LONDON FOREST STRIKE OF 1991

BY

KEN FULLER

Page 257

FOREWORD

When I was at our union's Bienniel Delegate Conference in July, 1991 and the National Secretary of our Passenger Services Group approached the General Secretary and myself to draft a message of support for the workers at London Forest Travel, I was delighted to do so. Not only did I welcome the opportunity to encourage the members in their struggle, but I saw the issue in terms of the wider conflict. For a decade, market forces - not the country's needs - had governed the passenger services industry. Here at last a stand was being made. The workers were not about to pay the price for a crisis engineered by the Tories' ideological obsession.

For much the same reasons, I was pleased to be invited to write the forward to this publication. Our members' achievement in defeating a proposal for a drastic wage cut and obtaining a guarantee of jobs for all those who wished to remain with London Buses displays for the whole industry a forward looking, unblinkered approach to the ever-changing labour market.

Having defined a strategy which can only lead to victory over the forces which threaten wages and conditions in London Buses in particular, I am sure that such a united and determined group of members can maintain the recruitment efforts called for following such upheaval, and that they will mobilise in the political campaign that is needed to finally defeat deregulation, privatisation and tendering. To that end, you have my fullest support.

With all good wishes,

BILL MORRIS
General Secretary (Elect)

PREFACE

There are any number of reasons which could be advanced for the production of a pamphlet of this nature. For example, the London Forest strike of 1991 was not only important in its own right, but it occurred exactly 100 years since the first industrial action of any magnitude by London busworkers: in June, 1891 staff employed by the London General Omnibus Company had struck over a series of demands and had achieved - albeit only briefly - the twelve-hour day.[1] Thus, the London Forest strike may well become known as the Centenary Strike.

The conflict in London Forest, involving over 1,200 workers for a period of nineteen days, was the longest official strike of London busworkers for 33 years - since the seven-week wages strike of 1958. It is important that such disputes are recorded as fully and as accurately as possible. In this particular case this is even more important for, apart from those directly involved, there is an insufficient appreciation of the consequences of the strike and of its achievements. To an extent, this is understandable, for the tactics employed by the TGWU were somewhat unconventional. Why were other groups of London busworkers actively dissuaded from taking industrial action? What was behind the apparent decision to favour the private sector (as the contracts involved were finally awarded to private companies)? Can the apparent "loss" of jobs be truthfully portrayed as a victory?

More than anything else, this pamphlet has been written to answer such questions - and one other, even more important one: what lessons does the dispute hold for busworkers as a whole?

The title chosen for this publication perhaps needs a brief explanation. "CHAMPION!" featured as a headline in a newsletter issued to staff by London Forest shortly after the company had been provisionally awarded the contracts for the routes in the Walthamstow network. The use of such a headline was, the union felt, indicative of a self-delusion which knew no bounds, for the company had before it the task of persuading its workforce to accept drastically reduced wages and conditions. Our own use of the title is therefore ironic, contrasting the company's initial confidence with the TGWU membership's celebration of a famous victory.

The decision to publish this pamphlet was taken by the TGWU's Operating Staff Committee in London Forest - Pat Caughlin (Ash Grove), Steve Cushion (Chair), Eddie Hayes (Clapton), Lucien Hoebeeck (Walthamstow) and Bill Knowles (Leyton). It is to these leading lay members, their engineering counterparts (particularly Larry Laurent and Steve Robbins) and to the lay membership as a whole that this pamphlet is dedicated.

KEN FULLER,
TGWU District Officer,
January, 1992.

CHAPTER ONE:
BACKGROUND TO THE DISPUTE

THE TENDER TRAP

The London Forest strike of 1991 was a direct result of the London Regional Transport Act, 1984. This Act compelled London Regional Transport (LRT, which now, confusingly, has once more taken to calling itself London Transport) to periodically put bus routes out to tender. Once the tenders are advertised, London Buses, Ltd. (LBL, the operating subsidiary of London Transport) then bids along with the private operators for the routes. As, all other things being equal, the contracts are awarded to the lowest bidders, it was always obvious that route-tendering was going to be a recipe for cutting wages and worsening conditions within LBL.

At first, LBL was prepared to honour its agreements with the TGWU, bidding on the basis of existing wages and conditions. This lasted until LBL had lost a significant number of routes to the private sector. Then, without prior discussion with the union, the company bid for routes operated from Potters Bar and Hounslow garages on the basis of dramatically reduced wages and conditions.

This time around, however, there was no dispute. At Potters Bar all staff were offered the choice of the new terms and conditions and a series of compensation payments, or the relatively generous terms of the voluntary severance package. The vast majority of staff opted for the latter, allowing the company to recruit new staff on the revised conditions. At Hounslow, a new subsidiary - Westlink - was opened on a green-field site; thus, existing staff were not affected.

The first dispute over tendering occurred when the network of routes operated at Norbiton garage was won by the incumbent, London Buses. This time, there was no green-field site, no voluntary severance payments. Therefore, the TGWU members at the garage, supported on occasion by action elsewhere in the LBL fleet, put up a fight with a series of strikes. Also, the TGWU funded a court case in which it was argued that the terms of the agreement for dealing with staff made surplus as a result of conversions to One-Person Operation should be applied in the present circumstances as well.

Predictably, the court case was lost. While the industrial action pressurised LBL into stretching the available cash to the limit, the wages and conditions were still considerably worse than those currently in force (although current staff were offered a series of compensation payments). At the end of the day, the TGWU faced a dilemma.

On the one hand, the union was confronted with a quite blatant worsening of wages and conditions. On the other, if it forced the issue and the contracts were re-awarded to the private sector, the private operators who had bid for the routes would pay even less!

This same dilemma would be faced time and again, all over London, in the years which followed. Until the summer of 1991.

One problem faced by some companies which won tenders in the intervening years was that, as they were paying low wages, they either had difficulty in recruiting staff or they had to allow long hours to be worked in order to provide a living wage. This was especially apparent when the London labour market was buoyant. This illustrated the central contradiction within the route-tendering system: the routes are awarded to the lowest bidder, but labour gravitates to the highest bidder. Thus, an employer may win a contract but he may have less success in recruiting the staff. This contradiction had, however, never made its way into the bargaining arena.

Until the summer of 1991.

LONDON FOREST - A DIFFERENT KIND OF COMPANY

In April, 1989, LBL was split into thirteen operating subsidiaries – London Central, Selkent, London General, South London, London United, Centrewest, Metroline, Leaside, London Northern, London Forest, East London, Westlink and London Coaches. This development was part of the government's preparation for the deregulation and privatisation of all London bus services. Each of the thirteen subsidiaries was provided with its own directors, who were recruited by advertisement. Thus, while most came from within LBL, there were a number of appointments from elsewhere in the industry. Understandably, this has resulted in recognisable fluctuations in performance between the subsidiaries in the spheres of operated mileage, financial performance and industrial relations.

London Forest Travel (LFT) was one of the smallest subsidiaries, commencing with just three garages: Ash Grove, Leyton and Walthamstow. Its Managing Director, Thomas Young, was recruited from outside LBL. Roger Torode, the Commercial Director, had little previous sharp-end experience of either bus operations or industrial relations. After a while, the company's Engineering Director, Peter McMahon, departed for a more secure future with London Underground, leading to the appointment, from outside LBL, of Peter Duff.

From the outset, Thomas Young let it be known that his company was going to be different, that his way of doing things would not necessarily be the traditional LBL way. This was reflected in the managerial appointments made at garage level, some of which caused eyebrows to be raised on both sides of the industrial relations fence within the LBL network.

And things certainly were different.

The TGWU found that in the early days of the company there was a lack of respect for agreements and procedures. Often, this was born of ignorance, as many managers and directors had little knowledge of these agreements and procedures. But this was coupled with an unusually parsimonious approach to such matters as time off for trade union duties. The company was proud of its slim administration at head office level; in practice, this meant that agreements reached at the regular (increasingly irregular, in fact) meetings between the company and the TGWU would not be implemented for months, as such matters were given low priority when it came to allocating tight administrative resources. The company certainly gave the impression that it accorded little importance to good industrial relations, leading Ash Grove Branch Chairman Ken McMahon to quip: "It seems we have to continually draw ourselves to their attention." This impression was strengthened by the fact that the Managing Director rarely attended meetings with the trade union.

It might have been expected that, given its proud reputation as a tight employer, LFT would be a sound financial performer. Such was not the case. The first set of annual accounts reveal that LFT, with a staff total of 1,407, made a loss of £2,158,000. Neighbouring East London, with fifty percent more staff, managed to record a lower loss-figure. To an extent, LFT's unnecessarily high overheads were to blame. The forecourt of Clapton Garage, originally closed some years earlier, was opened up in 1989 when the company commenced two midibus routes. The following year, the whole of Clapton was re-opened when route 38 was transferred from Leyton. Given the fact that LFT had lost tendered routes to East London and Kentish Bus, it was essentially a three-garage company at this stage; but it insisted on being a four-garage company. The fact that a large proportion of LFT's work was tendered should have meant that its financial performance was healthier, as LBL's subsidiaries are required to make a profit of at least five percent on tendered and commercial operations. The figures quoted above, then, were indicative of impending crisis.

The bulk of LFT's tendered work was at Walthamstow Garage. In 1988, the Walthamstow network of routes had been the subject of negotiated contracts with LRT. These were awarded to Eastern National and Forest District (the forerunner of LFT). At the time, the basic wage-rate at Walthamstow Garage was maintained, although the anniversary date was moved from March to November, hours were lengthened and changes were made to some other elements of pay.

Normally, London Transport will extend contracts if the incumbent operator is performing satisfactorily. However, in early 1991 the routes at Walthamstow were put out to tender as the initial three-year contract drew to an end. LFT invited the TGWU to enter pre-tender discussions, but the union responded by advising the company not to bid on the basis of reduced wages and conditions.

In the weeks which followed, LFT made ominous noises to the effect that if it retained the contracts there would need to be some hard talking once the results were announced. The company appeared to take no note, however, of the fact that it would be confronted with a workforce which, for the reasons outlined above, had become extremely disenchanted with its employer. London Forest was about to make the biggest blunder it is possible for an employer to make: having alienated many of its workers over the previous two years or more, it was about to make outrageous demands of them and, in so doing, give them the opportunity to play for keeps.

Demonstration outside 'The Slaughterhouse', Monday, 15th July, 1991

CHAPTER TWO:
THE STORM-CLOUDS GATHER

"CHAMPION!"

In early 1991 the TGWU and LFT's Commercial Director spent a considerable amount of time collating all current agreements and procedures covering the operating staff. This exercise was conducted at the union's suggestion, the aim being to make a joint presentation of the most important of these documents to a seminar of managers and union representatives in an attempt to ensure that the agreements were understood and respected. The last meeting on this matter took place on 27 February.

In the meantime, the deadline for the submission of the Walthamstow bids was 18 March. As it was thought that the results would be announced in early May, LFT arranged to hold a meeting with all staff representatives and union full-time officers on 2 May. When the results were delayed, the company postponed this meeting. A month passed. Then the news broke: LFT had been re-awarded the Walthamstow routes.

LFT immediately published a special issue of its in-house journal, Rumours, sporting the self-congratulatory headline: "CHAMPION". The result was described as "really welcome news for everyone who has anxiously awaited the result of the Walthamstow retenders..." Tucked away in the bottom righthand corner in extremely small print was a paragraph which read: "Another Rumours Special will be published shortly, outlining the detailed changes being discussed with your representatives." Those representatives found this publication to be little more than an exercise in bad taste; but it was consistent with LFT's management style.

Rumours
LONDON BUSES
NEWS FOR EVERYONE AT LONDON FOREST TRAVEL
Special Issue 27

CHAMPION!

Today, 31 May, we have learned that London Forest has been awarded the contract' by London Transport to continue to run all eleven of the Walthamstow Area tendered services. This is really welcome news for everyone who has anxiously awaited the result of the Walthamstow retenders which - at 90 buses, 300 jobs and a complete garage - have a major impact on the whole of the London Forest company.

WALTHAMSTOW TENDERS SPECIAL 31 MAY 1991

LONDON FOREST

"An exercise in bad taste"

The company's meeting with staff representatives on the morning of 5 June was brief enough. Managing Director Thomas Young explained that the contract-prices on which LFT had won the tenders had due regard for the realities of the "market-place". In 1989/90 the company had lost work by tendering on the basis of the current package of wages and conditions enjoyed by the staff at Walthamstow. The retention of the Walthamstow network now meant that around a half of the company's work was tendered. Once the whole of LBL was in a similar position, all eyes would be on the cost of the remaining "block-grant" routes (i.e. those in receipt of straightforward subsidy), and it was possible that LBL would implement a system of internal tendering. Better for us, said Young, to lower our costs now than to submit to internal tendering.

The company would be looking to reduce costs in three areas: labour, support costs (principally engineering) and overheads. With regard to labour, LFT would be seeking to negotiate new wages and conditions for all operating and skilled engineering staff, with the first meetings being held that afternoon. Eighteen non-skilled engineers' jobs would be shed. Leyton Garage would close.

6

The real enemy, said Young, was the competition. By reducing costs now, jobs would not only be preserved in LFT but could be increased: routes operated by Thamesway and Leaside were up for tender at the moment and LFT would bid at the same price as it had for the Walthamstow routes, so there was an excellent prospect of success.

Young was heard out in stony silence. When he was through, it was pointed out from the floor that it was all very well for him to brand the competition as the enemy, but it was almost certain that his staff would have a different view once they heard the company's proposals for wages and conditions. During a brief question-and-answer session, Young confirmed that the contracts had been awarded to LFT on a provisional basis, subject to the company demonstrating that it could get enough staff to work under the new conditions.

THE FIRST SKIRMISH

The TGWU was already in a combative mood and its London bus membership was already being mobilised, the mood being sharpened, due to the government's Green Paper on deregulation which had been issued in March. The Union's London Divisional Committee had drawn up a response to this and hundreds of members had attended a rally at Transport House on 7 May, prior to accompanying Deputy General Secretary Bill Morris when he presented the document to the Department of Transport. A public campaign was being planned , with petitions and posters being produced.

Now, the TGWU representatives absorbed the morning's news. Although Young had not spelled it out, it appeared that the company would be proposing wage-cuts at all four garages, not just Walthamstow. The true extent of this insult was only apparent when one realised that the original purpose of the afternoon meeting had been to negotiate a wage-increase for staff on the block-grant routes at Ash Grove and Clapton, the submission for which had been sent to the company in January. Even so, the hand of the TGWU would be greatly strengthened if all four garages were involved as the company would be unable to isolate Walthamstow.

The longer the representatives discussed the matter, the higher the stakes appeared. If LFT succeeded in imposing the wage-reductions, it would be in a position to win practically all future tenders in north and east London. It would not do so, of course, because all other companies would be forced to reduce their wages to the same level. Thus, victory for the company would mean an acceleration in the downward spiral for wages and conditions. Conversely, a victory for TGWU members in LFT would be a victory for all London busworkers.

That afternoon's meeting between the TGWU operating staff representatives and LFT was an ill-tempered affair. The union began by reminding the company that the annual wage-increase for block-grant staff was overdue and suggested that LFT put forward a realistic offer. Commercial Director Roger Torode (Young was not in attendance) stated that this could not be done; he then confirmed that the company wished to discuss wage-cuts at all garages and began, with the assistance of his colleagues, to outline the proposed changes. The basic week (for pay purposes only) would be increased from 38 to 40 hours. There would be no agreed limits on schedule conditions other than those provided by the law. Holidays would be reduced to 15 days, rising to 20 days after two years' service (as opposed to 20 days, rising to 25 days after five years' service). The day in lieu for working on a public holiday would be withdrawn. There would be no unsocial hours' payments, other than for night duties. No sick pay would be paid during the first year's service or at any time for the first three days of sickness; after the first four weeks of sickness, it would only be paid at management's discretion; the rate of sick pay would be reduced by 20 percent. No overtime would be paid until 40 hours had been completed, and then only at time-and-a-quarter (as opposed to time-and-two-thirds for weekdays and double time at weekends). Hourly rates would be £5.20 (OPO drivers), £4.60 (midibus drivers), £4.60 (crew drivers), £4 (existing conductors) and £3.50 (new conductors). In return for an extra payment of seven minutes, drivers would be expected to take their vehicles through the fuel bay and the wash.

In addition, there were proposals to introduce changes in industrial relations procedures, with most of these being concentrated at garage level. The quarterly Joint Consultative Committee meetings would now be held "as necessary". Changes were proposed to the disciplinary procedure - including the right of a manager to increase the penalty of a member of staff on appeal! A final clause stated: "All existing agreements, procedures and practices are cancelled except where stated above." Thus, the agreements and procedures so painstakingly collated by both the TGWU and LFT until as late as February were now being thrown out of the window!

Needless to say, the monetary aspects generated most anger on the union side. Even with the additional hours which some operating staff would be expected to work, the average reduction was 20 percent. The most dramatic cut was proposed for the 32 drivers on Leyton's "heavy" rota - 26 percent, or £72.90 per week! For most other staff, apart from Night Bus drivers, the weekly reductions would be between £40 and £50. Rubbing salt into the wound, LFT proclaimed: "There will be no fixed anniversary date: the rates of pay and conditions will be reviewed as deemed necessary by management. The Trade Union will have the right to request a review." However, staff with ten years' service would receive full compensation for their financial loss - although for the first year only. All other staff would be compensated for ten percent of their loss for each year of service - again, for one year only.

Both the document which outlined these proposals and the performance of LFT's representatives that afternoon were particularly inept. A member of the management team, seeing from the TGWU's reaction that the proposal he was outlining was considered to be particularly outrageous, actually snorted with laughter! The document itself was little more than a suicide note. It is of course common for both managers and trade unionists to commence negotiations by adopting an exaggerated position. But LFT's proposals were so obscene that they could not be taken seriously. That is not to say that most of them were not seriously intended: indeed, the TGWU could see that some of the procedures the company wanted to change were the very ones over which there had been differences in the past. As we shall see, the document was not even accurate with regard to the loss of earnings it calculated for Walthamstow staff. But the greatest error from the company's point of view was that the proposals and the way in which they were presented engendered in the union side the feeling that there was now nothing to lose, and that for the first time in over two years individuals might just as well speak and act as their feelings concerning London Forest Travel dictated. There was little point in being constrained by a concern for the future of the union's relationship with the company, because it was quite apparent that the relationship had no future.

Now the company suggested that it would be willing to consider the TGWU's initial comments and hold a further meeting. In response, the union expressed amazement at the fact that LFT appeared to be playing games on such a vital issue. Were the proposals serious or not? What the membership required was a document outlining the definitive proposals, so that they could decide what they thought of them. "Don't you realise," the prophetic question was put to the LFT team, "that the future of your company is hanging by a thread? We're not here to play games, so give us the bottom line so that we all know where we are!"

LFT replied that the proposals were negotiable, but only within the confines of the package which had been outlined. Thus, improvements in one area would imply a worsening in another. That seemed clear enough. The TGWU stated that, given the depth of the cuts, such "negotiations" would be meaningless and that its members would now be consulted.

THE TGWU STRATEGY

It was at this point that the union began to pay serious attention to the contradiction inherent in tendering. LFT's low bid had - at least for the moment - won the contracts but, given such a drastic reduction in wages and conditions would the company get staff to work the routes? More to the point, the contracts had been awarded provisionally. If, therefore, it could be demonstrated that LFT could not persuade its workforce to accept the new conditions, London Transport would re-award the contracts to the company which came second.

In an undertaking the size of London Transport, there have always been leaks of sensitive information. One such leak now provided the union with the knowledge that in second place for the Walthamstow routes had been not one but three companies. Ensign Citybus (hereafter called Citybus, as the company has recently changed its name to Capital Citybus) had come second on all the big-bus OPO work, while County Bus and Thamesway had come second for the midibus routes. It was easy enough to discover what wages and conditions they were offering. County Bus and Thamesway were TGWU-organised and their agreements were common knowledge. Citybus, however, was a non-union company. But in the previous months the TGWU had been recruiting members there, and TGWU District Officer Ken Fuller had already met the Managing Director to discuss the way in which recognition might be approached. During the ongoing recruitment exercises, Citybus drivers quoted the wage-rates which the company had been planning to pay on the Walthamstow routes. This information was later confirmed by the company itself.

All three companies were offering rates which were clearly in excess of those proposed by LFT. This placed the union and its London Forest members in an extremely strong position. A campaign of industrial action could be commenced with the aim of forcing LFT to increase the wage-rates. If this failed, or if the action itself caused London Transport to re-award the contracts, there would still be jobs with the other companies and the rates would be superior to those proposed by LFT.

Given that the only "negotiations" which LFT was prepared to enter would have consisted of juggling the various elements of the package, there seemed no point in delay. Therefore, the four Branches arranged meetings at which the Branch Representatives would report back to the members, and a ballot for industrial action was planned for Friday, 14 June . The engineering staff representatives agreed to adopt the same programme .

In one sense, the strategy adopted was completely new. Never before in the London area had the TGWU been in a position to "play the market", using as a benchmark the wage-rates paid by unsuccessful tenderers . In effect, the TGWU was putting LFT out to tender! This lent a special irony to Thomas Young's statement that his proposals had due regard for the "realities of the market-place". For years, London busworkers had been lectured about the need to "consider the realities of the market-place". Now, in somewhat different circumstances than those envisaged by those giving the lecture, they were to do precisely that.

The union's strategy also made a clean break with the past in another sense. Previously within LBL, with very few exceptions the media had been kept at arm's length during industrial disputes . In the run-up to the dispute in LFT, however, it was decided to make full use of the newspapers, television and radio, utilising the contacts made on the deregulation issue and cultivating new ones. If the dispute was protracted, media exposure would bolster morale and, in view of the issue, would win widespread public sympathy.

THE FIRST BALLOT

Before the ballot on 14 June, the propaganda war commenced, with LFT issuing a circular to all staff in which it listed the wage-rates paid by some other operators.[2] Either by accident or design, the information given was neither fully correct nor comprehensive. The rate quoted for Citybus took no account of the 1991 wage-rise or the weekly bonus, and no mention was made of the superior conditions (for example on sick-pay) available at County Bus. Also, the rate shown for County Bus was the big-bus wage, whereas it was on the midibus routes that this company was in the running. Four other companies were listed, none of which had been serious contenders (if they had bid at all!) for the Walthamstow routes. A further circular, issued the day before the strike ballot, threatened that staff refusing an offer of continued employment on new terms would have their employment terminated, with no redundancy payments, at the expiry of "the due notice period". Any industrial action, the company warned, would constitute a breach of contract and staff could be dismissed.

The results of the operating staff's ballot made it quite clear that the TGWU members were not about to be swayed by either threats or misleading information. First, those voting were asked whether they wished the TGWU to continue negotiations within the limits set by the company's proposals. Only 83 voted "Yes", while 627 voted "No". With regard to industrial action, the results were as follows.

ACTON SHORT OF STRIKE	Yes	No
ASH GROVE	265	1
CLAPTON	151	14
LEYTON	70	49
WALTHAMSTOW	146	8
TOTAL	632	2

STRIKE ACTION	Yes	No
ASH GROVE	267	1
CLAPTON	158	8
LEYTON	118	3
WALTHAMSTOW	47	8
TOTAL	690	20

Larry Laurent, Inside Staff Convenor

Thus, the union was given an overwhelming mandate to take both forms of action (and even the large "No" vote for non-strike action at Leyton was explained by the fact that members there were determined that nothing short of a strike would do). On a turnout of over 70 percent, slightly more than 97 percent were in favour of strike action. For the engineers, the result was 93 percent. This was a vivid illustration of the depth of the members' anger and determination. As we shall see, however, this same anger had led to undue haste in the construction of the ballot-paper, and this would be challenged by the company.

THE COMPANY SHIFTS ITS POSITION

On Monday, 17 June, the TGWU faxed a letter to the LFT Managing Director, outlining the ballot result and making the following demands:

a) that LFT's proposals be dropped for all operating and engineering staff;

b) that the current wages and conditions of staff employed within the Walthamstow network continue unchanged, subject to the annual increase due in November;

c) that a wage-increase be agreed for those whose rise was due in May.

Young faxed a reply in which he undertook to withdraw the present proposals and leave the rates and conditions intact at Walthamstow until November. However, new contracts would still be required at this garage. Separate negotiations were proposed for staff on the block-grant routes, "in accordance with the anniversary clauses in current agreements, and taking account of our business situation."[3]

Broadening its strategy, the same day the TGWU wrote to the Office of Fair Trading, pointing out that the sequence of events in LFT (principally the collation of existing agreements, the failure of LT to announce the tender results in early May and then, following the announcement weeks later, the proposal that most of the collated agreements be ditched) led to a number of questions. Was it the case that LFT's original bid had failed and that the company was then allowed to change that bid? Was London Transport really motivated by a desire to prepare its own subsidiaries for deregulation? In this regard, *Bus Business* in its issue of 15 June had reported: "Young says the approach to cost cutting followed by Forest must be followed by similar moves by other LBL subsidiary operators if they too are to become competitive in the run-up to privatisation and deregulation." Finally, had LFT been awarded the Walthamstow network in return for a pledge that the wages and conditions of all staff, not just those on the tendered routes, would be reduced?[4] Weeks later, the TGWU received a reply from the OFT which indicated that this was a matter solely for London Transport, but that the contracts appeared to have been awarded fairly;[5] by this stage, however, the dispute was well on the way to being resolved by other means.

This same afternoon, the TGWU held a press conference at its Grays Inn Road office at which the ballot result was announced. That evening there was an opportunity to see if this media treatment was having the desired effect, as the Shop Stewards and District Officer Ken Fuller met at Ash Grove to plan the dispute. Several people at the meeting reported that their members had seen the early-evening report on *Thames News* and were buoyed up by the exposure.

At the meeting, it was decided that the concessions made by Young earlier that day were too vague. Thus, a one-day strike was planned for Thursday, 20 June, when a mass meeting would be held at the Hackney Empire at 11 a.m. Here, the members would be asked to give the Joint Shop Stewards Committee the authority to organise an indefinite strike in the near future. In the meantime, the company would be pressed to make substantial improvements in the Walthamstow package and to table a firm wage increase for all other staff.

LAWYERS ACHIEVE PYRRHIC VICTORY

The following day, District Officer Ken Fuller and he TGWU's convenor Steve Cushion were due to meet LFT's Roger Torode for one of the regular meetings to discuss matters of company-wide concern. It had already been decided that the subject matter should be switched and the meeting devoted to injecting some clarity into the undertakings faxed over by Young the previous day. Arriving early at the LFT headquarters (dubbed "the slaughterhouse" by Cushion after his first few visits there), Fuller was told that his office wished to speak to him urgently. Telephoning Headland House, he heard that a fax had arrived from LFT which claimed that the paper used in the previous Friday's ballot had been defective and that legal action would follow unless the strike was called off. Why LFT had faxed him at 12.55 p.m. when it was known that he would be at its offices for a 2.30 meeting remains a mystery!

When Cushion arrived, he and Fuller repaired to the former's home in order to speak to the union's Legal Department without the risk of being overheard. The advice received was that the ballot paper was indeed defective, leaving no alternative: the strike and the mass meeting would have to be called off. Despite a shaky start to the afternoon, the immediate task was still to force the company into making as many concessions as possible. The Branch Representatives were contacted and told to convene at LFT's headquarters.

Sometime later than anticipated, and with almost the whole of the TGWU's team for the operating staff present, the meeting with the company got underway. Much of the time was spent in attempting to get the company to place a sufficiently clear and unambiguous interpretation on Young's letter of the previous day (Young himself being absent from the meeting). This was finally achieved, and in the early evening the TGWU side emerged with a letter signed by Torode which gave the union negotiators all they could have hoped for at this stage.

> "Firstly, our document on revised wages and conditions for London Forest Operating Staff has been withdrawn.
>
> "Secondly, wages and conditions of all operating staff on block grant routes at Ash Grove and Hackney [Clapton] are guaranteed subject to the negotiation of a wage increase to be back dated to the anniversary date.
>
> "Thirdly, platform staff at Leyton will not be compulsorily transferred to worse pay and conditions at another garage, when Leyton closes.
>
> "Fourthly, we will meet at 08.30 on Friday next, 21 June, to discuss platform staff pay and conditions at Walthamstow when we will commence negotiations afresh."[6]

The TGWU then typed up a notice to be displayed alongside this letter in all four garages. This explained why the strike had been called off and continued:

> "...the company has shifted its ground considerably and this constitutes a major victory for the TGWU and its members.
>
> "However, we still have a long way to go with the negotiations for Walthamstow and other negotiating groups. We trust that our members will remain firm in their resolve to defend wages and conditions."

As is evident in the tone of this notice, the union was, after a nerve-wracking start to the afternoon, confident that it had regained the initiative. The company, on the other hand, appeared to be lulled into a false sense of security.

ROUND TWO

On Friday, 21 June the TGWU's team of Fuller, Cushion, Eddie Hayes and Lucien Hoebeeck met LFT, taking up the company's offer to start again with "a clean sheet of paper" with regard to the Walthamstow contracts.

Torode announced that, while no movement could be made on the midibus hourly rates (which would affect Clapton as well as Walthamstow), the rate for big bus drivers could be increased to £5.55 per hour. A further 2.5 percent was available if the members were prepared to forego any further increase until September, 1993. Sick pay would now suffer a reduction of "only" ten percent. Alternatively, the £5.20 per hour could remain as originally proposed, in return for an unsocial hours' premium of 15 percent on weekends, public holidays and after 8 p.m. on weekdays. In return for either of these options, the compensation package would be reduced, with a maximum of £1,000. Although the proposal for reduced annual leave entitlement would remain, no current staff would lose their existing entitlement. It was further proposed that there be a system of heavy and light rotas, with the heavy rota featuring work of up to 45 to 50 hours' time on duty (excluding non-productive "spreadover" time and meal reliefs), while the light rota would contain work of around 35 hours' duration (in return, of course, for only 35 hours' pay). London Transport's Tendered Bus Division, explained Torode, required a firm assurance by 5 July that the routes could be operated by LFT. The company would prefer to negotiate the change in contracts rather than issuing staff with notices of termination.

Fuller asked Torode if he would give an assurance that wages and conditions would not be reduced in this fashion in future in order to win tenders. Torode replied that he was unable to give this assurance. Fuller then asked if further improvements in the package were possible, to which Torode replied that no further funds were available.

During the adjournment, Steve Cushion remarked that the "clean sheet of paper" looked remarkably like the old sheet of paper, apart from the extra 35p on the big bus rate, and even this had been achieved partly at the expense of the compensation payments! The new rate was then compared with what Citybus would pay, using both long and short jobs as examples. On both counts, Citybus came out way ahead - significantly so in the case of the long job. It was at this point, by poring over the figures, that LFT's blunder was discovered. Surely, the union team thought, £1,000 could not compensate in full for the loss of earnings! The document tabled by LFT on 5 June was consulted once more - and there was the answer. The company had used the wrong figures! The "current" rates it had used for Walthamstow were in fact a year out of date, taking no account of the 9.3 percent wage-rise in November, 1990. Thus, the original proposal would have meant a reduction for big bus drivers of £2,907 a year, not the £1,880 claimed by the company! Similarly, the true loss for midibus drivers was not 8.7 percent as the company had claimed, but 16.6 percent! Even with today's extra 35p per hour, Walthamstow big bus drivers were still being asked to take a reduction of 16 percent in rostered earnings for a 40-hour week - over £2,180 a year. The more the union negotiators analysed the figures, the angrier they became.

Following the adjournment, the company representatives were given both barrels.

History, the union reminded them, usually repeated itself first as tragedy and then as farce. In LFT, it was the reverse. Tuesday had seen the farce, with the company negotiators walking out after Eddie Hayes had lost his temper - despite the fact that it was LFT which was desperate for an agreement! Today, it was the turn of tragedy - but it was a tragedy for the company, not for the TGWU or its members.

Earlier in the week, the company had introduced the law into industrial relations. If that was the way LFT wanted it, so be it: in future, any infringement of the drivers hours' regulations would be reported to the Department of Transport.

Now, LFT was proposing to reduce wages by 16 percent or more, its original figures having been just as misleading as the rates for other companies which it had circulated to staff earlier. The TGWU membership at Walthamstow would not accept such a reduction. Moreover, the members at the other garages had not been reassured that they would not be subjected to similar treatment in the future. Therefore, there would be report-back meetings at all four garages, with a further ballot for industrial action on Friday, 28 June.

The real tragedy, the union concluded, was for the managers and directors of the company, as it was their jobs which were at risk. The drivers would be needed elsewhere if the routes were re-awarded - and on better terms than LFT was offering. The reputations of management could be rescued, however: by publicly resigning, publicly denouncing the auction of jobs, wages and conditions that was tendering and by joining with the TGWU in its demand for a public inquiry into bus operations in London.

After a further brief adjournment, the company representatives declined to follow this advice and indicated that there was no money left for further improvements.

In preparation for the report-back meetings at the garages on 25 June (where the formal decision on a further ballot would also be taken), the TGWU issued a four-page booklet which outlined the situation and corrected the misleading information circulated by LFT concerning the rates paid by other companies. The booklet concluded:

> "Needless to say, there is a clear risk that London Forest will now lose the Walthamstow contracts. That prospect should frighten no one but the directors and managers of London Forest. Our members at Walthamstow and those on the tendered routes at Clapton will still have jobs - even if their employer changes.
>
> "Until this dispute is settled, no one should resign from the company or even think of doing so. If the time comes when you need to seek employment with other operators who may be awarded the Walthamstow contracts, the TGWU will move heaven and earth to see that you are accommodated.
>
> "UNTIL THEN, SIT TIGHT AND REMAIN FIRM IN YOUR RESOLVE!"7

ENTER THOMAS YOUNG

Until this point, LFT's Managing Director had played no part in the negotiations, leaving this to Roger Torode, his Commercial Director. Torode was also assigned the thankless task of explaining to the media why LFT was reducing wages and conditions. Young's absence came to play a part in the propaganda war. When he was quoted in *Bus Business* as saying that LFT was "up against a union which doesn't care about its members' jobs"[8], Fuller wrote to put the record straight and, in so doing, pointed out that "We fail to see how Mr. Young could have arrived at his conclusion anyway, as he had not seen fit to attend the meetings which had taken place prior to the publication of your story."[9]

"A widely held view"

14

In its own contribution to the propaganda war, the company had less regard for the truth. In the minutes it produced of the meetings of 18 June and 21 June, comments made by the TGWU's Fuller were distorted. For example, he was alleged to have said: "So what, I don't care about their (the members') jobs."[10] Needless to say, this comment was never made. The minutes, however, were not submitted to Fuller for agreement, and even before he had seen a copy a junior manager read them aloud in the canteen at Walthamstow! He was quickly pulled up by Lucien Hoebeeck, the local TGWU Rep. From this, the reader should be able to gauge the level of professionalism displayed by London Forest and to gain some insight into why the bitter resentment of the staff ran so deep.

Finally, Thomas Young put in an appearance - deciding, with the second ballot approaching, that he had better call another meeting. Although Fuller was on annual leave this week, he had not gone away and the company had his number. But he received no call. Instead, Young suggested the further meeting to Oli Jackson, the union's Regional Passenger Officer, who happened to be in his office on a disciplinary appeal. Oli, however, made it clear that he would be playing it straight, telephoning Fuller in Young's presence. Asked if he thought if there would be merit in another meeting, Fuller said there would be - but only if new money was available; and if there was, Young should be told to stop buggering about. Oli then asked Young if there would be new money on the table. Young was heard to say that there would be. Thus, a meeting was arranged for the afternoon on 27 June, the day before the second ballot.

The meeting began with Fuller explaining the agreed constitution of the negotiating committee to Young: this provided for the attendance of the Managing Director at all meetings, not just on those occasions when the union's Regional Officer was present. Furthermore, it was pointed out that the minutes of previous meetings had been distorted and circulated before they had been agreed. (The company not only ignored this complaint, but distorted the minutes of the current meeting so that Fuller was alleged to have said that he did not want Oli Jackson present!) It also emerged that LFT had completely ignored the negotiating machinery, having held a meeting between the Commercial Director and the three Walthamstow Branch Officers the previous day. One can only assume that this was an attempt to introduce divisions in the trade union side; if so, this met with failure. The company had used the meeting to ask what kind of package the Walthamstow membership would find acceptable, in response to which the Branch Officers had stated that current earnings should be protected. LFT had said that it would consider this, and arranged for all three Branch Officers (instead of just the Branch Representative) to attend the meeting of the negotiating committee the following day.

As the meeting got underway, Torode announced that the company could now present a package which protected earnings. This would mean, however, an average rostered week (excluding meal reliefs and non-productive "spreadover" time) of 48 hours. The maximum spreadover would be 14 hours a day. A further £2 per day would be paid to all staff who arrived on time and completed a full duty. There would be a review of wages in November, 1992, said Young, although this would be "not contractural but agreed" - whatever that meant!

Thus, whereas at first the company had been demanding a reduction in earnings of around 20 percent, they were now prepared to guarantee current earnings - if staff would agree to work 20 percent longer instead! This package, claimed the company, represented "a lot of fresh thinking". When asked if the weekly earnings could be guaranteed for an average working week of less than 48 hours, LFT said that it could not: this was as far as the company could go. Indeed, the directors said, in order to win future tenders it might not be possible to guarantee such terms.

Oli Jackson reminded Young that he had promised "new money" at this meeting and invited him to identify it. Young was unable to do so.

Once again, the union's negotiating team compared what was on offer with what the competing companies could offer. Once again, LFT came up short. After an adjournment, the TGWU put forward the view that it had been duped into the meeting. New money had been promised, but it could not be identified. Even if it was there, it was clearly insufficient. Therefore, the union indicated that the ballot would go ahead the following day. The company might be prepared to mislead the union, but the TGWU was not prepared to mislead its members. For Young's benefit, the union repeated the advice offered at the previous meeting - that LFT's directors should rescue their reputations by resigning.

That evening, the Walthamstow Branch Officers reported back to their Branch Committee on both the "unofficial" meeting with Torode and the negotiating meeting. The Committee rejected the latest offer.

THE MEMBERSHIP REMAINS FIRM

On 28 June, the day of the second ballot, LFT issued a circular to staff in a clear attempt to influence the vote. This claimed that the TGWU had on various occasions either "refused discussions" or had turned down proposals "without discussion". This theme was pursued by the company throughout, obviously believing that the word "negotiation" could only be applied to circumstances in which the union accepted that the total size of the package was not negotiable! "Your Union," the circular went on, "tell you to 'stand firm' but they won't lose their jobs out of this - you may well do so." The document then promised guaranteed earnings of £270 for big bus drivers and £225 for midibus drivers - but the length of the working week received no mention! Moreover, the company claimed that "THE RATES WE NOW OFFER ARE HIGHER THAN THOSE OF THE COMPETITOR QUOTED TO YOU BY YOUR UNION."[11] This claim was simply untrue.

For a number of reasons, this dishonest attempt to influence the vote met with abject failure. First, the membership knew it was dishonest. Secondly, the TGWU had ensured that its LFT membership was kept fully-informed at every stage of the proceedings, involving them in the decision-making process at Branch Meetings. Thirdly, the union's decision to make full use of the media, issuing regular press releases and maintaining contact with the local newspapers, was paying off. Not only were the members gratified to see their case reported, but morale was significantly boosted by members of the public who, having picked up the story from the media themselves, went out of their way to express their support to individual drivers or conductors.

The TGWU conducted the second ballot on two separate bases: staff on the Walthamstow network were asked whether they wished to take strike or other industrial action concerning the immediate threat to their wages and conditions; staff elsewhere in London Forest were asked the same question but in relation to the company's refusal to give an undertaking that wages and conditions would not in future be subject to this kind of attack. This ensured that those staff outside of the Walthamstow network knew precisely what they would be striking for.

The results were remarkably similar to the first ballot. With a 65 percent turnout of voters in the Walthamstow network, 93 percent were in favour of strike action and 92 percent in favour of other forms of industrial action. Elsewhere, the turnout was 73 percent and the "Yes" votes were 97.1 percent and 92.3 percent, respectively, with a similar result for the engineers.

Thus, the membership had heeded the TGWU's advice to "stand firm"!

BEFORE THE STORM

On Monday, 1 July, the TGWU's Fuller wrote to Young to advise him of the ballot result and to ask that the proposals for Walthamstow be withdrawn and that an undertaking be given that wages and conditions elsewhere would not be reduced in order to win or retain future tenders. Torode replied two days later, advising the union that Young was on holiday. Both requests were turned down.

Also on 1 July, LFT wrote to all Walthamstow drivers, setting out the revised proposals and giving them notice of termination of their contracts of employment. This was obviously an attempt to panic staff into accepting the new terms on an individual basis and to demonstrate to London Transport that the company would have enough staff to operate the new contracts from 23 November. Each member of staff was asked to sign to accept the new conditions by 5 p.m. on Friday, 12 July. The document made it clear that the overtime rate would only be paid after the completion of 48 hours. Staff who did not wish to work 48 hours (with a maximum spreadover of 60 hours) for £270 could volunteer to work for less: for example, 44 hours for £242 or 40 hours for £214.

The TGWU advised its members by circular that, on the basis of a 48-hour week, the package was even worse than it seemed at first sight. Assuming that Walthamstow drivers would otherwise have received a five percent wage rise at their November anniversary date, the proposal meant that big-bus drivers were being asked to work 20 percent longer and receive 9.57 percent less than 48 hours would generate at current rates. The loss for midibus drivers would be over six percent. The union also pointed out that LFT appeared to be offering different hourly rates, depending on the length of the working week: £5.62 per hour for a 48-hour week, £5.50 per hour for a 44-hour week and £5.35 per hour for a 40-hour week. The TGWU's circular to Walthamstow members warned that:

> "In the days ahead, the managers and directors of London Forest will pull every trick to demoralise and weaken your resolve...
>
> "You have now given us a mandate for strike and other industrial action. This will commence as soon as the necessary authority is received from our General Secretary.
>
> "In the meantime - STAND FIRM."

In fact, it was announced on the afternoon of 2 July that TGWU General Secretary Ron Todd had given the authorisation for the action to commence. The strike could now proceed quite lawfully.

The shop stewards decided to call a one-day strike on Thursday, 4 July. This would be followed by a further strike on 11 July, when a mass meeting would be called at the York Hall, Bethnal Green. At this meeting a recommendation would be made for an indefinite strike.

In the meantime, the union attempted to bring whatever legal pressure it could on the employer, arguing that the two weeks which Walthamstow staff had been given to make up their minds was inadequate. The company, however, indicated that its own legal advice did not support this contention. The definitive view of the TGWU's Legal Department arrived on 9 July, five days after the one-day strike, pointing out that staff who did not accept the new contracts and who were thus dismissed on 22 November "may, depending on the circumstances, have a claim for unfair dismissal." If staff accepted the terms of the new contract, "the courts are reluctant to find a consensual variation of a contract of employment where an employee is faced with the alternative of dismissal and the variation is contrary to his or her interests. It is possible that there may be grounds for claims of unfair (constructive) dismissal at a later date."[12]

The choices, therefore, were: go ahead with the strike or attempt to sort the whole matter out by means of several hundred Industrial Tribunal applications at a later stage. Quite obviously, the strike would go ahead.

In fact, it would commence a day earlier than planned.

CHAPTER THREE: THE STRIKE

"TIES AND CRAVATS OPTIONAL"

On 10 July, Walthamstow drivers received another letter from LFT and a stamped, addressed envelope by means of which the new terms could be accepted by post. This was presumably motivated by the fact that very few drivers had so far signed and by the hope that while staff might be wary of handing their forms in at the garage, they might be willing to use the post. Angered by this latest ploy, Walthamstow Branch Representative Lucien Hoebeeck called his members in off the road and during the course of the day the other three Branches followed suit.

The longest London bus strike since 1958 had commenced.

In the weeks leading up to the strike LFT, with its usual deft approach to industrial relations and impeccable timing, issued an instruction that all company-issued neckwear must be worn. Now, the wag at Ash Grove who drafted the circular inviting all strikers to the York Hall mass meeting concluded it with the words: "Ties and cravats optional." Such humour would be a common characteristic of the dispute.

The mass meeting had been called for 11 a.m. By 10.30, only the front rows of seats in the hall were occupied and the organisers were understandably nervous. Half an hour later, however, there was hardly a seat to be found as almost a thousand striking busworkers and engineers crammed into the hall. At this time, the TGWU's policy-making Biennial Delegate Conference was meeting in Blackpool. The mass meeting heard a message, faxed over the previous day, from the conference's passenger transport delegation which stated: "Your stand in defence of your wages and conditions, and for public transport safety, demands the respect and support of all TGWU members both on and off the buses."

A further message was signed by Ron Todd (General Secretary), Bill Morris (General Secretary Elect) and Graham Stevenson (National Secretary, Passenger Services Group). On behalf of the whole BDC (which the following day would collect £700 for the LFT strikers), this message read:

"The strength of feeling, the certainty of purpose displayed by members at London Forest, in secret ballot, testifies to the unreasonableness of your employer's intentions. The 34th Biennial Delegate Conference has heard in a variety of debates of the many assaults on busworkers' wages and conditions. At a time when we ought to be seeking a reduction in scheduled hours of work, to lessen the burden of stressful duties upon busworkers, it is outrageous for a public transport company to seek to balance the consequences of the iniquitous route tendering system either by slashing wages or forcing long hours of work."

"Mass Meeting, York Hall, 11th July, 1991"

These messages of support did much to stiffen the morale and confidence of the strikers, as did the fraternal addresses at the mass meeting itself from a health worker, a local authority worker and Councillor Gerry Ross, the Mayor of Hackney.

The platform speakers gave a detailed account of the negotiations that had taken place. A key feature of any prolonged strike, it was pointed out, would be fund-raising. Thus, Branch Officers should telephone all TGWU Bus Branches in London, asking that collections be held regularly; moreover, Branch Committee members should be despatched to all London bus garages each Friday in order to raise support for these collections. In addition, each picket-line should have collection-buckets for use among the public. Quite apart from strike action, further activity was suggested, such as a demonstration of strikers' spouses outside LFT's headquarters.

"The Platform, York Hall – left to right: Pat Caughlin, Ken Fuller, Ken McMahon, Gerry Ross (Mayor of Hackney), Eddie Hayes and Bill Knowles

Most importantly, the meeting was told quite clearly that, as it seemed unlikely that LFT would improve its offer, the tactic must be to ensure that the contracts were re-awarded to the competitor-companies. At this stage, LT's Tendered Bus Unit was due to make a final decision on 18 July, so any strike would last until at least that date. If the contracts were re-awarded, the next stage of the battle would be to ensure that all staff at Walthamstow secured employment, either by transfer within London Buses, or with the companies which took over the contracts. Attempts would also be made to ensure that any staff forced to leave the employment of LBL on 22 November received redundancy payments. These tactics were clearly spelled out to the meeting and were fully accepted.

It was stressed by the platform, however, that even if all these objectives were achieved, the strike would still only have been a partial success. Why? Because the Walthamstow members would obviously like to continue on their current wages and conditions, operating their current routes at Walthamstow. That option was not on offer, due to the tendering process. A complete victory would be an end to tendering. Such a victory was not possible by strike action. This could only be achieved by a mass political campaign, involving busworkers and the public. Such a campaign should have as its focus the TGWU's call for a public inquiry. The strikers were therefore urged to take away copies of the anti-deregulation poster produced by the union and the petition produced by the Capital Transport Campaign, using these on the picket-lines (in the one-day strike the previous week, the Clapton Branch had collected 1,000 signatures in this way).

The major decision before the mass meeting- was, of course, on the recommendation that the strike be continued indefinitely. When this was put to the vote, there were just three votes against! The strikers left the hall in fighting mood.

ORGANISING FOR VICTORY

The most active participants in the LFT dispute were to rapidly learn one important lesson: that being on strike can be much harder work than driving or conducting a bus! The way these members acquitted themselves of the responsibilities before them should, however, serve as a lesson to trade unionists everywhere.

"Strike Office, Hackney"

A Strike Office was quickly established when the Hackney Trade Union Support Unit made available a room and a telephone. Deserving special mention in this regard are Tom Seabury and John Ballantyne of the Ash Grove Branch, who often put in extremely long hours, seven days a week. It was at this office that most of the work of organising "flying collectors" was done. Collectors visited public meetings in various parts of London as well as travelling to all LBL garages each Friday to assist in collections.

On the picket-lines, collecting buckets were much in evidence, as were the petitions calling for the public inquiry into London's bus services. The Ash Grove Branch was particularly brazen in its approach to fund-raising, their pickets walking up and down the lines of traffic in Mare Street with their buckets. The police did nothing - apart from sounding their horns in support! Members of the Walthamstow Branch made several visits to the local greyhound track, persuading punters to put a quid or two on the striking busworkers. This Branch also kept its spirits high by plastering the front of "the slaughterhouse" with slogans based on puns of the LFT directors' names, such as "WE'RE ON TORODE TO RUIN" and, in an allusion to the Wandsworth brewery, "YOUNG MAKES US BITTER."

Also deserving of mention with regard to fund-raising is TGWU District Officer Pat Mahon, who circulated his Branches in south London as soon as he heard of the decision of the mass meeting to go for an indefinite strike.

The union's Regional Office also circulated all Branches with a financial appeal. Thus, all possible steps were taken to ensure that the strikers' financial suffering was eased. By the time the last donations had arrived, a total of just over £60,000 had been collected. In addition, the Strike Headquarters in Hackney drew up guidelines for claiming from the DSS and members also received £24 per week in official strike pay from the TGWU.

Apart from arranging financial support, the strike organisers also realised the importance of keeping morale as high as possible by ensuring that members were regularly involved in various events; and if they chose not to be involved, they would see from the media that something was happening. So an "event" - demonstration, march or mass meeting - was held every few days. For example, on Monday, 15 July, four days after the first mass meeting, a demonstration was held outside "the slaughterhouse", with spouses of the strikers in attendance. The Walthamstow Branch also made doubly sure that the public knew why their buses were off the road, issuing a leaflet explaining the main issues of the dispute. This was produced with assistance from the Waltham Forest Trade Union Support Centre which, towards the end of the strike, also began to assist in the formation of a Busworkers' Support Group.

"Raising Funds"

UNCONVENTIONAL TACTICS

Predictably, TGWU members at LBL garages not directly involved in the dispute began to talk in terms of taking action in support of the LFT strikers. Such demands were vociferous in garages (particularly West Ham) in the neighbouring LBL subsidiary of East London. A West Ham driver asked to speak at the 15 July demonstration, expressing the view that his Branch should be on strike as well. In Leaside, the Stamford Hill Branch curtailed its route 253 buses at Clapton Pond for several days, a display of solidarity which did much for the morale of the strikers in Hackney.

The TGWU actively dissuaded non-LFT Branches from taking industrial action. This was due to several factors. The most obvious was that, as LBL was now composed of several separate subsidiaries, such action would have been unlawful. In order to escape a whopping fine, the union would have been required to publicly repudiate secondary action, and this would have done little for morale. But it was also pointed out that LBL's division into subsidiaries actually worked as much in favour of the trade union as it did against it. *It simply did not matter if other subsidiaries continued to run their normal services as long as London Forest remained isolated.*

Similarly, after a few days London Transport asked private operators to provide some form of service on LFT's tendered routes. Such services were provided by County Bus, Kentish Bus, Citybus and London Buslines. Where TGWU members refused to operate such services, these gestures of support were gratefully received. Thus, the Central Bus Committee at Thamesway decided that a service on route 251 specially funded by LT for the duration of the strike should not operate, a decision which was immediately implemented by the Branch Officers. The fact that other operators were providing a service (albeit extremely patchily) at first caused concern among the strikers. It was explained, however, that traditional notions of "strike-breaking" did not necessarily apply where tendered routes were concerned. *Again, it did not really matter, as long as London Forest did not operate the routes and thus was penalised financially by the tendering authority.* This is but one example of the new tactics which the tendering regime allows trade unionists to adopt, strengthening their hand in any dispute with their employers.

Such complexities were discussed at an all-London conference of LBL delegates held at Transport House on the evening of 17 July, where calls came from the floor for support for the LFT strikers which was "more than just financial." Apart from the arguments outlined above, it was pointed out that any secondary action would both shift the spotlight from the LFT strikers and reduce the capacity for fund-raising. These arguments were accepted by the conference, which agreed to hold weekly collections and to support a march on LFT headquarters planned for the following week.

"Ash Grove workers were so incensed by management conduct that, when the need for strike action came a day earlier than expected, it would have been more difficult for the Branch Officers to keep them working than it was to pull the buses in off the road. It was very soon obvious that no one at Ash Grove, including those few workers with a previous history of refusal to co-operate with industrial action, had any intention of going to work. The picket line was therefore relaxed and informal from the start, varying in number from three or four at 4.30 am to a hundred or more later in the day."

"A barbecue made by engineering staff was lit every morning providing sausages and burgers,often with home-made bread rolls supplied by conductor Blanchard's wife. Later everyday The Rose & Crown public house supplied a large tea urn and two loaves of sandwiches. Driver Mulla's family provided limitless flasks of tea.

"Driver Mulla's family also manufactured two immaculately sewn banners which, together with a whole array of placards, left the passing traffic outside the garage in no doubt as to the existence of and the reasons for the dispute. As peak hour traffic built up motorists and passers by were given the opportunity to contribute to the strike fund as strikers walked up the queues with buckets. Many hundreds of pounds were collected this way from local people who were more than willing to give support.

"At about 8 am every morning the paper sellers of various persuasions would turn up. Most persistent was WRP's Newsline that always carried a quote or two and a photo of bus strikers in the hope that at least those in the photo would buy the paper. The SWP offered more substantial assistance with a continuous flow of money from collections at meetings, schools, hospitals and local government offices and invitations to speak. All paper sellers were eager to engage in argument and harangue which provided pleasant sport for pickets.

"The pickets were further entertained by the company's inspectorate. With even less to do than usual they were bored to the point of lunacy. One displayed considerable skill upon roller skates on the garage forecourt at 4.30 am, whilst another goose-stepped back and forth with a false Hitler moustache and a broom stick over his shoulder.

"By midday the more courageous and articulate went off to address lunchtime meetings of teachers at a series of local schools. Hackney teachers on one-day strike invited a bus worker to address their mass meeting at Stoke Newington Town Hall, following which they contributed generously. In the evenings various Trade Union organisations were visited by Bus Workers. Experiences were shared and useful discussions about strategies for dealing with tendering took place. Driver Clyndes turned up at a meeting addressed by former GLC leader Ken Livingstone where he publicised the Forest dispute.

"Another delegation of Bus Workers set off to demonstrate at the G7 meeting of Prime Ministers. Although they failed to attract the attention of Soviet President Mikhail Gorbachev, they did meet Labour's transport spokesman John Prescott who was persuaded to sign the Capital petition against deregulation.

"The atmosphere on the picket line was never other than determined, confident, friendly and light-hearted. Three weeks of blue skies and sunshine helped. For any worker sat at home getting depressed by financial worries and concern about future job prospects, a visit to the picket line, an hour or two catching coins thrown by passing cars or collecting signatures, was guaranteed to raise morale. The picket line experience brought workers at Ash Grove together in a way that nothing had before."

KEN WARD, Ash Grove

AN ILL-TEMPERED EXCHANGE

On 12 July, the day after the decision to prolong the strike indefinitely, the TGWU's Ken Fuller advised LFT's Managing Director of this fact, pointing out that "the Walthamstow membership have made it absolutely clear to me that the package of wages and conditions currently on offer is unacceptable. This implies that the dispute may be resolved in one of two ways:

a) the company makes more funds available for a significant improvement... We have always made it clear that we would negotiate if additional funds were made available;

b) the Tendered Bus Unit re-awards the contracts and the surplus [of staff] within London Forest is dealt with by means of transfers and voluntary severance.

"As the company would presumably wish to avoid the second of these scenarios, I would again ask if additional funds are available for a negotiated settlement to be attempted... Such a settlement would hopefully assist in resolving the dispute in the other three garages."[13]

Young's reply was faxed to Fuller three days later. This began by asking if the strike had been declared official and "the exact nature (reasons for and demands of) the dispute" at each of the four locations. (This led the strike leaders to wonder whether Young had been paying attention for the previous five or six weeks!) He then asked Fuller to let him know by 5 p.m. that day if there was any point in him cancelling an appointment the following day in order to make way for negotiations. Young then became provocative, repeating the threadbare claim that the TGWU had "avoided any attempt at negotiation" and insisting that a "complete and full return to normal working" was a pre-requisite of any formal discussions."[14] In his reply the next day, Fuller expressed surprise "that you urge me to contact you by 5 p.m. on 15 July in view of the fact that I was outside your premises with several hundred members and their families (this was the day of the demonstration) when your letter was being typed. Obviously, I could have been contacted."

Fuller went on to charge that "an objective observer would conclude that London Forest, and not the TGWU, is the party which refuses to meaningfully negotiate" as no real improvements had been offered. With regard to the demand for a return to work, "your company has consistently misjudged the mood of our members since 5 June." Thus, there was no chance of a return to work until LFT had made real concessions. Fuller took exception to Young's implication that the TGWU had been neither "serious" nor "honest".

"Since 5 June, we have made our position perfectly clear - seriously and honestly. It would seem, however, that the company has either not heard correctly or it has chosen to disbelieve what it has been hearing. Equally consistently ... London Forest's behaviour has been characterised by dishonesty and intimidation in an attempt to frighten our members into accepting its conditions. It should be apparent by now that this has been counter productive."[15]

"Idle Hands"

This exchange is quoted at some length as it illustrates a number of points. Despite the fact that from the first meeting the TGWU had made it perfectly clear that it was deadly serious, there seemed to be a reluctance on the part of the company to believe this. Instead, it maintained an almost pathetic claim (in reality little more than a forlorn hope) that the union was in some way misrepresenting the views of its members - despite the fact that LFT must have received intelligence reports about the level of feeling at the garages and the good attendance at report-back meetings. Young's letter speaks volumes about the company's approach to industrial relations: days into a strike, with only a handful of staff crossing the picket line at Walthamstow, with the other three garages rock-solid, he was demanding a return to work before further negotiation. With London Transport about to make a decision on the future of the Walthamstow contracts (and therefore on the future of the company), Young was attempting to score points by questioning the basis of the strike and whether it had been declared official!

"The Spouses Demo" 15th July, 1991

TALKS RESUME

Needless to say, Young had to swallow his pride: talks resumed on 17 July with the strike still in progress. Meeting at the union's office at Headland House, Kings Cross where the TGWU's London bus officers are based, the company's team was joined by Jeff Porter, LBL Personnel Manager and a non-executive director of LFT. Oli Jackson headed the union's team. The Branch Representatives were absent from the first stage of the meeting, as this constituted "talks about talks". Young began by stating that the meeting provided an "avenue of discussion, if not negotiation". London Transport, he said, would already have made up its mind about what it wanted to do regarding the Walthamstow contracts and other current contracts. He wanted, however, to reach a sensible agreement on future tendering which could settle the dispute at the other three garages. Contradicting himself, Young then said that the Walthamstow contracts could be saved and "We will see if there is scope within the package price to address the problem areas."

Tom Holland, District Officer for the TGWU's engineering staff, stated that it had always been known that there would come a time when a tender price was too low to be accepted by the staff. That point had been reached at Walthamstow. As for the future, the engineering staff would be prepared to have prior discussion of tenders. Fuller agreed, pointing out that the most that could be hoped for from this meeting was a way forward for the future. This should be accompanied by an agreed package of safeguards in the event of routes being lost to tender in the future; such a package should be applied to the Walthamstow staff in November, as it was evident that the gulf between the two sides was too wide to bridge and that the contracts would therefore be re-awarded to the other companies.

It then became even more apparent that Young's primary mission was not, as he had initially claimed, to secure agreement on future tendering but to rescue Walthamstow. The company, he said, was prepared to look again within the total package; perhaps by reducing some support facilities more could be made available for wages. He also stated a desire to examine some form of differential between existing staff and new starters. Then again, he might be able to persuade LT to relax, at least for the first year, the five percent profit margin which all LBL subsidiaries were required to make on tendered and commercial work. More worryingly, he said that he would need a facility whereby tendered routes 48 and 56 (operated by Leyton) and D1 (operated by Ash Grove) would be "on arrangements we agree with you." Thus it appeared that he wished to widen the discussions to encompass reductions on other contracted routes.

In the afternoon session, with the Branch Representatives now present, all the emphasis was on Walthamstow, however. The offer which Young now put forward was £5.73 per hour for big bus drivers for a 40-hour week, with an overtime rate of £7.16 per hour (time-and-a-quarter) thereafter. This was achieved by incorporating the attendance allowance and assuming a four percent profit in the first year. Current average earnings could be maintained by working an extra 4.7 hours a week. For midibus drivers, the new offer amounted to £4.70 per hour; again, current earnings could be maintained by working an extra 4.7 hours a week.

Young went on to explain that new entrants would start at £4.50 per hour (midibus) and £5.20 per hour (big bus). This differential would be permanent-leading, the union realised, to a situation in the course of time when everyone would be on the lower rate. The rates for all staff, Young continued, would be reviewed in November, 1992 and each November thereafter. The fact that unproductive "spreadover" time would be unpaid would be tackled by eliminating it wherever possible.

Oli Jackson then argued that if there was to be a two-tier rate, new entrants should be given the opportunity of gaining the full rate after a given period; Fuller agreed, pointing out that anything else would be a recipe for division at the garage.

In an adjournment, the union side consulted the figures and discovered that the current average rostered earnings for a Walthamstow midibus driver was not £216 as claimed by the company but £220.74. The new proposal meant that such a driver would earn £32.74 (or 14.83 percent) less for 40 hours. A big-bus driver would earn £33.80 (12.85 percent) less. But one also had to take into account that the wage-increase which should have been paid in November, 1991 would not be there. Assuming a rise of five percent, this made the losses 15.57 percent and 13.5 percent, respectively. Even this took no account of the loss of the current attendance allowance (a potential of some £200 a year) or the fact that overtime earnings would be reduced by 17.4 percent on weekdays and 31 percent at weekends (again, these calculations took no account of the loss of the 1991 increase).

After the adjournment, Oli Jackson stated quite plainly that the proposal could not be recommended as it stood. After a further adjournment, the company agreed that new entrants would graduate to the full rate after one year's service . In May, 1992 there would be a further review of all rates, and if more were available it would be paid. Also by that time, certain drivers would qualify for a further modest increase under the DECAS (Driver

Competence Assessment Scheme) scheme. Young stressed, however, that everything put forward so far would have to be subject to thorough scrutiny by the auditors.

During the next adjournment, the TGWU negotiators took a sober look at the package. The midibus rate still did not equal that on offer at County Bus. The big bus rate meant that, considering the whole package, Citybus was still in front, although the gap was closing. Quite apart from this, though, the union team was deeply suspicious of LFT's tactics. The company was desperate for a return to work, for an agreement which would satisfy LT's Tendered Bus Unit that LFT would be able to operate the contracts from 23 November. Young had laid great emphasis on the role of the auditors. Was there a danger that, following a return to work, the company would then announce that the auditors had cried foul, and that the agreed rates would have to be reduced? Even if such a danger did not exist, working for an operation with such a tight budget would be sheer hell, with wages being stopped for the most minor infraction of the rules.

By now it was gone 6 p.m. and it was decided that Oli Jackson would depart for Transport House, where the conference of LBL delegates referred to above was awaiting a report on the state of play. Due to this fact alone, it was Fuller who led the union team after the adjournment, repeating that the improvements made by the company were still not sufficient to secure a resolution of the dispute. Nevertheless, there still remained the need to resolve the other issues in the dispute, and the union side was prepared to stay for as long as that took.

LFT's Managing Director expressed his disappointment. With regard to Fuller's suggestion that the meeting discuss a civilised way of handling the surplus which would arise at Walthamstow, Young said that the staff there had already determined their own future. "Without Walthamstow," he continued, "there's nothing we want to talk to you about." The decision of LT, he threatened darkly, would not just be about Walthamstow but would concern other tendered routes currently operated by LFT. Thus, when all else had failed, the company once again resorted to scare tactics.

Fuller charged that it was Young who was now refusing to negotiate. "You're cutting off your nose to spite your face." If the company was indeed concerned about its other

"Organising for Victory at Ash Grove"

contracts, surely it made sense to continue talking about the other aspects of the dispute, seeking an agreed method of discussing future tenders. With regard to the staff at Walthamstow, if the company was unwilling to discuss the problem further, the union would seek legal advice regarding redundancy payments.

It was at this point that a concerned Jeff Porter suggested a final adjournment. After the break, however, there was no noticeable change in the company's stance. Out came the scare tactics again. All of LFT's contracted work would be up for review tomorrow, said Young. The union, alleged Torode, had lied to staff about Citybus - for example, claimed the Commercial Director, this particular company would have no need to recruit any engineering staff as it had an all-in engineering contract. In finality, Young suggested a further meeting at 8.30 a.m. the next morning as the company was "prepared to continue until the very last moment."

The union stated that it would be reporting the details of the negotiations to a mass meeting at Walthamstow in due course.

IN THE COLD LIGHT OF DAY

The following morning both teams were back at Headland House - with the exception of Young, who was delayed with travel problems. In the previous twelve hours, the company had attempted (albeit at a perilously late stage!) to sow division in the TGWU ranks: at least one local manager had claimed to a Branch Officer that he had been told that the negotiations on the previous day had taken a turn for the worse with the departure of Jackson and Fuller's assumption of the leading role. This, the union team decided, needed to be brought into the open this morning.

So the meeting began with Fuller slamming the scare tactics which management had employed throughout the dispute. With regard to Torode's claim that Citybus would have no vacancies for engineers, Fuller had taken the precaution of speaking to that company's Managing Director within the last twelve hours. He had confirmed that Citybus had had an engineering contract - but that it had been with Ensign Engineering, a sister company. Moreover, even this had been terminated some time ago and so the company would need some thirty extra engineers if it was awarded the Walthamstow big bus contracts! As for the breakdown of yesterday's negotiations being due to the wicked Fuller, Oli Jackson had himself made it clear to the company before his departure that the proposals were not acceptable - and the only improvement the company had offered since that statement was that new entrants would move up to the full rate after a year. With regard to the overnight break, said Fuller, it seemed that the company had hoped that the union side would wake up in a different frame of mind. But in the cold light of day the offer still looked the same. And it still could not be recommended. However, the union was still willing to discuss an overall resolution of the dispute.

Torode explained that the management team had thought that "we were getting somewhere" at a certain stage in the negotiations of the previous day. He then confirmed the union's worst fears by stating that LFT had "moved further than we believe we were able to" and that the revised offer presented a number of "management challenges".

After the briefest of adjournments, Torode asked if this was really the end of the road, to which Jackson replied that there had to be further improvements in the offer. Torode then indicated that his team would leave for its meeting with LT. The company would be seeking a return to work but he was not in a position to discuss this at the moment.

REJECTION

Originally, LFT had scheduled a meeting for the same morning with the TGWU's engineering representatives. Obviously, the company had been banking on securing agreement with the operating staff, for this meeting was now cancelled. Then, mysteriously, it was reconvened at "the slaughterhouse" that afternoon and improvements similar to those made for the operating staff were put forward.

Quite soon, the pieces of the puzzle came together.

Without informing the TGWU, on 18 July the company again wrote to all members of Walthamstow's operating staff, outlining the latest offer and giving drivers until midday on 22 July to sign the acceptance form (the Tendered Bus Unit's decision on the future of the contracts having been postponed until 23 July). It seemed reasonable to assume, then, that LFT was hoping to conclude a settlement with the engineers and to boost the number of acceptances among the operating staff by means of this second letter. Around this time also, a driver on annual leave crossed the Walthamstow picket line and was given access to a telephone and the telephone numbers of striking drivers; he then commenced ringing around, appealing to his colleagues to join him in ignominy. Clearly, the company was pulling out all the stops.

On 19 July, a mass meeting of Walthamstow staff was held at the Waltham Forest Trades Hall. To most, it came as a complete surprise to learn that the company was proposing that new staff commence on lower rates of pay, as the letter they had all received from LFT the previous day had simply failed to mention it. Fuller alluded to the tactics being employed by the company and, to some amusement, read aloud Jack London's *The Scab.*[16] The latest offer was reported in detail, following which Fuller explained the fundraising measures which had been agreed by the Transport House conference two nights earlier and the fact that the union's Regional Committee had donated £5,000 to the strike fund. If the company would only realise that it had lost the Walthamstow contracts, he said, the union would discuss a formula for a return to work. The membership could not afford to lose its nerve now. Earlier, the TGWU had pledged that as long as the members stood firm, the union would stand firm alongside them. That pledge was firmer than ever.

When the chairman called the vote, not a single hand was raised in acceptance of the latest offer.

CLUTCHING AT STRAWS

On the Sunday evening the union's London Divisional Committee (which oversees the interests of all TGWU busworkers in London) met to review the fund-raising situation and to make the final arrangements for a march planned for the following Thursday. So far, the Strike Fund contained over £20,000 - and this after just one round of garage collections the previous Friday (some of the proceeds of which had not yet reached the fund although, equally, a good deal of the £20,000 came from street collections).

The following day, 22 July, negotiations with LFT resumed at the TGWU's Regional Office as, in Young's words, the company felt it was "worth one last throw of the dice". He said that he recognised that some of the phraseology in the proposed new contract had caused anxiety ("mirth" would have been a more appropriate word, as the document had stated that the company could change its terms by giving a mere 28 days' notice, something which, if the changes were significant, would be unlawful!). The company was prepared to look at this and to increase the hourly rate for big bus drivers by a further 7p an hour. As part of the DECAS scheme, some drivers might qualify for a further 15-20p an hour in 1992 - but there was an element of "swings and roundabouts" here, as the scheme would replace the existing safe driving allowance; moreover, this proposal could not be tied to the Walthamstow package as to do so "would not serve our purpose with the auditors." Asked what assurances he could give regarding the auditors, Young stated that the company had gone over the figures again and "we're still only just within the rules." But he could not guarantee the view of the auditors.

Oli Jackson then pointed out it should be possible to reduce the hours while maintaining earnings by eating further into the profit margin; also, an overtime rate of time-and-a-quarter was too low to be recommended. Staff would rather work for another operator than for an employer who had reduced their conditions after, say, 20 years' service. Young replied that the company's loyalty to long-service staff was demonstrated by LFT's attempt to save their jobs. "There is no need for anyone to take a cut in pay as long as they work the hours we want them to." Staff, he said, would have a choice of working light, heavy or medium rotas. The light rota would consist of mainly 40-hour duties; the heavy rota would consist of 15 duties, most of which would have a time on duty (excluding meal relief and "spreadover" time) of 48 hours, 45 minutes, each paying £295.44.

Drivers, protested Jackson, would want to earn more than that if they worked a time on duty of 9 hours, 45 minutes a day. Other LBL subsidiaries, said Ken McMahon, could win tenders against the same competition and on better terms than this; if Young went down to the garage gates at Walthamstow, said Ken, he would be told that the members were not prepared to accept such conditions.

"I know," said Roger Torode. "That's what I've been told."

After two adjournments, it was clear that no further progress would be made . Young indicated that the extra 7p per hour could be allocated on, say, the overtime rate rather than the basic rate if that would be preferable. Oli Jackson made it clear that the union was prepared to continue negotiations -everyone on the union side had commitments that afternoon, but the meeting could be reconvened in the evening if necessary. Following a further adjournment, Young said that the company would make itself available if "any issues emerge on Walthamstow." As far as the other three garages were concerned, "we anticipate a submission from you", and a further meeting was agreed for two days hence. Jackson later repeated that the TGWU was willing to continue discussing Walthamstow if more money was available. In response, Young at first indicated that no more resources were available: the hours could be reduced, but only at the expense of earnings. Oli therefore suggested that the meeting on Wednesday be scheduled at 2 p.m., whereupon Young startled the union side by asking: "You say you want more money. Can you put a figure on it?"

This triggered a barrage of contributions. Fuller reminded Young that ever since 5 June the TGWU had been asking one question over and over again: "Is that it? Is there any more? Are you saying this is your final offer?" Steve Cushion stated that the magic figure was £266 (current average earnings for a big-bus driver) for less hours than the company was proposing. Jackson invited Young to make a further offer if he had one. Walthamstow Rep Lucien Hoebeeck pointed out that staff were fed up with the threats and the generally intimidating approach which the company's managers had adopted throughout the dispute, and for this reason alone they would not be amenable to any reduction.

It was clear, said Young, that there was no basis for further discussion, and on that note the meeting ended.

ONWARD TO VICTORY

That afternoon, a further mass meeting of all LFT strikers was held at Hackney Town Hall. After Fuller's report of that morning's negotiations, the Walthamstow engineers left for a meeting of their own back at the garage where they considered their own latest offer - and rejected it.

Steve Cushion told the meeting how, finding his members on strike on his return from holiday, his girlfriend had jokingly remarked that this demonstrated that he had been holding them back for years! Referring to this, Fuller said that the strike leaders would be holding the members back if there was a failure to further develop the level of their understanding. During the thirteen days of the strike, that level had been raised considerably, especially concerning the tendering system. What was needed now was a much firmer understanding of how to end that system and a commitment to political activity in order to do so, using the petition and becoming involved in the local campaigns against deregulation. Not since 1958 had there been such a strike. Given the proximity of a decision on the Walthamstow routes by LT's Tendered Bus Unit, the march planned for Thursday could well be a victory march.

So onward to victory!

LT DECIDES, LFT DELAYS

London Forest's strategy had failed. Although some 50 Walthamstow drivers had signed the new contract, 38 of these had remained on strike. The engineering staff had rejected the offer put to them. Thus, when the Tendered Bus Unit met on Tuesday, 23 July it was clear that LFT would be unable to operate the Walthamstow contracts; the decision was taken, therefore, to re-award them to Citybus, County Bus and Thamesway.

For once, the media got it wrong, one TV station in particular announcing that the strikers at Walthamstow had been sacked. Despite the fact that Fuller corrected this misunderstanding in an interview the same day that the story was carried, the false version continued to be aired as this was clearly considered to be more newsworthy. On this same day - 24 July - LFT telephoned Oli Jackson's office, postponing the meeting arranged for that afternoon until the Friday while the company "took advice". The union issued a press release pointing out that the company had thus quite unnecessarily prolonged the strike for a further two days.

The lay members at the Strike Office in Hackney issued their own notice to the membership, which read:

"We have won a battle, but the war is still not over... We need to raise three demands:

1. An undertaking that a Walthamstow type package will NOT be used in future by London Forest.
2. That the company agree a transfer/separation procedure which would be used if London Forest loses tenders in the future AND WHICH SHOULD BE APPLIED TO WALTHAMSTOW STAFF IN NOVEMBER.
3. That current agreements be honoured.

"...You have NOT been sacked. Employment law has deteriorated considerably in recent years, but you can't be sacked by television, you must get a letter. Mr. Torode has confirmed that no-one has yet been dismissed."[17]

Bill Knowles, Leyton Rep.

THE VICTORY MARCH

At 10 a.m. on Thursday, 25 July, hundreds of strikers and their supporters from other bus garages around London assembled outside the Leyton & District Trades Hall in Leyton High Road. Two of their

30

number were despatched to collect General Secretary Elect Bill Morris, who had a prior meeting at Smithfield Market. Shortly after Bill's arrival the march set off, with the Walthamstow Branch Officers and strikers given pride of place at the head of the column, followed by the other LFT strikers and then the representatives of the other TGWU Branches.

Perhaps symbolic of this stage of the dispute (given that there were issues still to be settled), rain threatened but held off, and the march proceeded in high spirits towards Walthamstow. Along Hoe Street, support from the local community became obvious, as cars sounded their horns and the marchers passed shop windows displaying the TGWU's anti-deregulation posters. Passing "the slaughterhouse" in Chingford Road, the marchers observed directors and managers of LFT viewing the procession from a first-story window, with one of the managers taking photographs; charitably, the strike leaders assumed that he was merely recording history.

"Victory March, 25th July, 1991 – left to right: Lucien Hoebeeck, Ken Fuller, Bill Morris, Bob Barwell (Branch Secretary, Clapton)"

The march ended with a rally in the car park outside Walthamstow Swimming Pool, where local authority workers had rigged up a lorry with a public address system, allowing the strike leaders to address the marchers. Among the speakers was the Mayor of Waltham Forest, who extended his support to the strikers. Bill Morris pledged the TGWU's full material support to the dispute and urged the strikers to involve themselves in the political campaign to defeat tendering and the plans to deregulate London's bus services. Ken Fuller and Steve Cushion emphasised the fact that the reawarding of the Walthamstow contracts only meant that LFT's wage-cutting proposal had been defeated - a lot still needed to be done to ensure that every Walthamstow striker had either a job to go to or was provided with severance payments.

"An attentive audience at the rally, 25th July, 1991"

"On 6 June the Leyton Branch held a special meeting to consider management's proposals. All the buses were run in for this, and after we told the members of the plans to close the garage, the proposal from the chair to return to work was unnanimously overturned. So the buses stayed in. That's how the dispute started for us."

"We always thought that a picket line was a place of fear, of drivers moaning, of members of the public jeering. Wrong. During the Forest dispute the Leyton picket line was a place of friendship, of drivers wanting to help and the public being on our side for a change but it was also a place of 14 hour days and hard work.

"We had a 'battle wagon' from which tea and coffee was served, a grille which served bacon, sausages and eggs. We're grateful to R. Moore for providing the wagon and to everyone who provided the food."

"On one occasion while collecting, a lady came up and, explaining that she had no change, donated a bottle of wine. Other bottles were to follow. We then decided to get some cheese and one of our members who lived nearby went home to get wine glasses. Imagine management's reaction when they came out expecting to find a dispirited picket line and found, instead, everyone sitting on the battle wagon, drinking wine and sampling various cheeses! Another time, an old lady left a note with 9Op, saying she apologised for being unable to give more and that she supported us in everything we did.

"What stands out most is the way all groups among the members came together as one - black, white, Muslim, Jew, etc. Friends were made."

"We had collection tables set up at the Baker's Arms, where we also used the petitions against deregulation. The response was marvellous - cash in the buckets and signatures on the petitions. Police would come along occasionally and wonder what sort of management we were dealing with. Ambulances pulled up and poured money into the collection buckets. The Fire Brigade did the same."

"We regret that two garages closed, but we do not regret the closure of London Forest. We were proud that we were not defeated. The fight must continue. The original proposal to close Leyton was a major issue at this garage. After it was all over, the joke went around: 'If you had not tried to close Leyton, none of this would have happened.' We referred to ourselves as the KLO (Keep Leyton Open)!"

Bill Knowles, Leyton.

"The Picket Line at Leyton"

BACK TO WORK

A start was made on the outstanding tasks the following day, when the TGWU team met with the LFT directors at the union's Regional Office in order to arrive at a formula for a return to work. Early in the afternoon, Young indicated that he thought it would be a short meeting. At 9.20 p.m. that evening, the TGWU emerged with a signed document which, it felt, would guarantee a return to work. Signed by Young on behalf of LFT, Oli Jackson for the TGWU and Peter Lesurf on behalf of the craft unions, the document provided that:

a) ongoing attempts would be made to arrive at a formula for the future discussion of tenders;

b) the provisions of the LBL voluntary redundancy scheme would apply to all surplus engineering staff who could not be accommodated by transfers;

c) attempts would be made to accommodate all surplus staff by means of transfer to other LFT garages and other LBL garages (with disturbance allowance being paid in each case), with an above-establishment figure being accepted "within reasonable limits" and, where possible, transfer to other positions within LFT or LBL;

d) in addition, drivers who had signed to indicate their acceptance of the proposed new wages and conditions at Walthamstow would have the possibility of leaving under the terms of the voluntary redundancy package; the TGWU was of the view that this should apply to all staff and had written into the document its intention to "pursue this matter through legal channels".

LFT also agreed to issue clear instructions to its managers and supervisors "that there should be no attempt at retribution or victimisation of strikers upon resumption of normal working" and gave an undertaking that the block-grant wage negotiations should resume as soon as possible.

Within the TGWU team, there was discussion as to whether it would be possible to prolong the dispute until LFT had agreed to extend the possibility of redundancy payments to all Walthamstow drivers who remained surplus on 22 November. This had taken up more time than any other single item during the eight hours of negotiation, and it was clear that the company was not going to shift its ground by negotiation alone. Its somewhat illogical view was that people who had not signed the new contract had sealed their own fate and thus, if they could not be transferred to another location, they would leave with nothing on 22 November. This ignored the fact that the vast majority of those who had signed had also remained on strike. Nevertheless, it was the view of the TGWU's team that it would be impossible to maintain the strike on this basis alone, as the picket lines at all four garages would almost certainly be crossed, converting what promised to be a memorable victory into a nightmare. Thus, in the interests of unity it was decided that the question of redundancy payments would have to be pursued at an Industrial Tribunal; given the strength of the union's case, the chances of success here would be excellent, anyway.

At the final mass meeting the following morning at the Waltham Forest Public Hall, copies of the document signed by the union and LFT were handed out and the recommendation for a return to work based on its contents was moved by the platform. There was some nervousness on behalf of some Walthamstow members concerning the absence of redundancy payments if no jobs could be found for the 160 or so drivers who had not signed the new contract, but it was argued successfully that rather than the members losing more earnings in pursuit of this aim, the TGWU's resources could be used to achieve it. Bill Morris had, after all, pledged full material support for the strikers and such a pledge would not have been given lightly.

At the end of the meeting, the overwhelming majority of the hundreds of strikers present (including a majority of those from Walthamstow) voted for a return to work on Monday, 29 July.

Thus ended the longest London bus strike since 1958 - and it had ended in victory!

But there was still much to do, and further dramatic developments were in the offing. As a result, by the time the last bus ran out of Walthamstow on 22 November, the union would have achieved every objective it had set itself in the dispute.

"Surprise Guest at Mass Meeting, 27th July, 1991 (the poster reads: 'A Nightmare On Chingford Road: London Forest Makes More Cuts Than Freddy Krueger')

CHAPTER FOUR
MOPPING-UP OPERATIONS

LFT PETTINESS

At Ash Grove, Clapton and Leyton, the return to work went smoothly enough, with amicable union-management relations being swiftly re-established. At Walthamstow, however, it was a different story.

The returning strikers were immediately upset by the news that management had granted the dozen strike-breakers a week's paid leave. This, and the fact that some drivers had left during the strike, would have meant that the company would have been hard-put to staff the Walthamstow services. This problem was then compounded by LFT's decision to allow no overtime or restday working at the garage. The company explained this by stating that the strike had meant that it had been penalised financially by LT's Tendered Bus Unit while the overhead costs still had to be met; thus, savings had to be made. This argument conveniently ignored the fact that, although there were tendered routes at all the other garages, no prohibition on overtime or rest-day working existed; furthermore, the decision not to cover the Walthamstow services on overtime would attract further penalties. To the union, and particularly to the Walthamstow Branch, this appeared to be an attempt at petty victimisation - and a breach of the return-to-work agreement.

The TGWU immediately wrote to Joan Ruddock,MP, Labour's spokesperson on transport in London. Joan fired off a letter to the Tendered Bus Unit, triggering a response from the TBU's R.J. Bourne which (with diplomatic vagueness) assured her that "These short-term staffing difficulties have now been resolved by London Forest."[18] Rest-day and overtime working at Walthamstow was resumed.

A further example of the depths to which the company had sunk came to light when the TGWU negotiators spotted a notice in LFT's headquarters building. This had been on display in Walthamstow Garage during the strike and was executed in the form of a redundancy-payments chart, with zeros where the numbers of weeks' pay should have been. A paragraph at the foot of the table read:

"A special 'one-off' (the wrist) payment of sweet fuck all will be made to all ex drivers who are queer, lesbian or members of the union. Staff who fall into more than one of these catogaries [sic!] may apply to thier [sic!] local manager for a double payment. All staff wishing to work for other bus companies may rely on London Forest for an accurate reference."

The gutter humour and the spelling give one a fair idea of both the educational attainments and the humanity of the person responsible. The fact that this was allowed to remain on display in LFT's headquarters also provides a valuable insight into the company's sensitive approach to industrial relations.

But illiteracy and boorishness were the least of LFT's problems: in early August the Metropolitan Police and LBL's auditors arrived on the scene, the gentlemen from the former organisation arresting an LFT accountant in connection with the disappearance of tens of thousands of pounds.

A WAY FORWARD ON NEW TENDERS

On 6 August, the TGWU met LFT in order to begin discussion on the matters outstanding from the strike. Top of the agenda was, of course, the method of avoiding disputes like the one which had just finished. At the last meeting on 26 July, the union had put forward a document which, amended slightly by LFT, suggested discussion between the parties once tenders had been advertised and the specifications were known. Where the route was not currently operated by LFT or another LBL subsidiary, the aim would be to agree a total package of wages and conditions. In such cases, the work would be offered to specially-recruited staff or to volunteers from among current staff. Where the route was currently operated by LFT or a sister-company, the document stated that "the detail of wages and conditions will be discussed with the aim of retaining the work while protecting earnings and hours of the staff."

The TGWU had argued that this document should have been a component of the return-to-work formula. On 26 July, however, Young had stressed that such a document should give examples of the items which could be discussed and provide some idea of the scale and scope of the changes which might be possible. It seemed to the union that Young wanted a detailed agreement, rather than a mechanism for arriving at such an agreement. Young also asked what would happen if agreement on a tender was not forthcoming to which the TGWU replied that, if the company went ahead regardless, there would be another Walthamstow. In the end, Young indicated that he would want his Commercial Director, Roger Torode, to be party to the discussion of any such formula (Torode was at the time on annual leave).

Now, on 6 August, Torode commented that the company "wouldn't win any tenders on the basis of this document" and that the only work worthwhile going for would be non-LBL routes. To this Fuller replied, alluding to the recent strike: "You won't win it any other way." Eventually, Young and Torode agreed to the document with just two technical amendments and one addition - that, where non-LFT or non-LBL routes were won on tender and it was not possible to avoid existing staff being allocated to them, "discussion will take place regarding the terms upon which" this would occur.

Thus, a satisfactory mechanism was arrived at which - had LFT survived -may have proved beneficial to both sides.

HANDLING THE SURPLUS

The meeting on 6 August also began the discussion of how the staff surplus at Walthamstow would be handled. It was pointed out that there would in fact be a phased handover of the routes, with Citybus receiving routes 97A and 215 on 14 September, route 123 on 26 October and the remainder on 23 November. It was anticipated, said Torode, that there would be no staff surplus on 14 September; if there was such a surplus on 26 October, those staff who wished to go could be released to Citybus. Young pointed out that if individuals could not start when Citybus wanted them, they would be "passed over".

This could have developed into a major problem. All along, the union had assured its members at Walthamstow that there would be sufficient jobs at both Citybus and County Bus to accommodate them. In strictly mathematical terms this was quite true. Countybus had won 70-odd jobs' worth of midibus work and Citybus would need some 150 big-bus drivers; the latter company had also won 40 jobs' worth of midibus work in the tendered Wood Green network (the results of which were also announced in July, although these contracts would not commence until February, 1992). By this time Citybus had agreed (as had County Bus) that all Walthamstow drivers would be granted an interview and that the TGWU would be recognised at the company's new Northumberland Park depot, where it would trade under the name of Capital Citybus. The problem, of course, was that Citybus would need drivers before 23 November, and anyone who left Walthamstow before that date would be relinquishing an opportunity to pursue a claim for redundancy payments at the Industrial Tribunal. With this in mind, the TGWU advised staff not to leave prematurely. Citybus itself placed local newspaper advertisements advising Walthamstow drivers not to bale out early; in practice, the company accepted short-service staff, as these would have little or nothing to lose in the way of redundancy payments. It was also felt that LFT would anyway attempt to avoid releasing staff early, as this would benefit LBL's competitors. Then again, Thamesway lost work in the tendering process and, rather than face life on the dole, a sizeable number of its drivers made their way straight to Citybus, even though some of them would have qualified for redundancy payments.

It was clear that, especially for the long-service staff at Walthamstow, this dilemma would have to be addressed by the TGWU. It was - and with great success.

On 6 August, the mechanics of transfer within LFT and to other LBL subsidiaries were discussed and it was agreed that staff would be asked to list their priorities. The TGWU pursued at some length the question of why LFT was so insistent in closing Leyton at a later date than Walthamstow. Roger Torode replied that the two matters were entirely separate and the company did not want the "chaos" of organising transfers from two garages on the same date. It was clear to the union, however, that if both garages were closed on the same date it would be practical to treat staff on an equal basis, thereby strengthening the TGWU's claim for everyone to be given the opportunity of a job or a redundancy payment.

EXIT THOMAS YOUNG

On 20 August, LBL's Public Relations Office issued a terse announcement that Young had resigned as Managing Director of LFT and that Graham Elliott, LBL's Network Services Manager, had been appointed as Acting MD. The grapevine soon made it clear that most major decisions had been frozen. Two days later, Fuller and Cushion dropped in for an informal discussion with Elliott, during which the new man intimated that his job was basically to decide whether it was worth keeping LFT afloat. Diplomatically, he said that he was heartened by the enthusiasm of those who wanted to "make a go of it".

CONCILIATION? WHAT CONCILIATION?

On 30 August, the TGWU and LFT visited the conciliation service of ACAS in an attempt (by the TGWU) to resolve the question of redundancy payments. The union made a detailed presentation of its case but came up against a brick wall. The arguments of LFT, as relayed by the ACAS officer, included "It's not the money, it's the principle", and the feeling that it would not "be appropriate to reward those who brought about the end of the contracts." The company even refused to consider the possibility of arbitration.

At this stage, then, it appeared as if there would be a host of Industrial Tribunal applications after 22 November. It seemed to the union that, the spite factor to one side, the company's position was probably dictated by LBL, which would have wished to avoid a situation whereby staff went on strike, ensured the loss of contracts, received a handsome payout in recognition of past services and then walked straight into a job with the successful competitor. It would have made an interesting Industrial Tribunal case, but events were to take another course entirely.

BLOCK GRANT WAGES SETTLED

Originally, it will be recalled, it had been LFT's intention to reduce wages at all four garages. While the immediate threat to staff at Ash Grove, Clapton and Leyton was seen off even before the strike, still unresolved was the question of the wage-rise which staff at Clapton and Ash Grove should have received in May.

After LFT had retreated from its threat to immediately cut the wages at these two garages, the first wage negotiations had taken place on 2 July. By this time, most of LFT's sister-companies were offering a basic five percent, or more with conditions. But LFT had to be different. Roger Torode said that the company found "untenable the differences between tendered and non-tendered routes" and that "the overall position of the company" was "not as good as we had hoped." Therefore, he wanted to make progress towards eliminating the differences between wages on tendered and non-tendered routes. The company was offering an increase of five percent on all elements of pay in return for no sick pay for the first three days of sickness (currently achieved after five years' service) and payment of public holidays at source (i.e., eliminating the day in lieu). More was available if schedule conditions could be relaxed.

For the TGWU, Fuller indicated that the union would have difficulty in handling two disputes with the same company at the same time but, nevertheless, special meetings would be called at both garages and the company would be advised of the outcome.

The company-wide strike then intervened. Following this, one might have expected the company to have mellowed. It may have done, but its Managing Director had not. Young chose to be present at the next meeting on 8 August and began by asking if the TGWU intended to pay for the signs which had been defaced outside the building during the strike. He was given a suitable reply. By the end of the meeting, the company's offer had been completely revised - but was just as unacceptable. On the table now was a zero award on the basic rate and the withdrawal of the proposal on sick pay. Instead, the current attendance allowance of £200 per annum would be amended to a weekly payment of £20, subject to full attendance; as previously, public holidays would be paid at source.

On 22 August, after Elliott's appointment, Fuller wrote to advise him that the offer had been rejected by meetings at Clapton and Ash Grove. In his reply of 3 September, Elliott offered a straight five percent with no strings. This was accepted overwhelmingly at the membership at the two garages.

Another loose end had been tied up.

CATERING STAFF

The five percent offer also applied to catering staff, but there was a further unresolved matter concerning this group. During the strike, some catering assistants at Ash Grove had been told to either take annual leave or be locked out. Fuller wrote to the company, pointing out that its action was almost certainly unlawful and demanding that the staff concerned be paid. Months later, this was agreed and implemented, as it emerged that the original decision had been made locally.

LONDON FOREST - THE FINAL CHAPTER

On 16 September, it was announced that London Forest Travel would cease to exist as a bus operating subsidiary of LBL at the close of play on 22 November. Moreover, Leyton would remain open, with Ash Grove closing instead . Leyton would pass to LBL's East London subsidiary, while Clapton would come under the wing of Leaside.

Of course, no one was happy with the announcement concerning Ash Grove. But then the members at Leyton had not greeted the prospect of the closure of their own garage with equanimity - in fact, they had been prepared to fight the proposal. In this situation, however, the TGWU saw its opportunity to solve the last problem posed by the strike. Ash Grove and Walthamstow were to cease operations on the same day. Here was the chance to ensure that everyone was either given a job or offered the relatively generous terms of the LBL Voluntary Redundancy Scheme.

Already, a problem had been nipped in the bud with regard to the handling of surplus staff at Walthamstow, when it had emerged that LFT intended to give priority to those staff who had signed the new contract when it came to allocating jobs. The TGWU was able to point out, however, that the minutes of the meeting of 26 July (which had arrived at the formula for a return to work) recorded Young's undertaking that, with regard to transfers, all Walthamstow staff would be treated equally. The company had no alternative but to honour this.

On 24 September, the TGWU met with directors of LFT, East London and Leaside to negotiate a mechanism for dealing with the movement of staff following the closure of LFT. The number of surplus staff would be considerable, as not all routes were being transferred to the neighbouring subsidiaries route 6 would go to Willesden (Metroline) and route 35 would transfer to Camberwell (London Central). At this stage, the overall surplus was estimated at 134 OPO drivers, 20 crew drivers and 62 conductors. Thus, a sizeable task lay ahead.

The TGWU was a little taken aback when the meeting commenced with LFT inviting the union to put forward its own ideas for handling the surplus. It was then the company's turn to be surprised as the TGWU put forward a six-point plan, involving transfers and voluntary redundancies, which its negotiating team had formulated during a pre-meeting discussion. Furthermore, the union argued that the Walthamstow surplus should now be considered anew, with this group of staff being placed in the "same pot" as the Ash Grove staff in an attempt to ensure that all Walthamstow staff who so wished were given jobs. With the offer of suitable alternative employment, there would be no need for the large number of Industrial Tribunal applications which would otherwise arise.

Early on in the meeting, LFT's Graham Elliott agreed that the Walthamstow staff would be brought back into the redeployment process, although voluntary redundancy payments would still not be offered to those who had not signed the new contracts. At the end of the day, an agreement was signed between the three companies and the TGWU regarding the mechanism for transfers. A subsidiary agreement between LFT and the TGWU introduced the subject of voluntary redundancy payments; staff at Ash Grove and (if they had signed the new contracts) at Walthamstow would be able to express a preference for redundancy. This meant that if there were sufficient volunteers for redundancy payments everyone else would be guaranteed a job.

In the period following this meeting, the TGWU issued a circular to the Walthamstow membership, announcing the achievement of these agreements and pointing out that if anyone was denied both a suitable transfer opportunity and a redundancy payment the TGWU would support an Industrial Tribunal application

JOBS FOR EVERYONE

At this point, the long saga appeared to be over. But then a problem appeared which threatened to wreck the whole understanding.

At the meeting on 24 September, the TGWU had suggested that a "logic tree" be drawn up to ensure that there was mutual understanding on how applications for transfer and/or redundancy would be handled. At the time, LFT's managers were of the view that the document would need to be lengthy and the hour was getting quite late. In late October, however, they drew up a "memorandum of understanding" which was faxed to the TGWU's Ken Fuller for approval. He could find no problem with it. It then transpired that LFT were attempting to discriminate against Walthamstow staff again. The document stated that, after the first attempt to allocate staff to vacancies, and before staff were selected for redundancy payments, "those at Walthamstow will be dealt with on the basis of the arrangements already notified to them." To the TGWU, this merely meant that only those who had signed the new contract would be considered for redundancy payments. The interpretation of LFT, however, was that at this stage all Walthamstow staff unallocated or ineligible for redundancy payments would leave with nothing on 22 November.

Quite clearly, this was not what had been agreed on 24 September. Fuller telephoned the directors of Leaside and East London who had been present and found that they agreed with him. On 24 October, therefore, a grim-faced TGWU team arrived at "the slaughterhouse" for the final battle. But Graham Elliott agreed without further argument to "go along with" the union's interpretation. In all probability, there were two reasons for this: the numbers involved were not so great and Elliott had almost certainly made the same telephone calls as Fuller!

In the weeks which followed, the tortuous job of slotting staff into vacancies took place. From this point on, management and administrative staff from LFT and the other LBL companies which assisted were extremely helpful and cooperative. From the TGWU, Steve Cushion (Larry Laurent for the engineers) spent long hours persuading management to be more flexible over this or that individual. To understand what this cost Steve, it must be recalled that it was he who coined the phrase "the slaughterhouse", and it was at "the slaughterhouse" that all these discussions took place.

At the end of the process, everyone who wanted a job had one. Thus, just over five months from the time London Forest had first outlined its draconian wage-cutting proposals, the dispute and the consequences to which these proposals had led had been settled. All along, the TGWU had warned the LFT directors and managers that the drivers' jobs were safe and that it was their own jobs which were at risk. More than anyone could have predicted at the time, this proved to be correct.

CHAPTER FIVE
THE LONDON FOREST STRIKE: ACHIEVEMENTS AND LESSONS

ACHIEVEMENTS

It should not be forgotten that the London Forest strike was conducted in a period when the TGWU was, just like most other unions, increasingly concerned about the decline in national membership since 1979 and was in the process of implementing a series of measures to address the financial problems arising from this. A more opportunistic trade union may well have been more concerned with safeguarding 300 weekly dues-payments at Walthamstow and thus may have attempted to persuade the members to accept the deterioration in their wages and conditions. That this did not happen must rank as an achievement. Instead, this problem was addressed in reverse, by seeking an undertaking from Citybus that the union would be recognised at its new Northumberland Park base.

The financial protection of the membership should rank as a further achievement of the strike - and one for which TGWU busworkers all over London, along with other trade unionists, are responsible. Of course, it was impossible to fully compensate for the loss of wages during the strike; but the combination of strike pay and the proceeds from fund-raising made a big difference to a lot of people.

Next, as we have seen, the TGWU succeeded in securing jobs for everyone who wanted to remain within LBL. Despite the advice of the union, some members at Walthamstow baled out early - but, of course, they did so in order to go to other jobs. The union's original objective was to ensure that all Walthamstow staff secured jobs at either County Bus or Citybus and to secure redundancy payments via the Industrial Tribunal if necessary. What the achievement of so many jobs within LBL did was to give members the choice to leave if they so wished. Moreover, LFT's desire to ensure that strikers did not receive redundancy payments and then walk straight into a job with the competitor was not realised - although the strikers concerned tended to come from Ash Grove rather than Walthamstow.

A further achievement was the agreement of the framework for the discussion of future tenders. This enshrined maximum protection for current wages and working hours. It had also been the intention of the TGWU in such discussions to ensure that LFT did not bid on the basis of undercutting the wages at non-LBL companies. However, this particular achievement was shortlived due to the early demise of LFT (something which some hailed as an achievement in itself).

The major achievement of the dispute was, of course, the defeat of LFT's proposed wage-cuts. For Ash Grove, Clapton and Leyton, this was achieved even before the strike commenced by the collective anger of the membership as expressed in the first ballot. The defeat of the Walthamstow proposals was not merely a victory for the Walthamstow members, but a victory on behalf of all London busworkers. Indeed, shortly after the strike an LFT director let it be known that if the proposals had been accepted the company would have also been awarded contracts in the Wood Green network and for some routes operated by Thamesway.

A victory for the company would have meant that all other bus companies in the area would then have screwed down the labour elements in their own tender bids, leading to a downward spiral in wages and conditions throughout the London area. The London Forest strike demonstrated that there is a point beyond which busworkers will not be pushed. Certainly it is very doubtful whether any other LBL subsidiary will repeat the mistakes of LFT.

LESSONS

On an organisational level, the unity displayed throughout the strike between operating, engineering and craft grades did not materialise out of thin air. From the moment London Forest came into being as a subsidiary company, all the stewards and Branch Officers from all trades had met as a "Joint Shop Stewards Committee". In the many minor skirmishes with the company, each group had respected the others' picket lines and the solidarity this built was a major factor in winning the dispute.

Many of the other lessons arising from the dispute will have been self evident in the foregoing pages. Some, however, deserve to be underlined.

The major immediate lesson is that, given the right combination of circumstances, it is possible within the route-tendering system for busworkers to "play the market" in much the same way that the tendering authority does - except that in this case the workers are interested in finding the company which will bid the highest for their labour. That the LFT strikers were willing to learn this lesson was in itself no mean achievement, as throughout LBL there has been a tendency to look upon the company in much the same way that previous generations of passengers looked upon the red bus - as the embodiment of security, reliability and comfort.

However, there is a more fundamental lesson that is still in the process of being learned: that the long-term common interests of London busworkers dictate that all busworkers in the London area should be recruited into the TGWU. As long as the division between union and non-union persists the government, the tendering authority and the more unscrupulous employers will be able to play off one group against another (to the detriment of both!), persuading busworkers to look upon colleagues who happen to be employed by another company as "the enemy."

The truth is that the current system of route-tendering can only work as a method of cutting wages and worsening conditions as long as busworkers go along with it. And it must be noted here that although the strike of 1991 defeated LFT's wage-cuts, the Walthamstow routes went to other operators who, while paying more than LFT had proposed, still pay less (when considering the package of wages and conditions as a whole) than the Walthamstow drivers previously received. The TGWU's experience in Liverpool is important in this regard. In that city, the union has not only organised thousands of contract cleaners, but it has established a "going rate" and a system whereby if a company wins a cleaning contract from a rival, the workers employed by the incumbent simply transfer to the new employer on the same terms and conditions.

With a lot of hard work in the fields of recruitment and organisation, there is no reason why such a system should not be evolved by London busworkers -or, indeed, busworkers anywhere. This way, tendering would cease to be a wage-cutting mechanism and employers would be forced to compete on grounds of quality and efficiency.

Even so, it is well-known that route-tendering breeds other evils, such as the violation of drivers' hours regulations: at the time of writing, more than 200 summonses have been issued at Armchair, a non-union company in west London. To an extent, some abuse of the regulations is understandable, if not forgivable, due to the financial pressure on the companies to ensure that the contracted mileage is actually run. Thus, if a company is short of staff (as it might well be if it pays low wages) or a number of vehicles are off the road with mechanical faults, the temptation to break the law must be considerable.

It is therefore in the interests of busworkers to both work for the organisational strength in the manner outlined above and at the same time to campaign politically for an end to the current tendering system.

But the government has also stated its intention to deregulate London's bus services as soon as possible after the next general election (if, of course, the Tories are re-elected). Deregulation would make the current system of tendering look like a picnic. It should be recalled that LFT's Managing Director suggested that all other LBL subsidiaries would have to follow his example of wage-cutting in the approach to deregulation and privatisation. Thus the current system and deregulation are clearly linked. The government's Green Paper on deregulation certainly made it clear that the last five or six years should be seen as the period of London's "preparation" for deregulation.

But tendering and deregulation are also linked in another way: in the campaign which the TGWU and the Capital Transport Campaign are currently waging, the main demand is a halt to the plans to deregulate and the establishment of an independent public inquiry. At such a public inquiry, the union would like to see an honest and thoroughgoing appraisal of London bus services since the 1984 London Regional Transport Act. This should include taking evidence concerning abuses of the drivers' hours and other regulations, with all parties granted immunity from prosecution arising from such evidence. Only in this way will the whole truth about tendering come out. With deregulation halted and tendering discredited, the way would then be open for the discussion of a sane and civilised framework for the operation of bus services in London which would benefit both the travelling public and London busworkers.

In finality, then, all London busworkers should be encouraged to campaign for this goal with the same tenacity and courage which the TGWU members in London Forest displayed in the strike of 1991. Only when this aim is met will the achievements of the London Forest dispute be overshadowed by a greater victory.

NOTES

1. Ken Fuller, *Radical Aristocrats : London Busworkers From the 1880s To The 1980s*, Lawrence & Wishart, 1985, pp. 20-23 .

2. "News For Drivers At Walthamstow", LFT, 10.6.91. The same circular was issued at the other three garages.

3. T. Young to K. Fuller, 17.6.91.

4. K. Fuller to the Office of Fair Trading, 17.6.91.

5. Tim Goodship (Competition Policy Division, OFT) to K. Fuller, 26.7.91.

6. R. Torode to K. Fuller, 18.6.91.

7. "The Current Dispute With London Forest - A Message From Your Trade Union", TGWU, July, 1991.

8. *Bus Business*, 29.6.91.

9. *Bus Business*, 13.7.91.

10. "Minutes Of A Meeting Held At 1430 Hours On Tuesday 18 June 1991 At Tramway Offices To Discuss Negotiations On Revised Rates Of Pay And Conditions Of Service Of Platform Staff Within London Forest Travel Limited." These minutes were never agreed. Fuller sent these back to Torode, stating that "certain passages belong to the realm of fiction. It is beyond me what the company can hope to achieve by such dishonesty." Torode then agreed to some changes, but not all those requested by Fuller. In his reply of 8 August, Torode provided a wonderful illustration of the double standards being employed by advising Fuller, in response to a request to amend one of Torode's own minuted comments, "I do not need your assistance in quoting what I have said . . . " ! Fuller wrote again on 16 August, remarking: "To a certain extent, I am prepared to accept that your approach is a result of inexperience. But I think that the interest of all parties will be best served when petulance is replaced by professionalism." The issue was never resolved .

11. "It's Time To Decide", LFT, 28.6.91.

12. A. Blyghton, TGWU Legal Secretary, to K. Fuller, 9.7.91.

13. K. Fuller to T. Young, 15.7.91.

14. T. Young to K. Fuller, 15.7.91.

15. K. Fuller to T. Young, 16.7.91.

16. "After God had finished the rattlesnake, the toad and the vampire, He had some awful substance left with which He made a SCAB. A SCAB is a two legged animal with a corkscrew soul, a water-logged brain, and a combination backbone made of jelly and glue. Where others have hearts he carries a tumour of rotten principles.

    "When a SCAB comes down the street men turn their backs and angels weep in heaven, and the devil shuts the gates of hell to keep him out. No man has a right to

SCAB as long as there is a pool of water deep enough to drown his body in, or a rope long enough to hang his carcass with. Judas Iscariot was a gentleman compared with a SCAB. For betraying his Master, he had character enough to hang himself. A SCAB HASN'T.

"Esau sold his birthright for a mess of pottage. Judas Iscariot sold his Saviour for thirty pieces of silver. Benedict Arnold sold his country for a promise of a commission, in the British Army. The modern strikebreaker sells his birthright, his country, his wife, his children, and his fellowmen for an unfulfilled promise from his employer, trust or corporation.

"Esau was a traitor to himself, Judas Iscariot was a traitor to his God. Benedict Arnold was a traitor to his country.

"A STRIKEBREAKER IS A TRAITOR TO HIS GOD, HIS COUNTRY, HIS FAMILY AND HIS CLASS!"

Jack London, quoted in Philip S. Foner, *Jack London: American Rebel,* New York, 1964, pp. 57-58.

17. "Splinters - A Newsletter From Your Negotiators".

18. R. J. Bourne to Joan Ruddock, MP, 14.8.91.

Lightning Source UK Ltd.
Milton Keynes UK

174624UK00002B/43/P

9 784871 876759